Impeaching Clinton

STUDIES IN GOVERNMENT
AND PUBLIC POLICY

Impeaching Clinton

Partisan Strife on Capitol Hill

Nicol C. Rae & Colton C. Campbell

University Press of Kansas

Published by the University Press of Kansas (Lawrence, Kansas 66049), which was organized by the Kansas Board of Regents and is operated and funded by Emporia State University, Fort Hays State University, Kansas State University, Pittsburg State University, the University of Kansas, and Wichita State University

Library of Congress Cataloging-in-Publication Data

Rae, Nicol C.
   Impeaching Clinton : partisan strife on Capitol Hill/Nicol C. Rae & Colton C. Campbell.
      p. cm. — (Studies in government and public policy)
Includes bibliographical references and index.
   ISBN 0-7006-1281-5 (alk. paper)—ISBN 0-7006-1282-3 (pbk. : alk. paper)
      1. Clinton, Bill, 1946– —Impeachment.   2. United States—Politics and government,1993–2001.   3. United States. Congress—History—20th century.
4. Political parties—United States—History—20th century.   5. United States. Congress. House. Committee on the Judiciary.   I. Campbell, Colton C., 1965– II. Title. III. Series.
   E886.2.R435   2003
   320.973'09'049—dc21   2003007157

British Library Cataloguing-in-Publication Data is available.

Printed in the United States of America

10 9 8 7 6 5 4 3 2 1

The paper used in this publication meets the minimum requirements of the American National Standard for Permanence of Paper for Printed Library Materials Z39.48-1984.

For BW

—N.C.R.

For Marilyn

—C.C.C.

Contents

List of Tables and Figures   ix

Preface   xi

1. A Rancorous Partisan Atmosphere   1

2. Congressional Guillotine   23

3. Ignoring Electoral Outcomes: Republican Members of the House Judiciary Committee   55

4. Standing by Their Man: Democratic Members of the House Judiciary Committee   75

5. House Floor Debate   97

6. Herding Cats to Trial   122

7. Conclusion: Lessons Learned   151

Appendixes   159
    Methodology   159
    Congressional Time Line: Impeachment and Trial   160
    President Clinton's Response to Questions by Chairman Henry J. Hyde (R-Ill.)   161
    Articles I, II, III, and IV   174
    Senate Vote on Article I: Perjury   177
    Senate Vote on Article II: Obstruction of Justice   179
    Quantifying the Impeachment Proceedings   180

Notes   181

Bibliography   209

Index   225

Tables and Figures

Tables

Congressional Resolutions Alleging Offensive but Not Necessarily Illegal
 Behavior by Presidents   26
Congressional Resolutions Alleging Violations of Statutory or
 Constitutional Law by Presidents   27
American Impeachment Experience   35
Impeachments: Dates of Consideration in the House and the Senate   36
Impeachments: Days of Consideration in the House and the Senate   38
Impeachment Data   47
Congressional Attempts to Censure Officials in Other Branches   50
Ideological Leanings of House Judiciary Republican Committee Members,
 1974 and 1998   59
General Election Winning Margins of GOP House Judiciary Committee
 Members, 1996 and 1998   66
1996 Presidential Election Results in GOP House Judiciary Committee
 Members' Districts   67
Losses by the President's Party in Midterm Elections, 1862–1998   78
Ideological Leanings of House Judiciary Democratic Committee Members,
 1974 and 1998   87
House Vote on Articles of Impeachment against Clinton   119
Presidential Victories on House and Senate Votes, Eisenhower through
 Clinton   149

Figures and Charts

Party Unity Votes in Congress, 1953–1998   18
Draft of Democratic Censure Proposal   93
H. Res. 614   118
Party Unity and Polarization in Senate Voting, 1977–1998   124
Internal Leadership Memorandum Outlining Senate Deposition
 Procedures   138

Preface

This book is concerned with the congressional aspect of the Clinton impeachment drama, that is, the pattern of events from the time Independent Counsel Kenneth Starr submitted his report in September 1998 until President Bill Clinton's acquittal by the Senate on February 12, 1999. Our subject matter is the "political" dimension of the case rather than the legalities or the moral issues involved. Our account demonstrates that political factors were central to the decisions as to whether or not the president should be impeached, and that the partisan political context of congressional politics during the decade of the 1990s more or less determined the pattern of events from the decision to open an impeachment inquiry to the eventual acquittal of the president. The Clinton impeachment was an essentially political rather than a legal proceeding from beginning to end, and we believe that rather than being an exceptional event in the context of American politics in the 1990s, it provides a fascinating case study of how the American political system operated during that decade and the critical factors underpinning the political process: the influence of single-issue and ideological activists on both parties, high levels of political partisanship and polarization, low citizen political participation and mobilization, the growing irrelevance of elections, and the pervasive influence of partisan and nonpartisan media of communication in the shaping of public opinion and political outcomes.

While much excellent work has already appeared in print from journalists, jurists, and political scientists on the events we discuss, we believe that the most significant and visible aspect—the impeachment proceedings in both Houses of Congress—has not been set in its proper political context. That is the gap that this study aims to fill. To that end, our opening chapter chronicles the intense polarization and partisanship that now characterizes Capitol Hill. Chapter 2 sketches the genesis and evolution of the impeachment process in United States history and underlines the essentially political nature of the process, particularly as it applies to presidential impeachments. Chapter 3 is based on personal interviews with Republican members of the Judiciary Committee that conducted the impeachment inquiry, and explains the forces that determined the committee members' decision to vote for four articles of impeachment in defiance of public opinion and following a significant electoral setback. Chapter 4 discusses the Judiciary Committee proceedings from the point of view of the Democratic minority, who found themselves unable to prevent the impeachment of the Democratic president, but whose tactics and rhetoric during the inquiry helped to shape the media and public view of impeachment and the eventual Senate outcome. Chapter 5 deals with the final impeachment votes on the House floor and how the influence of party leaders was decisive in the final result, together with some reflections on debate and deliberation in the contemporary House. Chapter 6 deals with the Senate trial and how, despite the predetermined nature of the final acquittal of the president, the chamber was able to bring political resolution and closure to this highly sensitive and polarizing proceeding, while still doing so in a highly partisan context. Finally, chapter 7 concludes the work with some final reflections on the Clinton impeachment, the factors underlying that event, and its significance for the future evolution of the American governmental process more generally.

Scholarly writing is often considered to be a solitary endeavor when, truly, it is a collective enterprise. The publication of this book would not be possible without the generous financial support of the Everett McKinley Dirksen Congressional Leadership Center as well as the cooperation and kindness of so many individuals. At Florida International University, once again, the Jack D. Gordon Institute for Public Policy and Citizenship Studies, under the steadfast leadership of John F. Stack, Jr., made enormous contributions. The continuous commitment, support, and encouragement of Provost Mark B. Rosenberg are especially appreciated. We gratefully acknowledge the contributions of Arthur W. Herriott, former Dean of the College of Arts and Sciences, Joyce Peterson, Associate Dean of the Biscayne Bay Campus, and graduate student Yagmur Sen, along with our colleagues in the Department of Political Science. And we value the interest and insight of our students, both graduate and undergraduate.

We acknowledge many individuals at the University Press of Kansas. Fred M. Woodward, director, agreed that an understanding of Congress necessitates a detailed account allowing for nuance. Next, we wish to thank Marie Blanchard for helping us to prepare the manuscript for publication.

We thank those members of Congress and their political aides for taking time out of their crowded schedules to meet with us. Mark Twain was fond of cartoonishly poking fun at lawmakers. He would ask audiences to imagine themselves in two different worlds, one in which they were idiots, the other in which they were members of Congress, only to then apologize for repeating himself. The picture of Congress conveyed in the contemporary news media is scarcely more flattering. To be certain, numerous flaws can be identified in members' personal or public behavior, in their priorities, and in their law-making practices. But careful observers also will discover much behavior in Congress that is purposeful and principled, with the public spirit in mind.

We also would like to acknowledge the United States Senate Historical Office. The Historical Office serves as the Senate's institutional memory, collecting and generously providing information on current and past Senate activities. This is largely due to the two historians, Senate Historian Richard A. Baker and Associate Historian Donald A. Ritchie, who are students of the Senate in the highest sense of the word. Their assistance and patience is limitless.

We continue to learn from our colleagues in the congressional scholarly community; there are too many to list here, but we owe special gratitude to Larry Dodd of the University of Florida, and to Roger Davidson (emeritus) of the University of Maryland, College Park, for their thoughtful and constructive reviews of the manuscript.

The American Political Science Association and its congressional fellowship program deserve particular acknowledgment. This invaluable program gave us the privilege of working in Congress and meeting many of the people who were a part of the congressional impeachment process, as well as observing firsthand how events unfolded. In the case of one author this meant the chance to meet his future wife.

Our deep appreciation for our families, for their unconditional love and support, cannot be adequately expressed in words. Nicol Rae is grateful to Bill Walker for his support during the completion of this project. Colton Campbell would like to give special mention to his patient wife Marilyn, whose own personal experience and insight into the historical impeachment of President Clinton contributed to a better understanding of congressional events.

To the reader: We hope our efforts will advance your understanding and appreciation of an institution that is never void of significant drama, the United States Congress.

1
A Rancorous Partisan Atmosphere

The prosecution of [impeachable offenses] . . . will seldom fail to agitate the passions of the whole community, and to divide them into parties, more or less friendly or inimical, to the accused. In many cases, it will connect itself with the preexisting factions, and will enlist all their animosities, particularities, influence and interest on one side, or on the other; and in such cases there will always be the greatest danger that the decision will be regulated more by the comparative strength of the parties than by the real demonstration of guilt or innocence.
—Alexander Hamilton, *The Federalist* No. 65

This book is about the December 1998 impeachment of President Bill Clinton by the U.S. House of Representatives, and his subsequent trial and acquittal by the U.S. Senate in February 1999. In contrast to most of the other writings on this subject our focus is on the congressional aspect of the Clinton impeachment rather than the details of the Lewinsky affair and the legalistic aspects of the case against the president.[1] Since the two chambers of Congress made the ultimate political decision on whether or not to impeach and convict the president, we believe this approach is entirely justified. Moreover, our argument in this book is that impeachment is an inherently political matter—as indicated by Alexander Hamilton above—and that the Clinton impeachment was the culmination of two decades of increasingly intense partisanship and polarization on Capitol Hill and therefore stands as an excellent case study of the Washington political process during the 1990s.

We argue further that the electoral/political environment in which the contemporary Congress operates created the context for the impeachment of President Clinton, and the Lewinsky affair was merely the catalyst. From the moment Independent Counsel Kenneth Starr submitted his report to Congress in September 1998, impeachment became inevitable (provided the Republicans retained control of the House), despite the ostensible opposition of the majority of the public as expressed in polls and unanticipated Republican losses in the 1998 midterm congressional elections. Impeachment happened because, for the Republican congressional leadership, the political costs of desisting from impeachment outweighed those of proceeding, while the Clinton White House for largely legal, but also to some extent political, reasons could not afford to give the House Republicans the kind of admission of "guilt" on the charges of perjury and obstruction that would have provided the Republicans political cover with their grassroots supporters.

Of course this raises some fundamental issues with regard to the representativeness of the Congress and the quality of democracy and democratic deliberation in the American governmental process today. The new partisanship and polarization on Capitol Hill is a product of an electoral process that has become much more contingent on "mobilization"—getting a party's own committed base of supporters to the polls—as participation rates have declined among the public in general.[2] As a consequence, these committed supporters who tend to have a more polarized view of political life exercise a disproportionate influence in the modern American electoral and governmental process. The congressional impeachment of Bill Clinton stands as an extreme example of this disproportionate influence.

SUMMARY OF EVENTS

On May 6, 1994, a former Arkansas state employee, Paula Corbin Jones, sued President Clinton for sexual harassment based on an incident in a Little Rock hotel room almost exactly three years previously, while Clinton was governor of Arkansas. The White House attempted to delay the Jones suit until Clinton had left office, arguing that it would detract from his duties as president. After the case had worked its way through the federal courts, the Supreme Court decided on May 27, 1997, in a nine-to-nothing decision that *Jones v. Clinton* could go forward. In their preparation for trial Jones's lawyers (provided by a conservative public interest law firm, the Rutherford Institute) sought depositions from other women alleged to have been sexually involved with the president, in an effort to demonstrate a pattern of behavior.

On December 19, 1997, Monica Lewinsky, a former Clinton White House intern and later full-time employee, then working at the Pentagon, was subpoenaed to give testimony in the Jones case. Lewinsky would sign an affidavit on January 7, 1998, denying having had a sexual relationship with the president, but five days later, a workmate and confidante of Lewinsky who also had previous experience working in the White House, Linda Tripp, contacted

Whitewater Independent Counsel Kenneth Starr and provided him with twenty hours of taped telephone conversations with Lewinsky. In these conversations the former intern gave intimate details of a series of sexual liaisons with the president from 1995 to 1997, and more recent efforts made by the president's friend, Washington attorney Vernon Jordan, to find Lewinsky a job, which had borne fruit with a job offer from Revlon Corporation on January 7, 1998. In that the tapes indicated possible "obstruction of justice" by President Clinton in an effort to influence Lewinsky's testimony, Starr was granted permission by Attorney General Janet Reno to extend his investigation to cover the Lewinsky matter on January 15. The following day Starr's deputies and Linda Tripp confronted Lewinsky at the Ritz Carlton Hotel at the Pentagon City Mall, in Arlington, Virginia, and after questioning offered her immunity from prosecution for perjury in the Jones deposition if she would provide details of her affair and subsequent conversations with Clinton.

On January 17, 1998, the president inadvertently got himself into even deeper trouble by giving a deposition to the Jones lawyers denying a sexual relationship with Lewinsky, thus exposing himself to possible future perjury charges. The news media began airing the Lewinsky story on January 21, 1998, and a Washington feeding frenzy erupted. President Clinton publicly and categorically denied having any affair with Lewinsky, wagging his finger before television cameras on January 26. First Lady Hillary Rodham Clinton, in a television interview the following day, declared that she believed her husband, and attributed the whole Lewinsky matter to "a vast right-wing conspiracy" seeking to bring down his administration. These denials were sufficient to assure congressional Democrats and the president's cabinet that this was just another effort by the Republican right to undermine the president, which would founder as the other scandals had done, owing to lack of hard evidence and unreliable witnesses.

For the next few months the Lewinsky matter continued to dominate media headlines as Kenneth Starr's grand jury in Washington took testimony from Clinton's secretary Betty Currie, his aide Sidney Blumenthal, Vernon Jordan, and Secret Service officers who observed Lewinsky's visits to the Oval Office. In July Lewinsky and her attorneys finally reached an immunity deal with Starr, and she provided the independent counsel's office with a semen-stained dress, in addition to testimony before the grand jury on August 6, 1998. On August 17, 1998, Clinton testified before Starr's grand jury and admitted an intimate relationship with Lewinsky. In a nationally televised address later that evening Clinton publicly admitted to a relationship with Lewinsky that was "not appropriate."

On September 9, 1998, Kenneth Starr submitted his final report to Congress. Two days later the House voted 363 to 63 to release the report publicly, and a videotape of Clinton's grand jury testimony was released and broadcast on September 21. On Monday, October 5, the House Judiciary Committee voted 21 to 16 along party lines to open an impeachment inquiry. Three days later, the full House adopted the resolution by a 258 to 176 margin, with 31 Democrats joining all the Republican members in support. On November 3, the Republicans lost five House seats in the midterm congressional elections and Speaker Newt Gingrich (R-Ga.) resigned three days later, to be succeeded in the new Congress by Speaker-elect Robert L. "Bob" Livingston (R-La.).

On November 5, Judiciary Committee chair Henry J. Hyde announced that Kenneth Starr would be the only witness before the committee, and that the committee had sent the president eighty-one questions relating to the Lewinsky case. (Ironically, on November 13, the Jones lawsuit, which had started the whole proceedings, was finally settled out of court, with Paula Jones getting $850,000 but no admission of guilt or apology from the president.) Starr testified before the committee on November 19, and the White House responded to the questions on November 27. On Friday, December 11, the House Judiciary Committee voted 21 to 16 along party lines for two articles of impeachment against the president on the grounds of perjury before Starr's grand jury and obstruction of justice, and 21 to 17 for a third article alleging perjury in the president's deposition in the Jones case. The following day the committee voted in another party-line vote for a fourth article, "abuse of power," after rejecting a Democratic censure resolution. On Saturday, December 19, the House approved two of the articles of impeachment—Article 1, perjury before the grand jury (228 to 206), and Article III, obstruction of justice (221 to 212)—and rejected Article II, the Jones case perjury (205 to 229), and Article IV, abuse of power (148 to 285), along with the Democratic rules change to force a vote on censure (204 to 230). During the floor debate, Speaker-elect Livingston announced his resignation, after revelations that he had had an extramarital affair surfaced in the media. Representative Dennis J. Hastert, the Republican deputy whip from Illinois, rapidly replaced him as Speaker-in-waiting.

The Senate trial formally opened on January 7, 1999, and a bipartisan agreement on procedures passed by unanimous vote after a closed-door session the following day. For a week, from January 14 to January 21, the Senate heard arguments from the House managers and counsel for the president. On January 27 the Senate voted 56 to 44, after another closed-door session, to take testimony and not dismiss the case. The following week the House managers took videotaped testimony from Monica Lewinsky, Sidney Blumenthal, and Vernon Jordan. After the Senate voted to bar live testimony, snippets of the videotaped testimony were shown to the Senate on Saturday, February 6, 1999. On February 9 the Senate began deliberations behind closed doors, and on February 12 voted to acquit the president 45 to 55 on perjury and 50 to 50 on obstruction of justice, both well short of the two-thirds (sixty-seven votes) needed for conviction and removal from office.

PERSPECTIVES ON IMPEACHMENT

One study of the Clinton impeachment suggests that the current system of campaign finance enabled House Republicans to impeach the president while simultaneously providing them with the means to retain their majority in the House. Based on an examination of district-level voting patterns and campaign contributions, Irwin L. Morris argues that many potentially vulnerable Republican incumbents compensated for an unpopular position on the impeachment issue in their districts by receiving increased campaign contributions from political action committees (PACs).[3]

Others attributed lawmakers' voting behavior more directly to the high public salience of the impeachment issue.[4] It is a common assumption among political scientists that individuals' motives in the political arena are essentially the same as their motives in the marketplace, that is, they are based on rational calculations of self-interest.[5] Also important are the relationships that are assumed to exist between means and ends (and which enable the lawmaker to choose the most rational means for achieving the specified end) and the relationships between costs and benefits involved, in the interest of efficiency. Legislators are therefore ever mindful of the direct correlation between their individual performances and the voting booth, and thus structure their behavior toward the achievement of conscious goals.[6] Such congressional behavior is especially prevalent with issues that are likely to provoke controversy with voters. Challengers, after all, will gleefully remind citizens of an incumbent's record on a traceable issue like impeachment, for example.

Still other analysts, while acknowledging partisan and ideological goals, argue that in this case the timing of the votes strongly influenced the strategic decisions made by each representative.[7] According to this theory, electoral considerations played a greater role in the October 1998 vote on holding impeachment hearings than in the actual impeachment votes two months later—a difference attributable to where the two votes fell in the election cycle.

The presumption that members are constituency-minded is a useful place to start in understanding legislative behavior. But in direct conversation with members of Congress, the listener is frequently left with a different perspective, one that suggests many nuances to congressional politics and life on Capitol Hill.[8] In Congress it is not always possible to construct a purely rational decision-making process for any but the simplest, lowest-level decision. Often there is an elaborate maze of subtleties to be sorted out and disparate goals to be weighed. A methodological approach that reduces congressional structure and decision making solely to the calculation of optimal means may disregard much of the political nature of Congress. There are times when lawmaking emphasizes personal relationships between members with an assortment of goals and motives, behind-the-scenes maneuvering and informal arrangements, and accumulated practice. Often the best way to start examining Congress and its operations is to recognize former House Speaker Thomas P. "Tip" O'Neill's (D-Mass.) insight: politics is an art.[9] In short, politics matters. Or as Senator Bob Graham (D-Fla.) reminded a classroom of college political science students: "A physics exercise, if done correctly, will yield similar results every time. But government, especially Congress, involves people, with different ideas that you can't control for, which produces inconsistencies and unpredictability."[10]

Congress is very much a collection of individuals who happen to serve in it at any given time. Members' personal motives, goals, beliefs, emotions, and talents have a direct impact on how the institution operates. Based on the personal accounts of those lawmakers and legislative staff that we interviewed, the backdrop for impeachment was partisan animosity and the deep ideological chasm between the two parties.[11] One party's defense of the rule of law was the other party's idea of a witch-hunt or a legislative coup d'état. Nowhere was this more evident than on the polarized House Judiciary Committee, whose impeachment hearings were permeated by partisanship. Republicans cast themselves as the party of probity and portrayed Democrats as willfully closing their eyes to clear violations of the law. "The only way to avoid impeachment is to leave your common sense at the door," said Representative Lindsey O. Graham (R-S.C.).[12] Democrats accused Republicans of misusing the impeachment process in service of a personal and political vendetta against Clinton. "You haven't liked him from the very beginning," Representative Carrie P. Meek (D-Fla.) said to her Republican colleagues. "Too many of you have a 'gotcha' syndrome."[13]

Committees have long been referred to as "miniature legislatures" or "microcosms" of their parent chambers, and subject to the same influences.[14] The intense partisanship that now characterizes the House as a whole is a powerful factor in the explanation of the raucous nature of the Judiciary Committee.[15] Indeed, if the House has become partisan, the Judiciary Committee has become hyperpartisan. The Judiciary panel has become a bastion of each party's ideological philosophy rather than a cohesive bipartisan body working out necessary compromises in a complex decision-making process.[16] Congressional scholar Roger H. Davidson observed that Judiciary Committee Democrats were significantly more loyal to President Clinton and Judiciary Committee Republicans significantly less supportive of the president than their respective fellow partisans in House floor votes during the 105th Congress (1997–1999).[17] Davidson forcefully concludes, "It is no exaggeration to say that there were *no* moderates on the committee, at least as measured by the most commonly cited voting indices. There were, for example, none of the party mavericks—southern Democrats and moderate Republicans, among others—who had so enlivened the Watergate proceedings a quarter of a century earlier."[18]

The reasons for the Judiciary Committee's extreme polarization and partisanship are embedded in the two parties' policy priorities and committee assignment patterns, with the respective sides staffing the panel with staunch conservatives and equally staunch liberals committed to divisive issues that lie within the Judiciary panel's jurisdiction: gun regulation; anticrime legislation; constitutional amendments on subjects such as abortion, school bussing, school prayer, and flag desecration; and other matters such as church-state relations, civil liberties, affirmative action, and gay rights.

The underlying notion of partisanship igniting a constitutional remedy is not new, as is clear from the admonishments of Alexander Hamilton in Federalist No. 65 and the record of previous presidential impeachment proceedings in Congress. Andrew Johnson was impeached along party lines and sent for trial in the Senate on eleven counts. In 1868, like 1998, partisanship swept away nearly all semblance of political civility during the political quagmire. Like Clinton, Johnson was a southern Democrat who had risen from the class scorned as "white trash" and whose personal life inspired widespread snickering.[19] The Republicans who controlled Congress detested him. They investigated every aspect of his life and then voted to impeach him. With his fate in the hands of a few moderates, he hired a "claque of lawyers skilled in nitpicking and pettifoggery."[20] Though Johnson had opposed the secession of the southern states, he drew the ire of Republicans when he argued that the formerly Confederate states could be readmitted to the Union with little federal oversight. Almost immediately upon entering the White House Johnson fell foul of Congress, where the Radical faction of the Republican Party, bent on maximum vengeance on the South, promoted financial aid for freed blacks and a strong civil rights act. For Johnson, these measures were unfair and infringed upon states' rights. To the fury of the Radical Republicans, he vetoed them both. The congressional elections of 1866, in which Johnson sought to outflank his nominal allies by enlisting the support of northern Democrats, brought him only defeat and crushing repudiation. The Republicans' distaste for Johnson only grew. Their chance to remove him finally came when he fired his secretary of war, Edwin Stanton, in defiance of a law stipulating that such steps required congressional approval.

In the modern era, the intense congressional partisanship that led to the impeachment and trial of Bill Clinton was driven by a resurgence of partisanship in congressional elections that has also affected the institutional norms, structure, and decisions of both chambers of Congress. The one essential conclusion to be derived from the congressional impeachment of President Clinton is that, to paraphrase an oft-cited remark of Mark Twain, reports of the death of partisanship in American politics have been greatly exaggerated.

THE RENASCENCE OF PARTISANSHIP IN AMERICAN POLITICS, 1980–1998

The traditional view of America's two-party system has been to regard it as weak by comparison with other mature liberal democracies.[21] The American political culture has been antipathetic toward political parties since George Washington first warned about their baleful influence, in his farewell address, and various writers have commented on how parties have been distrusted due to America's individualistic or Lockean political culture.[22]

American parties were strong in terms of popular support in the period roughly from 1828 to 1948: the era of the great political machines. Participation in elections reached unprecedented levels in the late nineteenth century, and Congress was organized around strong parties, with Speakers Thomas Brackett "Czar" Reed (R-Maine) and Joseph Gurney "Uncle Joe" Cannon (R-Ill.) being regarded as the most powerful officers of the federal government at that time.[23] Party loyalty among members of Congress was also extremely high. But while parties commanded great popular support, this devotion appears to have been tied more to patronage and regional and cultural cleavages than to ideology in the European sense. The party machines came under assault from the Progressive reformers of the early twentieth century. These emergent upper-middle-class professional and media elites held partisanship and the party machines to be the major impediments to the efficiency and modernization of American government that they wished to achieve. Thus the Progressives introduced a variety of devices at the state and local level specifically designed to erode the influence of the parties.[24] The most important of these was the "direct primary," whereby party nominations were removed from the control of state and local party leaders and instead decided by an election of voters (usually those who had registered with the specific party).

The "decline" of American parties really starts from this period, although the party machines were initially powerful enough to resist the Progressive assault. In the longer term, however, the primary system became almost universal, participation rates in elections dropped precipitously, and the party cohesion characteristic of the late-nineteenth-century congresses eroded considerably.[25] In 1910 an alliance of Republican progressives and the Democratic minority executed a revolt on the floor of the House that stripped Speaker Cannon of his most significant powers over scheduling of bills and committee appointments, and replaced the strong Speakership with a new congressional power structure based on powerful independent committees with strong chairmen selected according to the seniority rule. This system—with some modifications—prevailed in both houses of Congress until the 1980s, and while the party was still significant on Capitol Hill for some organization purposes (e.g., selecting the Speaker), the needs of members' individual states and districts appeared to be far more significant in determining election and reelection to Congress as well as the success of congressional careers.[26]

The Progressive reforms and demographic changes also encouraged a decline in strong affiliation or "identification" with the major parties, but the result was that voters in congressional elections began to make decisions based more on incumbency, since the system gave voters an incentive to keep incumbents in power so they would accumulate seniority. Incumbents were likely to be able to raise more money and achieve more name recognition among voters than any putative challengers.[27] Getting elected on their own merits rather than based on party affiliation, members were also less likely to "go along to get along" and less likely to go along with the leadership of their parties. Party unity scores dropped to low levels, and on some of the most important issues facing Congress during this century—the New Deal, "court-packing," the struggle between isolationism and interventionism abroad, civil rights—congressional voting alignments did not fall along party lines.

The most famous cross-party alliance and one that determined congressional outputs most of the time from the mid-1930s to the mid-1970s was the so-called "conservative coalition" of Republicans and southern Democrats that first formed in opposition to President Franklin Delano Roosevelt's plans to reform the Supreme Court in 1937.[28] This alliance formed a majority in both Houses to oppose expansion of the federal government at home and keep civil rights off the congressional agenda. The fact that the most conservative and most liberal members of Congress during the New Deal and post–New Deal periods could be in the same political party seemed testimony to the increasing irrelevance of parties as agenda-setting or policy-making tools in American politics. Beyond "structuring" electoral choices there seemed to be little governmental relevance to American parties at mid-century.

This was also the time when the weakness of American parties relative to those in other advanced liberal democratic systems began to be noted by scholars and commentators.[29] The main difference between American political parties and those in Western Europe was the apparently very low salience of ideology, which had come to be the determining factor in European electoral cleavages by the mid–twentieth century. Maurice Duverger had contrasted the European ideological, centralized, and disciplined mass parties to the American nonideological, weak, and decentralized parties. He argued that the ideological prototype was derived from the socialist and communist parties of the left, whose political opponents had survived in the new mass politics by aping the centralized and ideological characteristics of the former. For Duverger, the absence of a mass socialist party in the United States accounted for the fact that American parties were premodern, loosely organized, elitist, and nonideological "cadre parties."[30]

Leon Epstein produced an eloquent defense of the American party model as the product of America's different pattern of socioeconomic development, but most scholars on both sides of the Atlantic adopted Duverger's perspective.[31] They also tended to bemoan the absence of strong parties as a major problem in the political system, arguing that this led to low electoral participation and thereby helped to entrench the power of economic elites who did not need strong mass organizations to exert their interests politically. By contrast, the "have nots"—lacking a serious socialist party in the American political context—were unable to organize effectively.[32] Weak political parties also led to divided government and a lack of accountability in the political system since voters increasingly divided their tickets for different offices. In the early 1950s the American Political Science Association recognized the decline of party as the most serious problem in the American governmental system and issued a controversial report entitled "Toward a More Responsible Two-Party System."[33]

By the mid-1970s a consensus had been reached in American political science that the parties remained pitifully weak and had been in decline since the end of the nineteenth century.[34] Voters became so detached from partisan affiliations that it seemed unlikely that strong parties could be revived. Moreover, the parties had so weakened that they appeared unable to serve as vehicles for political change through the periodic electoral realignments that had characterized American political history.[35] Citizen energies were more likely to be channeled toward single-issue groups than parties, and political change more likely to occur from strong executive or judicial action than from the implementation of a partisan manifesto. The political turmoil of the 1960s brought ideology into American politics, but ironically the rise of ideological activists on both the right and left side of the political spectrum appeared to be merely one more symptom of the decline of the traditional party. Indeed, the ideologues appeared to regard the party merely as an instrument to further their goals rather than an end in itself, and traditional partisan considerations such as the primacy of winning power at all costs was less significant to ideological activists, to whom it was more important just to be "right" on the issues they cared about.[36]

On Capitol Hill the Democrats' nominal majority from the New Deal era persisted, but in practice power seemed to have become even more fragmented due to the rise in the number of subcommittees in both chambers—a result of a revolt by junior Democrats against the committee chairs.[37] Nevertheless, as the party faded congressional elections were being increasingly characterized by the high return rate of incumbent members and a declining number of marginal House districts.[38] David R. Mayhew suggests that most of the organization and norms of Congress in the 1970s could be explained simply by the needs of members to get reelected, and they were doing so with increasing frequency.[39] Richard F. Fenno, Jr., argues that members successfully manipulated the electoral process by fashioning both a "home style" and a "Washington style," thereby explaining why the public continued to hold their own representatives in high regard while increasingly despising Congress as an institution.[40] All this meant that Congress was increasingly hard to lead. This was difficult enough when House Speakers had to attempt to corral committee chairs with independent bases of support, but with the arrival of incumbency protection and subcommittee government there were now even more power centers within the House that had to be brought along. And while the sway of the conservative coalition had been eroded somewhat by the civil rights revolution and the erosion of committee chairs' power, much legislative activity had come to resemble a series of ad hoc coalitions across party lines. The erosion of the committee-seniority system at the behest of the new wave of junior, largely northern Democrats in the early 1970s thus initially appeared only to exacerbate the centrifugal tendencies on Capitol Hill.[41]

But it was from this low point that a remarkable revival of congressional partisanship and congressional parties has taken place. Several factors have combined to bring about this change, factors that can be broadly grouped into two interrelated categories. The first encompasses changes in the electoral environment that have intensified partisan competition in congressional elections. The second category includes institutional change within the House and Senate in response to these electoral factors.

The first of the external factors is the electoral realignment in the southern states since the passage of the 1965 Voting Rights Act. The enfranchisement of southern blacks by a Democratic president (Lyndon B. Johnson) brought a new electoral base to the Democratic Party in the South and brought southern Democrats much closer ideologically to national Democrats. At the same time conservative southern whites were realigning with the Republican Party, which emerged as a significant electoral presence in the southern states for the first time since Reconstruction. Together, David W. Rohde suggests, these electoral changes had the effect of making congressional Democrats more consistently liberal across the country and Republicans more consistently conservative, thereby undermining the potency of the old conservative coalition in both the House and Senate.[42]

Similarly, both parties at their grass roots have become increasingly ideological, certainly more so than at any previous time in U.S. history. Throughout the 1960s and early 1970s ideological and/or single-issue activists became a more visible force in both major political parties. Demographic changes, increased education, and economic development created a larger class of highly educated, middle-class Americans who were attracted to this kind of political activity. The old party politics of following a boss-led hierarchy for patronage appealed little to this rising social stratum, but the power of ideas and issues did. The parties became vehicles for promoting those ideas and issues and giving them greater legitimacy on the national political stage. Barry Goldwater's capture of the GOP presidential nomination in 1964 and George McGovern's capture of the Democrats' in 1972 announced the arrival of the new ideological activists in both parties, and they eventually become so entrenched in each that they now define their respective parties.[43]

Thus American politics finally became ideological, if not quite in the manner envisaged by Duverger. Groups representing, or claiming to represent, certain interests now cluster together around the labels of the respective parties—minorities, feminists, gays and lesbians, teachers, labor unions, environmentalists in the case of the Democrats; conservative Christians, gun owners, small business groups, anti-abortionists, tax reformers in the case of the Republicans. These groups share membership lists with each other and provide a cadre of activists and fund-raisers for primary and general election campaigns. The increased "nationalization" of American politics also means that aspiring candidates for each party in any part of the country have to accommodate the same forces at the grass roots of their parties, be it in Maine, Mississippi, or Washington state. The crucial fact is that these energized activists vote, spend money on campaigns, and donate their time and services to them. Their support is essential to winning party nominations and their mobilization is essential to winning general elections. Given the low participation rates in American elections, their influence is further magnified.[44]

Related to the interest groups are their fund-raising arms, the political action committees, or PACs. These entities raise and dispense funds to favored candidates, and their rise to prominence was stimulated by the 1970s campaign finance reforms and subsequent court decisions that restricted individual donations to candidates but expedited those by PACs. In fact by the 1990s, PACs were more or less unrestricted on what they could spend "on behalf of" a candidate so long as this activity was not connected with the candidate's campaign.[45]

Increasingly during the 1980s and 1990s it became apparent that PACs were coordinating their activities in election campaigns and that the national party organizations—the respective national committees and House and Senate campaign committees—were playing an increasingly important role in that coordination process. The national parties themselves were now much more active in recruiting candidates for elections at all levels and channeling funds in their direction via a more integrated state-national party collaboration.[46] They made particularly creative use of loopholes in the campaign finance laws that permitted unlimited individual contributions if channeled through the state parties—the so-called "soft money" loophole. In all this activity national party committees worked naturally with single-issue and ideological groups closely associated with the party. In fact, by the mid-1990s it was questionable whether the distinction between national party committees and PACs was still viable.

As the scope of political debate became increasingly national, so national

news media became more significant in the political process. A prevailing—
if often unconscious—attitude in contemporary television news is that politics is and should be perceived in terms of a clash of ideas in the public arena.
Hence, even beyond the entertainment value generated by partisan or ideological spokespersons shouting at each other on television, the new ideological politics is highly congenial to electronic media outlets. The longer-term
effect of the news media's treatment of issues, however, is to exaggerate and
encourage polarization at the mass as well as at the elite level. Many talk
radio shows and cable television stations are targeted at specific ideological
audiences and perforce have an interest in keeping the ideological conflict
white hot. The advent of the Internet has encouraged further ideological "nar-
rowcasting" with like-minded activists talking only with themselves, and
political debate both inside and outside Congress is increasingly resembling
a dialogue of the deaf.[47]

A final factor that has contributed to enhanced partisanship, especially in
the House, is the congressional redistricting process. In order to conform with
federal voting rights legislation mandating a more proportional representation for minorities in state delegations to the U.S. House, mapmakers tend to
draw overwhelmingly black or Hispanic districts, which are invariably safe
(with the exception of the three Cuban-American majority districts in South
Florida) for the Democratic Party. Simultaneously, however, the packing of
minority voters into such districts reduces the Democratic base in the remaining districts and makes them safer for the GOP.[48] With most districts thus
being uncompetitive in general elections, the real competition comes in low-
turnout primary elections, where the electoral incentive is to try to outbid
one's opponents for the support of hard-core ideological activists, interest
groups, and PACs. For elected members it thus becomes far more electorally
rational to conciliate the base than to cultivate the political middle ground.[49]
(In the Senate, this factor is somewhat attenuated by the more diverse electorates of most states and the more competitive nature of Senate elections.)

PARTISANSHIP RETURNS TO CAPITOL HILL

The cultural factors discussed above have encouraged institutional changes
on Capitol Hill that have reinforced partisanship and party loyalty. In their
efforts to curb the influence of southern conservative committee chairs over
policy in the mid-1970s, the same junior, generally more liberal, northern
Democrats, who instituted the reforms strengthening subcommittees, also

instigated some changes in the rules of the House Democratic Caucus (generally unnoticed at the time) that had the potential to enhance the power of the party leadership. Most importantly, the House Speaker was given the power to name the Democratic members of the House Rules Committee, which had operated as a relatively independent fiefdom since the 1910–1911 Cannon "revolt."[50] As the Rules Committee controls the rules for floor debate and the scheduling of most legislation, this change significantly enhanced the power of a Democratic Speaker willing to exercise it. The power to make committee assignments was also taken away from the Democratic members of the Ways and Means Committee and given to a steering committee of the Democratic caucus chaired by the Speaker. Finally, the party caucus as a whole was given the power to remove committee chairs and elect new chairs regardless of the seniority rule.[51]

In addition, the House faced a simple "collective action" problem that made it likely that the power of party leaders would increase in both chambers. If members are more beholden to ideological and single-interest constituencies, then these constituents are going to want to see some return on their investment in terms of policy. In a highly fragmented and undisciplined Congress, however, such policy outputs are going to be almost impossible to achieve. Since the Speakership of Tip O'Neill (1977–1987), the party leadership has stepped into the vacuum and has increasingly exercised its new powers in an increasingly successful effort to corral fellow partisans behind agreed legislative initiatives and agendas. In exchange for increased party loyalty, members could look forward to favorable committee assignments and greater opportunities of advancement in the House. They also would be able to show they had "delivered" for their base supporters back in the district. This "principal-agent" relationship, as Barbara Sinclair notes, has resulted in a more active party leadership and a far more partisan House.[52]

As the Democratic House leadership during the 1980s was increasingly successful in organizing its liberal majority against the initiatives of conservative Republican presidents Ronald Reagan and George H. W. Bush, the overwhelmingly conservative Republican House minority found itself becoming progressively more marginal, as the Democratic leadership was consistently able to assemble winning majorities using their new prerogatives without Republican input. The reaction of the frustrated House Republicans was to become increasingly partisan and shrill in opposition to the Democrats. Frustrated and marginalized inside the chamber, the House GOP became more and more inclined to follow the lead of a young Georgia firebrand, Newt Gingrich (R-Ga.), who argued that since the Republicans were denied any serious influence inside the chamber, public attacks on the "corruption" of the Democratic majority and the use of ethics investigations against prominent Democrats was the only way that the Democratic grip on the House could be undermined.[53] Gingrich's policy claimed its most significant victim when Speaker James C. Wright (D-Tex.) was forced to resign in 1989 after a barrage of ethics charges generated by Gingrich drew significant media attention.[54] The overall effect, of course, was merely to exacerbate the partisan bitterness on the House floor.

In the Senate, the larger constituencies and the chamber's traditions of individualism and courtesy set parameters on the level of partisan intensity, but the same trend was nevertheless evident, in terms of both rising party loyalty and conflict. This became apparent in the bitter confrontations over the Supreme Court nominations of Robert Bork in 1987 and Clarence Thomas in 1991, where ideological and single-issue activists on both sides lobbied their respective parties furiously. Of course the fact that the contemporary Supreme Court is charged with the resolution of the extremely sensitive social and cultural issues that today divide the parties added to the bitterness of the furor. The irony of this situation in the Senate, however, is that given that chamber's supermajoritarian rules for the passage of most bills, increased partisanship is actually likely to make the Senate less effective in passing legislation. During the 1990s this proved to be the case, to the frustration of ostensible Democratic and Republican majorities in the chamber.[55]

By the start of the 1990s the House of Representatives was ideologically divided in a partisan way not seen since the Cannon Revolt—a situation only enhanced by the Republican takeover in the 104th Congress (1995–1997). Long-term effects of ideological realignment united and homogenized the parties on Capitol Hill, and increasingly seeped into the internal workings of the House.[56] The new conservative Republican House regime of 1994, at least initially, was structurally an exaggeration of its liberal Democratic predecessor.[57] Enthusiastically backed by the seventy-three overwhelmingly conservative freshmen, Speaker Newt Gingrich created a more powerful Speakership, weakened committee chairs, and drafted legislation by party task forces and interests affiliated with the party.[58] The razor-thin Republican majority in the following 105th Congress (1997–1999) raised the partisan stakes even further.

With the margin of control so finely balanced, polarizing forces particularly dominated the House during this period. Democrats and Republican party leaders were constantly engaged in constructing policy platforms, negotiating agendas, raising and dispersing campaign funds, recruiting and tutoring nonincumbent challengers, making committee assignments, scheduling floor debates, and rounding up votes.[59] In this sense, the parties began to resemble modern armies, continually drilling their troops to subordinate their narrow self-interest and goals for the betterment of the whole.[60] Party unity votes, defined by the *Congressional Quarterly* as those votes in which a majority of voting Republicans opposes a majority of voting Democrats, have been rising over the past twenty-five years. (See Figure 1.1.) Since 1992, for instance, GOP unity scores in both chambers have been well over 80 percent and occasionally climbing above 90 percent.[61]

A consequence of the last two decades of raw partisanship has been a depletion of the comity among members that helps to lubricate the mechanics of lawmaking.[62] Some members, particularly departing lawmakers looking back on their careers in Congress, viewed the impeachment saga as another installment of a steady march by both parties toward ever more partisan and personal attacks.[63] In an example of a "ratchet effect," party leaders have relied on this acrimony to claim, and often get, party loyalty on critical votes.[64] Of the nearly two thousand floor votes cast by the House and Senate members on articles of impeachment against President Bill Clinton, for example, 92 percent followed partisan lines.[65] Even traditionally nonpartisan positions, such as the office of Senate parliamentarian, the chamber's referee, have suffered collateral damage.[66]

The fine partisan balance in both chambers of Congress since 1994 has also helped to sustain partisanship—a factor that is easily forgotten, since the Democrats held such a dominant position in both the House and Senate for much of the preceding half-century. During this period, Congress was often portrayed not as a battlefield where two partisan armies fought each other, but as a marketplace where 535 individual entrepreneurs bartered with one another. Scholarly footnotes in legislative studies contain many references to economists, but none, as John J. Pitney, Jr., comments, to military strategists like Clausewitz or Sun Tzu.[67] Following the 2000 elections, after almost a decade of partisan warfare, Democrats and Republican numbers on Capitol Hill remained in exquisite balance. Both parties had sought power, but neither had firmly grasped it. Without working majorities, but rather, as Robin Kolodny finds, "pursuing" majorities, the parties are engaged in tactical and verbal jousting as both strive to compile records geared to the next campaign cycle rather than negotiating with each other to achieve results for the present.[68] In this climate, talk of "bipartisanship" tends to be a matter of posturing or short-term tactical advantage, as both sides routinely position themselves for coming political battles. In his departing observations Senator William S.

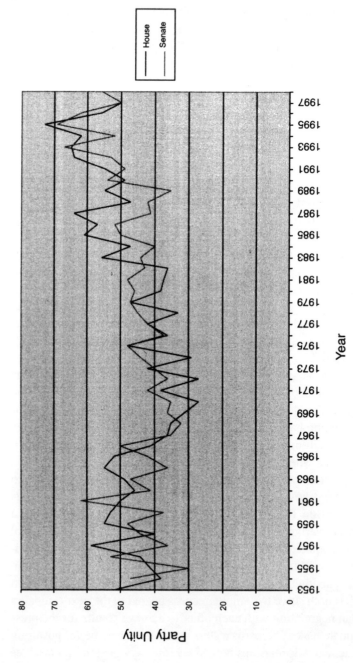

Figure 1.1. Party unity votes in Congress, 1953–1998. (Data derived from Norman J. Ornstein, Thomas E. Mann, and Michael J. Malbin, *Vital Statistics on Congress, 1999–2000* [Washington, D.C.: AEI Press, 2000])

Cohen (R-Maine) commented on the new partisanship on Capitol Hill as seen from the inside: "There is a dynamic force at work today that is producing a gravitational pull away from center-based politics on both the left and right. Those who seek compromise and consensus are depicted with scorn as a 'mushy middle' that is weak and unprincipled. By contrast, those who plant their feet in the concrete of ideological absolutism are heralded as heroic defenders of truth, justice, and the American way."[69]

CLINTON AND CONGRESS

William Jefferson Clinton took office in 1993 as the first Democratic president elected in sixteen years, in the midst of the upsurge of intense partisanship on Capitol Hill. Elected as a minority president in a three-way race, Clinton's background in the 1960s and his involvement on the margins of the antiwar movement and the so-called "counterculture" of that period earned him significant Republican enmity even though he ran as a moderate "New Democrat." The 1960s, however, had served as the catalyst for the cultural/ideological chasm that had opened up between the two parties in Washington and in the country as a whole.[70] Actually, this so-called "culture war" was an ideological struggle more between the mobilized interests and activists that rallied around both the Democratic and Republican labels than among the public at large. The latter was generally ambivalent about or uninterested in the highly sensitive moral and cultural issues that sustained the "culture war," such as abortion, gay rights, affirmative action, school prayer, and gun control, but because the ideologues were more mobilized and controlled the grass roots of their respective parties, the influence of their cultural conflict was greatly magnified politically.[71]

Clinton immediately discovered problems in getting some of his proposals past the Republican Senate, where Republican leader Robert J. "Bob" Dole of Kansas marshaled his troops in opposition to the new president's "jobs program" in 1993. Despite Democratic control in both Houses, Clinton's 1993 deficit reduction plan barely scraped through both chambers (Senate supermajority requirements do not apply to finance bills) and failed to attract a single Republican vote in either.[72] Under pressure from the party's ideological base, Clinton's policy in office had also taken an apparently greater liberal direction than implied by his "New Democrat" rhetoric in the 1992 campaign. Meanwhile the Democratic congressional leadership was hit by further scandals concerning the House bank and Post Office. In the wake of the failure in Congress of

Clinton's 1994 health plan, it appeared that the administration and the Democratic congressional leadership were in disarray. Then-Representative Newt Gingrich in the meantime successfully pushed aside the more conciliatory veteran minority leader Robert Michel (R-Ill.) and assumed control of the 1994 Republican congressional campaign, which depicted the Democrats and Clinton as "corrupt" and outmoded and promised a new Republican policy agenda, set out in their campaign manifesto, the "Contract with America."[73] Much to everyone's surprise, the Republicans took control of both chambers of Congress, the House for the first time since 1954.

The new Republican majority on Capitol Hill only succeeded in ratcheting up the partisan stakes even further. Gingrich and the Republicans interpreted their 1994 election victory as a mandate to implement their ideological program. Moreover, they organized the House in such a manner as to even further enhance the influence of the leadership. The new Speaker virtually appointed the committee chairs, and made significant decisions on legislation via "task forces," thereby bypassing the traditional committee system.[74] The Democrats, without control after forty years and seething with resentment against Gingrich, were totally excluded from a significant role in legislation. In the Senate the Democratic minority, led by Senator Tom Daschle (D-S.D.) found equally creative ways to frustrate the will of the majority, as had Bob Dole (now restored to the position of majority leader) two years previously. The partisan warfare culminated in a "shutdown" of the federal government at the end of 1995 as President Clinton refused to sign the Republican budget package and accompanying appropriations bills. With public opinion more inclined to side with the president against what appeared to be an ideologically strident Republican Congress, Gingrich was forced to back down.[75]

This did not endear Clinton to the congressional Republicans, who resented the frustration of their ambitions, and at the party grass roots the enmity toward the president intensified. Frustrated by the president's popularity and growing political skill, both House and Senate Republicans launched a series of investigations into various ethical "lapses" by him and his administration—the Whitewater land deal, the firings of personnel at the White House Travel Office, the suicide of White House counsel Vincent Foster, the "theft" of FBI files on prominent Republicans by Clinton White House operatives—but none of these had made much impact with the public.[76] In 1994, an independent counsel, respected New York attorney Robert Fiske, was appointed to investigate Whitewater and most of the associated scandals (he issued a report in June 1994 exonerating the White House from any involvement in the Foster suicide).

Later that year, however, the three-judge federal panel (consisting of two Republicans and one Democrat), required by statute to ratify Fiske's appointment, instead replaced him with former federal judge and then-U.S. solicitor general Kenneth Starr. Fiske's replacement by Starr was tainted by the partisanship emanating from Capitol Hill from the start. The chair of the three-judge panel, Judge David Sentelle, was a close associate of North Carolina Republican Senator Duncan McLauchlin "Lauch" Faircloth, who had publicly demanded that Fiske be replaced, and Judge Sentelle had shortly before been seen lunching with Faircloth and his fellow Republican North Carolinian, Senator Jesse Helms, the Senate's longtime archconservative and severe Clinton critic.[77] By early 1998 Starr's efforts had yielded no significant evidence of criminal behavior on the part of the Clintons, but the partisan background to Fiske's replacement by Starr in 1994 and the latter's service as solicitor general in the first Bush administration enabled Democrats to successfully portray his investigation as a partisan "witch-hunt" against the president.[78] The same applied to the investigations by the House Government Operations Committee led by the conservative Republican chair, Representative Dan Burton of Indiana, and Senate and House Banking Committee investigations into Whitewater headed up by Senator Alfonse M. D'Amato (R-N.Y.) and the more low-key Representative Jim Leach (R-Iowa) in the House.[79]

After the reelection of Clinton and the Republican Congress in 1996, further investigations were opened into the apparent fund-raising excesses of the Clinton reelection campaign in 1996, conducted by the Governmental Affairs Committee in the Senate, under Senator Fred Thompson (R-Tenn.), and by the relentless Representative Burton's committee in the House. While some of the details of these activities embarrassed the president and Vice President Al Gore, again the White House and their congressional allies succeeded in persuading the media and the public that these investigations were merely partisan and that there was no compelling evidence of criminal behavior on the president's part. In fact, as these investigations wound down, relations between Clinton and the congressional Republicans improved, as they compromised on the budget—the most significant accomplishment of the first session of the 105th Congress.[80]

The context was still ripe for a congressional impeachment inquiry against Clinton, however, should evidence of serious wrongdoing emerge in another context. Republican enmity toward him on Capitol Hill, but even more so at the grass roots of the party, was such that another major scandal might well precipitate such an inquiry even if the country, enjoying unprecedented prosperity, was generally happy with the incumbent. The conservative Republican network of interest groups, think tanks, talk show hosts, journalists, and ideological activists, frustrated by Clinton's success in maintaining public popularity and extremely distrustful of his "counterculture" background and sharp political skills (which they interpreted as "slickness" or even "deceit"), were certainly ready to exploit such an opportunity to the maximum.[81] The electoral influence that this network could exercise on Republican members of Congress on Capitol Hill meant that their views were likely to be listened to very seriously by the congressional leadership. All that was required was a pretext and the rest of the impeachment process would flow in clockwork fashion. The pretext came in the shape of former White House intern Monica Lewinsky's testimony in a civil lawsuit that had been bothering the Clinton White House for some time.

2
Congressional Guillotine

What then is an impeachable offense? The only honest answer is that an impeachable offense is whatever a majority of the House of Representatives considers it to be at a given moment in history; conviction results from whatever offense or offenses two-thirds of the other body considers to be sufficiently serious to require removal of the accused from office. Again the historical context and political climate are important; there are few fixed principles among the handful of precedents. . . . The President and Vice President, and all persons holding office at the pleasure of the President, can be thrown out of office by the voters at least every four years. To remove them in midterm—it has been tried twice and never done—would indeed require crimes of the magnitude of treason and bribery.
—Representative Gerald R. Ford (R-Mich.), House Minority Leader, requesting an impeachment inquiry into the conduct of Supreme Court Justice William O. Douglas, April 1970

Impeachment is a formal process the Framers provided lawmakers for investigating and trying allegations of wrongdoing on the part of the president, vice president, federal judges, and other "civil officers of the United States" for treason, bribery, or "other high crimes and misdemeanors."[1] The remedies of removal from office and potential disqualification from holding any future federal office testify to the seriousness of betraying the public trust; some consider impeachment to be the Constitution's substitute for the guillotine.[2] Alexander Hamilton referred to impeachment in *Federalist* No. 65 as "a method of national inquest into the conduct of public men."[3]

Ironically, as John Labovitz notes, despite the amount of time and attention the Constitutional Convention delegates devoted to the provisions concerning presidential impeachment, supporters of the Constitution believed it improbable for a corrupt person to ever become president of the United States.[4] As expressed by Hamilton in *Federalist* No. 68, the method of selection of the office of the president, through electors chosen by the states for that specific purpose, "affords a moral certainty," thus preventing any individual who was not to an "eminent degree endowed with the requisite qualifications."[5] Hamilton further declared: "Talents for low intrigue, and the little arts of popularity, may alone suffice to elevate a man to the first honors in a single State; but it will require other talents, and a different kind of merit, to establish him in the esteem and confidence of the whole Union, or of so considerable a portion of it as would be necessary to make him a successful candidate for the distinguished office of President of the United States."[6]

HISTORICAL ORIGIN

Hamilton and his colleagues at the Constitutional Convention understood impeachment as a constitutional process dating from fourteenth-century England, when Parliament introduced this legislative ability to curb and control tyrannical monarchs.[7] Impeachment enabled British legislators to discipline monarchial rule without directly confronting monarchical authority by indirectly removing the king's ministers.[8] The practice of impeachment fell into disuse in England by the mid–fifteenth century, but, in the early seventeenth century, the "excesses" of the Stuart kings prompted members of Parliament to revive their moribund power.[9] The Framers in Philadelphia enthusiastically followed the London impeachment trial of Warren Hastings, who was charged with oppression, bribery, and fraud as colonial administrator and first governor general in India, though he was eventually acquitted.[10] As Mary L. Volcansek notes, the lengthy Hastings trial, which lasted seven years from 1788 to 1795, undermined the practice of impeachment in Britain, which fell into disuse as monarchical power receded and cabinet ministers became subject to discipline in the House of Commons.[11]

The Framers emulated the British model of trial before the upper legislative body on charges brought by the lower house, but they did not adopt the practice of simultaneous removal from office and the imposition of criminal punishment; nor did they allow impeachment by the lower house for any crime or misdemeanor, regardless of whether the alleged offender was a fellow lawmaker or citizen.[12] Instead, the Framers' solution for misbehavior emphasizes removal from office rather than penal sanction invoked upon conviction of breaking the law,[13] thereby placing greater focus on the office than on the officeholder, which, as Michael J. Remington suggests, lends itself to protecting "public interest" as opposed to "punishing" the individual, with the focal point being the "offense" or "wrongdoing" that merits impeachment.[14]

The Constitution states that impeachment is appropriate for conduct amounting to treason, bribery, or other high crimes and misdemeanors. Treason is defined by the Constitution, and a definition of bribery was eventually supplied by statute. But toward the end of the Constitutional Convention, George Mason grumbled that simply barring those two misdeeds "[would] not reach many great and dangerous offenses," including "attempts to subvert the Constitution."[15] After discarding terms like "corruption," "maladministration," and "neglect of duty," for being too vague, the Framers added the much-interpreted phrase "high crimes and misdemeanors." Historically, this phrase has usually been defined by Alexander Hamilton's words, as "abuse or violation of some public trust."[16] That is to say offenses against the state, political institutions, or society as a whole, although no definitive determination has ever been made about what behavior will result in impeachment. For example, according to David Y. Thomas, the tenth article of impeachment against President Andrew Johnson charged him with high crimes and misdemeanors for speeches he made denouncing the Republican majority in Congress, even though these bore no relation with his official conduct, except insofar as he was "unmindful of the high duties of his office and of the dignity and proprieties thereof."[17] Congress has yet to enact a statute defining and cataloging impeachable behavior. Moreover, none of the previous impeachment cases explain legislative discipline of federal officials, largely because the Senate, which is the high court of impeachment, has failed to issue written opinions with its decisions.[18]

The individual actions that have produced resolutions of impeachment against presidents vary, but according to congressional scholars Steven W. Stathis and David C. Huckabee, they generally fall into three broad categories: actions that exceed the constitutional bounds of the powers of the office; behavior considered improper to the function and purpose of the office, but not necessarily illegal; and acts that defy statutory or constitutional law.[19] In addition, most resolutions are in the form of charges that are usually referred to the House Judiciary Committee, but some are in the form of resolutions of inquiry, seeking to authorize investigations to determine whether a formal impeachment inquiry by the House is warranted; the latter are usually referred to the House Rules Committee.[20] Tables 2.1 and 2.2 cite the formal impeachment charges that had been brought against eight presidents preceding President Bill Clinton.

Table 2.1. Congressional Resolutions Alleging Offensive but Not Necessarily Illegal Behav‹ by Presidents

Abused Power	Engaged in Misconduct	Made Bad Policy Decisions	Withheld Information from Congress	Failed to Exhibit Moral Leadership
John Tyler	John Tyler	Herbert Hoover	Harry S Truman	Richard M. Ni»
Andrew Johnson	Andrew Johnson	Harry S Truman	Richard M. Nixon	
Herbert Hoover	Herbert Hoover	George H. W. Bush		
Richard M. Nixon	Harry S Truman			
Ronald Reagan	Richard M. Nixon			

SOURCE: Adapted from Stephen W. Stathis and David C. Huckabee, *Congressional Resolutions on Presidential Impeachment: A Historical Overview,* CRS, Report No. 98-763 GOV, September 16, 1998, Washington, D.C. Congressional Research Service.

IMPEACHMENT IN THE HOUSE OF REPRESENTATIVES

Lodging a complaint of official misconduct in the House of Representative initiates the impeachment process. The House has no standing rule dealing with its role in impeachment, which effectively means "accusation" or "charge."[21] Since the Constitution only scantily describes the procedure, House impeachment actions are generally governed by the numerous precedents set in previous congressional actions as well as by the normal rules of the chamber.

Initiating the Inquiry

As a practical matter, various methods are available to trigger an impeachment investigation: charges made on the floor by any member or delegate; a resolution submitted by any representative and referred to a committee; a message from the president; charges transmitted from a state legislature, territory, grand jury judicial conferences, or independent counsels; or the action can result from facts developed by an investigation by the House. But while impeachment resolutions are easily filed, setting in motion impeachment proceedings is burdensome to members of Congress. The process can siphon away time from an otherwise crowded legislative docket, and the arcane nature of the process often deters Congress from poking into the business and personnel of the other two branches.[22] The final decision in all instances as to whether or not impeachment is appropriate rests with the full House.

The Nixon impeachment inquiry in the 93rd Congress (1973–1975) began in rather haphazard fashion when various members of the House, following the "Saturday Night Massacre," introduced resolutions calling for the im-

le 2.2. Congressional Resolutions Alleging Violations of Statutory or Constitutional Law
Presidents

lated tutory Law	Obstructed Justice	Defied Court Orders	Violated the United Nations Charter	Violated the U.S. Constitution
n Tyler	John Tyler	Richard M. Nixon	Richard M. Nixon	Grover Cleveland
drew Johnson	Richard M. Nixon		George H. W. Bush	Herbert Hoover
over Cleveland				Harry S Truman
rbert Hoover				Richard M. Nixon
rry S Truman				
hard M. Nixon				
nald Reagan				

JRCE: Adapted from Stephen W. Stathis and David C. Huckabee, *Congressional Resolutions on Presidential
eachment: A Historical Overview*, CRS, Report No. 98-763 GOV, September 16, 1998, Washington, D.C.,
ngressional Research Service.

peachment of President Richard M. Nixon or for an investigation to determine whether he should be impeached.[23] Speaker of the House Carl Albert
(D-Okla.) referred the impeachment resolution to the Judiciary Committee,
which had traditionally conducted impeachment inquiries, because almost
all previous inquiries had involved the conduct of federal judges. In the Nixon
case, however, Speaker Albert referred the resolutions calling for an investigation to the House Rules Committee.

Conducting the Inquiry

Before the creation of the Judiciary Committee in 1813, impeachment proceedings were referred to a special committee created for that purpose.[24] The
House also used a select committee (entitled the "Select Committee on the
Impeachment of the President") to consider the impeachment of President
Andrew Johnson in 1868. In modern practice, impeachment resolutions are
referred to the Judiciary Committee, while resolutions calling for an investigation by the Judiciary Committee, or a select committee, are referred to
the Rules Committee.[25] After submission of the charges, a committee investigation begins, with the panel deciding in each case whether the subject of
the inquiry has the right to be present at committee proceedings, to be represented by counsel, or to present and question witnesses. In some cases, an
investigative subcommittee might be charged with an impeachment inquiry,
but limited to the powers expressly authorized by the full committee.[26]

The committee can hold hearings and then debate and amend the resolution and articles under its normal internal procedures, which must be consistent with House rules governing committee action and also consistent with the resolution authorizing the impeachment investigation. Alternatively, the committee can, by unanimous consent, agree to vary these procedures by adopting formal changes to its written rules that specify procedures to be followed during the consideration of an impeachment resolution and articles. Such rules need to be approved in open session by majority vote and be published in the *Congressional Record* in order to be valid.[27]

The issue of committee jurisdiction in the House is frequently contentious, as documented by David C. King, with the tug-of-war demands from legislators seeking electoral and political benefits.[28] Under House precedents the reference of a measure to a committee, even if erroneous, effectively confers jurisdiction on the committee, a doctrine presumably equally applicable to impeachment resolutions.[29] Jurisdiction, however, does not guarantee a committee the authority to investigate with subpoena power, which is generally conferred on committees by House resolution. For instance, the resolution giving investigative power to the Rodino Judiciary Committee during the Nixon impeachment empowered the committee to issue subpoenas for investigations and inquiries within its jurisdiction as set forth in the rules of the House.[30]

There are different procedural models for impeachment investigations by House committees. The first is one patterned after a grand jury proceeding, in which the individual being investigated is prohibited from appearing before the committee, denied the ability to confront and cross-examine witnesses, and refused the right to introduce evidence in his or her own defense.[31] The earliest impeachment investigations by House committees were conducted in this manner, and the role of the House in impeachment is still frequently likened to that of a grand jury in a criminal prosecution. The second model provides the investigating committee a more adjudicative role, one that often renders a more adversarial investigative proceeding, in which that member of Congress who recommends impeachment brings forward charges against someone and introduces the evidence in support of such charges.[32] In turn, the official against whom the charges are made may seek to rebut the charges through examination of adverse witnesses and presentation of evidence in his or her own defense.[33]

The Decision to Impeach

Once an impeachment investigation is completed, the next procedural step is to vote on the articles of impeachment, which routinely coincides with the

House's vote on a resolution of impeachment, just as a grand jury indictment, with one or more "counts," goes to the trial court and jury, for final determination of guilt or innocence.[34] Before 1912, for example, articles were drawn up after the House had approved the resolution for impeachment.[35] Such measures are privileged for immediate consideration in the House, which is no more bound by the committee's recommendation on impeachment than it is by a committee's advice and action on any legislative matter.[36] For instance, in 1933 the House Judiciary Committee found insufficient grounds to recommend impeachment of District Judge Harold Louderback for the Northern District of California, but the House impeached him anyway. Articles of impeachment may also be amended on the House floor. For instance, when the articles of impeachment against Andrew Johnson were considered by the full House in 1868, two additional articles were adopted along with those recommended by the committee.

If the resolution and the article(s) are approved, precedent provides that the House then proceed to the adoption of privileged resolutions designating managers to conduct the trial on the part of the House and directing them to present the articles before the bar of the Senate. The House notifies the Senate of the adoption of articles and appointment of managers, and grants the managers necessary powers and funds; an odd number of mangers, ranging from five to eleven, have traditionally been selected, including members from both parties who voted in favor of impeachment.[37] The House, in effect, is the prosecuting party at the Senate trial, and the managers are the House's counsel. Until the 1980s, managers were chosen by the House in one of three ways: by election of the majority of the House, by resolution naming the slate, or by resolution authorizing the Speaker to appoint them.[38] The Constitution, however, does not require this, so it is possible that the House could appoint nonmembers, such as committee staff, to prosecute an impeachment. After the impeachment procedure, the managers return and make a verbal report to the House.[39]

Although the managers are the House's official representatives in the Senate proceedings, any House member may attend an impeachment trial. As one news print reporter observed throughout the trial of President Clinton, Representative Sheila Jackson-Lee (D-Tex.), herself a member of the House Judiciary Committee who voted against impeachment, kept vigil, scribbling a prodigious set of notes.[40] Every day, as she sat in the rear of the chamber behind Democratic Senators Joseph R. Biden of Delaware and Ernest F. "Fritz" Hollings of South Carolina, the normally boisterous Texan meticulously logged everything she heard and saw on the floor, making copious notations where she found conflicts between the House and Senate proceedings.[41] "My method is running the memory bank of the [House] Judiciary Committee proceedings with what I'm seeing," she explained.[42]

THE SENATE'S ROLE IN IMPEACHMENT

While the House decides and specifies the grounds for impeachment, the Senate is the final judge of whether to convict on any articles of impeachment. The Framers, however, were divided about whether the Senate should act as the court of impeachment. At the 1788 constitutional convention, the Supreme Court was originally vested with jurisdiction over impeachments of federal officers, with the exception of its own members (in which case the Senate would constitute the court of impeachment). But near the convention's end, delegates transferred all impeachment trials, including those of a president, from the Supreme Court to the Senate.[43] Opposing this role for the Senate, James Madison and Charles Cotesworth Pinckney asserted that it would make the president too reliant on the legislative branch, suggesting instead, as alternative trial bodies, the Supreme Court or the chief justices of the state supreme courts.[44] Hamilton and others counter argued that such bodies would be too small and liable to corruption. Hamilton explained the convention's decision in the following way: "The Convention . . . thought the Senate the most fit depository of this important trust. Where else than in the Senate could have been found a tribunal sufficiently dignified, or sufficiently independent? What other body would be likely to feel confidence enough in its own situation, to preserve unawed and uninfluenced the necessary impartiality between an individual accused, and the representatives of the people, his accusers?"[45]

Trial Preparation

Senate procedure governing the conduct of impeachment trials is specified by the "Rules of Procedure and Practice in the Senate when Sitting on Impeachment Trials," contained in the *Senate Manual*. These rules for judicial and presidential impeachment trials are both precise and vague, providing the Senate with an imperfect road map. After presentation of the articles and organization of the Senate to consider the impeachment, the Senate formally notifies the impeached person in writing of the charges brought by the House, and informs him or her of the date set by the Senate for the impeached official to appear and formally answer such charges. The impeached official may attend the Senate trial in person, may appear accompanied by counsel, or may appear only through counsel. In the event that an impeached person fails to answer the charges, the Senate infers the entry of a plea of not guilty and proceeds with the trial. Subpoenas may be issued for the attendance of witnesses and the presentation of documents.

Under its impeachment rules the full Senate may order the appointment of a committee to receive testimony and evidence concerning the charges in the articles of impeachment. In the 1986 impeachment trial of Federal District Judge Harry E. Claiborne for tax evasion, a special impeachment committee was established to receive evidence. This practice has continued in cases of judicial impeachments as a way of avoiding time-consuming trials before the full body, while giving the impeached judge an opportunity for an extended presentation of his or her case.[46] On such occasions the Senate committee conducts its business under the same procedural guidelines outlined for the chamber, reporting its findings to the full Senate, which then reviews the report to decide how competent and relevant the body of evidence contained in it is.

Generally speaking, the Senate continues its legislative and executive business responsibilities, but gives priority to the conduct of the impeachment trial. Under the impeachment trial rules, the Senate remains sitting as an impeachment court at noon daily, unless it orders otherwise. During the trial of President Clinton, for instance, Senate leaders pursued a dual track, with the Senate's routine work continuing in Senate committees before and after trial sessions.

Trial Procedure

In many respects an impeachment trial is conducted in a fashion similar to a criminal trial, with both sides presenting witnesses and evidence, and the defendant allowed counsel, the right to testify in his own behalf, and the right of cross-examination. But this is where judicial similarities end, as senators themselves decide whether and how to proceed, which evidence to consider, and what constitutes an impeachable offense. Even though the chief justice presides over Senate trials of the president, his rulings may be overturned by majority vote. The Constitution is silent on a presiding officer for lesser defendants, but Senate practice has been for the vice president or the president pro tempore to preside. The very first Senate impeachment rule, in 1798, handed down during Congress's first impeachment, against Senator William Blount, a Tennessee Federalist and signer of the U.S. Constitution, provided that the Senate keep silent as the House managers delivered articles of impeachment.[47]

This action followed a bitter floor debate that raised significant questions about the Senate's power to set its own impeachment rules. Federalist senators, who held a nearly two-to-one majority, contended that the Senate could establish such an oath of silence by simple resolution. The opposing Jeffersonian-Republicans, backed by several Federalists, responded that the Senate had no right to set its own oath. In their view such action should be accomplished, like any other legislation, by statute with the necessary involvement of the House and president. Otherwise, they cautioned, an impeached party might "deny the jurisdiction of the Senate, sitting under an oath of their own making," and some senators might decline to take an improperly established oath.[48] Citing state legislative precedents and the constitutional provision granting the Senate sole power to try all impeachments, the Federalists prevailed in their determination that the Senate should have complete authority to set the rules for such trials.[49] Like other Senate rules, those covering impeachment can be changed by a two-thirds majority vote.

Indicative of how much freedom the Senate has to plan its own trial proceedings is the duration of the period from the time senators are sworn in at the beginning of a trial until the final vote on the articles.[50] Based on one study, this has ranged from three days for Florida District Judge Alcee Hastings (1988–1989) to 266 days for Missouri District Judge James Peck (1830).[51]

The Supreme Court refused to review the Senate's procedures when an impeached judge, Walter L. Nixon, Jr., objected that although the full Senate had voted to convict him, the evidence in his case was taken by a committee rather than by the full Senate.[52] Delivering the opinion of the court for Associate Justices Stevens, O'Connor, Scalia, Kennedy, and Thomas, and for himself, Chief Justice William Rehnquist held the issue before them to be nonjusticiable, based upon the fact that the impeachment proceedings were textually committed in the Constitution to the legislative branch.[53] In addition, the court found the "lack of finality and the difficulty in fashioning relief counsel [led] against justiciability."[54] It argued that to open "the door of judicial review to the procedures used by the Senate in trying impeachments would 'expose the political life of the country to months, or perhaps years, of chaos.' "[55]

Judgment of the Senate

The Constitution does not address the standard of proof that is to be used in impeachment trials. The use of certain words such as "try," "convicted," and

"conviction" suggests that impeachment might be likened to a criminal proceeding, where the standard of proof is beyond a reasonable doubt. This position, according to congressional scholar Thomas B. Ripey, was voiced by the
Republicans of the House Judiciary Committee on the impeachment proceedings against President Nixon.[56] Not surprisingly, defendants in impeachment proceedings generally advocate for proof beyond a reasonable doubt,
whereas those prosecuting, the House managers, urge the lower standard of
preponderance of the evidence. In the final analysis, as Ripey suggests, the
question is one that historically has been answered by individual senators
guided by their own consciences.[57] And, as with so many decisions in the
political arena, personal motivations for or against conviction can be obvious, subtle, lofty, crass, or a complex mixture of all four.

The Senate makes all its decisions during an impeachment trial by roll-
call vote and without debate unless in secret session. But on the final question, guilt or innocence, each senator is given fifteen minutes of floor time
in secret session. The Senate votes on each article of impeachment separately, and, in accordance with the Constitution, conviction must be approved by a two-thirds vote. According to the Constitution, removal from
office results automatically from conviction, but, as congressional scholar
Elizabeth A. Bazen documents, the historical precedent suggests that the
Senate vote separately to bar the convicted individual from future public
office, provided that judgment is also deemed appropriate.[58] Only two of the
seven convictions have been accompanied by disqualification, which is
decided by majority vote rather than the two-thirds needed for conviction.[59]
The Constitution precludes the president from extending executive clemency
to anyone to prevent their impeachment by the House of Representatives or
trial by the Senate.

INFLUENTIAL CASES AND NEAR CASES

Impeachment activity commenced almost immediately after the Framers
finished the Constitution and has continued in intermittent fashion. Since
1789 impeachment proceedings have been initiated in the House sixty-two
times. Only seventeen federal officers have been impeached, of which fourteen were tried by the Senate; three were dismissed before trial because the
individual had left office, seven ended in acquittal, and seven in conviction.
The seven who were removed from office were all judges who, unlike executive officers, enjoy open-ended terms of office, and their errors included

drunkenness and senility, incitement to revolt and rebellion against the nation, bribery, kickbacks and tax evasion, conspiracy to solicit a bribe, and false statements to a grand jury.[60] Table 2.3 lists those individuals who have had articles of impeachment voted against them by the House for commission of a high crime or misdemeanor and have been tried by the Senate. Table 2.4 lists the dates of consideration of impeachment for those impeached by the House. Table 2.5 converts the dates in Table 2.4 into counts of days of consideration; also included are data pertaining to witness testimony in Senate trials. According to these studies, although the total elapsed time from when senators were sworn in as jurors until the trial was concluded has ranged from as few as three days to as many as 266 days, the average trial length was seventy-nine days.[61] The actual number of days that the Senate considered impeachment-related matters after being notified by the House of an impeachment was considerably shorter, ranging from six days to forty-eight days, averaging twenty-three days.[62]

Impeachments

At barely nine years old, Congress was confronted with its first impeachment and trial, involving Senator William Blount, who was found guilty of a high misdemeanor, inconsistent with the public trust and duty of his office. A year after becoming one of Tennessee's first two senators, Blount was accused of being active in a clandestine plan to assist the British in preventing Spain from ceding its territories of West Florida and Louisiana to France, a transaction that would have depressed the value of his extensive southwestern landholdings.[63] The House voted, without debate, to impeach Blount. The Senate concluded that Blount's behavior was unbecoming a member of the Senate, subsequently expelling him from the chamber the following day. Impeachment proceedings were subsequently dismissed. During the trial Senator Blount did not lose the support of his constituents, for they elected him to the state Senate of Tennessee, where he was also chosen to be president of that body.[64]

With removal from office no longer an issue, the House decided to activate a second element of the impeachment power: to disqualify Blount from again holding a post in the federal government.[65] Five articles of impeachment were adopted, with eleven managers selected to present the House's case to the Senate. With Vice President Thomas Jefferson presiding and Blount absent, the Senate formed itself into a high court of impeachment. The defense argued, among other points, that senators were not "civil officers" as understood under the Constitution and hence were not subject to impeachment proceedings.[66]

Table 2.3. American Impeachment Experience

	Official	Proceedings
Impeachment proceedings from 1797–1799	Senator William Blount (R-Tenn.)	Impeached by the House on five articles; Senate dismissed articles in response to a motion that moved that (1) Blount was not a civil officer, (2) had already been expelled, thus no longer impeachable, and (3) no crime or misdemeanor in the execution of the office had been alleged.
1803–1804	District Court Judge John Pickering	Impeached by House on four articles; convicted by Senate on every article.
1804–1805	Supreme Court Justice Samuel Chase	Impeached by House; acquitted by Senate.
1826–1831	District Court Judge James H. Peck	Impeached by House on one article; acquitted by Senate.
1862	District Court Judge West H. Humphreys	Impeached by House on seven articles; convicted by Senate on every article other than the second part of Article VI.
1867–1868	President Andrew Johnson	Impeached by House on eight articles; acquitted by Senate on every article.
1876	Secretary of War William W. Belknap	Impeached by House on five articles; acquitted by Senate on every article.
1903–1905	District Court Judge Charles Swayne	Impeached by House on twelve articles; acquitted by Senate on every article.
1912–1913	Appellate Court Judge Robert W. Archbald	Impeached by House on twelve articles; convicted by Senate on Articles I, III, IV, V, and XIII; acquitted on other articles.
1926	District Court Judge George English	Impeached by House on five articles; Senate dismissed articles at the request of House in light of the accused having resigned before trial.
1932–1933	District Court Judge Harold Louderback	Impeached by House on five articles; acquitted by Senate on every article.
1936	District Court Judge Halsted Ritter	Impeached by House on seven articles; convicted by Senate on Article VII; acquitted on the first six articles.
1974	President Richard Nixon	House Committee on the Judiciary House voted to report three articles of impeachment; Nixon resigned; House voted to take notice of these facts and to thank the committee, adjourning without voting on articles of impeachment.
1986	District Court Judge Harry E. Claiborne	Impeached by House on four articles; convicted by Senate on Articles I, II, and IV.
1988–1989	District Court Judge Alcee L. Hastings	Impeached by House on seventeen articles[a]; convicted by Senate on Articles I, II, III, IV, V, VII, VIII, and IX, and acquitted on other articles.
1988–1989	U.S. District Court Judge Walter L. Nixon	Impeached by House on three articles; convicted by Senate on Articles I and II, acquitted on Article III.
1998–1999	President William J. Clinton	Impeached by House on four articles; acquitted by Senate on every article.

SOURCE: Adapted from Stephen W. Stathis and David C. Huckabee, *Congressional Resolutions on Presidential Impeachment: A Historical Overview,* CRS, Report No. 98-763 GOV, September 16, 1998, Washington, D.C., Congressional Research Service.

[a]Article XVII was an omnibus charge that included all the others.

35

Table 2.4. Impeachments: Dates of Consideration in the House and the Senate

			HOUSE				SENATE		
	Office	Outcome	Investigation Begun	Committee Reported	Impeachment Floor vote	Articles Approved	Senate Notified	Trial Begins[a]	Trial Ends
William Blount	Senator (Tenn.)	Charges dismissed	7/3/1797	7/6/1797	7/7/1797	1/29/1798	2/7/1798	12/17/1798	1/14/1799
John Pickering	District Judge (N.H.)	Convicted	2/4/1803	2/18/1803	3/2/1803	12/30/1803	3/3/1803	1/4/1804	3/12/1804
Samuel Chase	S. Ct. Justice	Acquitted	1/7/1804	3/6/1804	3/12/1804	12/4/1804	3/13/1804	1/2/1805	3/1/1805
James Peck	District Judge (Mo.)	Acquitted	1/7/1830	3/23/1830	4/24/1830	4/26/1830	5/4/1830	5/11/1830	1/31/1831
West Humphreys	District Judge (Tenn.)	Convicted	1/8/1862	3/4/1862	5/6/1862	5/19/1862	5/7/1862	6/9/1862	6/26/1862
Andrew Johnson	President	Not impeached	1/7/1867	11/27/1867	12/6/1867				
Andrew Johnson	President	Acquitted	1/21/1868	2/22/1868	2/24/1868	3/2/1868	3/3/1868	3/5/1868	5/26/1868
Mark Delahay	District Judge (Kans.)	Impeached/ resigned	3/19/1872	2/28/1873	2/28/1873		3/3/1873		
William Belknap	Secretary of War	Resigned/ acquitted	1/14/1876	3/2/1876	3/2/1876	4/3/1876	3/3/1876	4/5/1876	8/1/1876
Charles Swayne	District Judge (Fla.)	Acquitted	12/10/1903	3/25/1904	12/13/1904	1/18/1905	12/4/1904	1/24/1905	2/27/1905

Name	Position	Outcome							
Robert Archbald	Court of Appeals Judge	Convicted	4/23/1912	7/8/1912	7/11/1912	7/11/1912	7/13/1912	7/19/1912	1/13/1913
George English	District Judge (Ill.)	Impeached/ resigned	1/13/1925	3/25/1926	4/1/1926	4/1/1926	4/6/1926	4/23/1926	12/13/1926
Harold Louderback	District Judge (Calif.)	Acquitted	6/9/1932	2/17/1933	2/27/1933	2/27/1933	2/28/1933	4/11/1933	5/24/1933
Halstead Ritter	District Judge (Fla.)	Convicted	6/1/1933	2/20/1936	3/2/1936	3/9/1936	3/12/1936	4/6/1936	4/17/1936
Richard M. Nixon	President	Not impeached	2/6/1974	8/20/1974					
Harry Claiborne	District Judge (Nev.)	Convicted	6/3/1986	7/16/1986	7/22/1986	7/22/1986	8/6/1986	9/14/1986	10/9/1986
Alcee Hastings	District Judge (Fla.)	Convicted	7/14/1988	8/1/1988	8/3/1988	8/3/1988	8/8/1988	10/18/1989	10/20/1989
Walter Nixon	District Judge (Fla.)	Convicted	2/22/1989	4/25/1989	5/10/1989	5/10/1989	5/11/1989	11/1/1989	11/13/1989
William J. Clinton	President	Impeached/ Acquitted	10/8/1998	12/12/1998	12/19/1998	12/19/1998	12/19/1998	1/7/1999	2/12/1999

SOURCE: Adapted from David C. Huckabee, *Impeachment: Days and Dates of Consideration in the House and Senate*, CRS, Order Code RS20018 GOV, January 13, 1999, Washington, D.C., Congressional Research Service.

[a] The "trial begins" column denotes when the Senate was organized for trial (i.e., when senators were sworn in as "jurors").

Table 2.5. Impeachments: Days of Consideration in the House and the Senate

			HOUSE			
			INTRODUCTION TO			
	Office	Outcome	Committee Report	Vote to Impeach	Articles Approved	Elapsed Time
William Blount, 1797–1798	Senator (Tenn.)	Charges dismissed	4	5	211	29
John Pickering, 1803–1804	District Judge (N.H.)	Convicted	15	27	330	69
Samuel Chase	S.Ct. Justice	Acquitted	60	66	333	59
James Peck, 1830–1831	District Judge (Mo.)	Acquitted	76	108	110	266
West Humphreys, 1862	District Judge (Tenn.)	Convicted	56	119	132	18
Andrew Johnson, 1867	President	Not impeached	325	334		
Andrew Johnson, 1868	President	Acquitted	2	4	11	83
Mark Delahay, 1872–1873	District Judge (Kans.)	Impeached and resigned	347	347		
William Belknap, 1876	Secretary of War	Resigned and acquitted	49	49	81	119
Charles Swayne 1903–1905	District Judge (Fla.)	Acquitted	107	370	406	35
Robert Archbald, 1912–1913	Court of Appeals Judge	Convicted	77	80	80	179
George English, 1925–1926	District Judge (Ill.)	Impeached and resigned	437	444	444	235

	SENATE						
	WITNESSES						
Days of Floor Consideration	Managers		Respondents		Total Days	Senate Notified to End	Total Elapsed Time
	No.	Days	No.	Days			
24	N/A	N/A	N/A	N/A	N/A	342	561
22	N/A	N/A	N/A	N/A	N/A	376	403
25	20	4.9	33	4.4	9.0	354	420
36	9	6.5	11	4.5	11.0	273	390
6	5	N/A	0	N/A	1.0	51	170
35	25	7.5	16	8.0	15.5	85	96
48	22	5.0	19	2.0	10.0	152	201
20	33	7.5	16	2.5	10.0	86	446
27	N/A	N/A	N/A	N/A	N/A	185	267
7	N/A	N/A	N/A	N/A	N/A	252	700

Table 2.5. Impeachments, *continued*

			HOUSE			
				INTRODUCTION TO		
	Office	Outcome	Committee Report	Vote to Impeach	Articles Approved	Elapsed Time
Harold Louderback, 1932–1933	District Judge (Calif.)	Acquitted	254	264	264	44
Halstead Ritter, 1933–1936	District Judge (Fla.)	Convicted	995	1,006	1,013	12
Richard Nixon, 1974	President	Resigned	196			
Harry Claiborne, 1986	District Judge (Nev.)	Convicted	44	50	50	26
Alcee Hastings, 1988–1989	District Judge (Fla.)	Convicted	19	21	21	3
Walter Nixon, 1989	District Judge (Fla.)	Convicted	63	78	78	13
William J. Clinton, 1998–1999	President	Impeached and Acquitted	66	73	73	37

SOURCE: Adapted from David C. Huckabee, *Impeachment: Days and Dates of Consideration in the House and Senate*, CRS, Order Code RS20018 GOV, January 13, 1999, Washington, D.C., Congressional Research Service.

By a vote of 14 to 11 the Senate dismissed the charges against Senator Blount for lack of jurisdiction,[67] accepting the argument that impeachment proceedings had breached Blount's right to a trial by jury, thus concluding the proceedings.[68] The Blount case addressed the question of whether members of Congress are subject to impeachment. Individual lawmakers accused of wrongdoing or ethical violations while in office have historically been removed from their position through other means. Constitutionally, both chambers of Congress have the authority to punish "Members for disorderly Behavior and, with the Concurrence of two thirds, expel a Member." The preferred type of sanction has his-

Table 2.5. Impeachments, *continued*

	SENATE						
	WITNESSES						
Days of Floor Consideration	Managers		Respondents		Total Days	Senate Notified to End	Total Elapsed Time
	No.	Days	No.	Days			
16	25	2.0	19	4.0	7.0	86	350
16	12	4.0	12	1.5	6.0	37	1,052
20	3	N/A	16	N/A	7.0	65	129
28	26	N/A	12	N/A	18.0	439	464
12	4	N/A	6	N/A	4.0	187	265
20	13	4	0	N/A	N/A	56	128

torically been expulsion or, for lesser offenses, a formal rebuke, such as censure, condemnation, denunciation, reprimand, or other forms of disciplining.[69] Since 1789 five representatives and fifteen senators have been expelled instead of being removed through the impeachment process, and many others resigned before the issue of their expulsion came to a vote.[70] In all its history, the Senate has managed to muster the necessary two-thirds vote to expel one of its members on only fifteen occasions, all of them for "disloyalty" to the United States, with fourteen occurring during the Civil War for "unfaithfulness" to the Union.[71]

The impeachment of John Pickering, district judge for New Hampshire, marked the first time a federal official was removed from office. The Pickering impeachment case had two important features, according to legal scholars Emily Field Van Tassel and Paul Finkelman: it reminded members of Congress that the Constitution makes no provision for removing a judge because of disability, and it occurred in part as "a test of a theory of impeachment held by the newly dominant states-rights party of Thomas Jefferson, the Jeffersonian Republicans."[72] Majorities of Jeffersonian Republicans in both houses of Congress were elected on the coattails of Jefferson, who challenged for the first time the Federalist Party's advocacy of commercial expansion and a strong national government. In light of this circumstance, the new majority Jeffersonian Republicans, who favored Congress, with its greater democratic nature, as the leading branch of government,[73] viewed the impeachment process as a means of bringing the federal judiciary—of which not a single member was of Jefferson's party—into partisan and ideological alignment.[74] This ensued following the Judiciary Act of 1801, enacted in the closing days of President John Adams's administration, which reduced the size of the Supreme Court from six to five members, thus delaying the opportunity for the Republican president, Thomas Jefferson, to make his own appointments. The "midnight judges act" also allowed the outgoing President Adams to appoint sixteen more Federalists to newly created circuit courts.

The impeachment articles brought against Pickering grew out of one confiscation case, *U.S. v. the Brig Eliza* (1802). The precise terminology of the charges—drunkenness, profanity, and senility—was significant but not the actual offense.[75] Instead, legislators decided that Pickering had violated a congressional statute, contrary to "his trust and duty" and had caused "manifest injury to the country."[76] With no way to relieve Pickering of his duty to hold court, and with no other judge capable of legally holding court in his place, impeachment was the only solution, other than resignation. On March 12, 1804, the Senate, by a strict party vote, found Federalist U.S. District Court Judge John Pickering guilty of decisions contrary to law. Because enough senators believed that drunkenness and insanity did not meet high crimes and misdemeanors, the Senate voted to remove him without finding that his behavior fell within the impeachment clause.[77]

For Federalists the impeachment and conviction of Pickering was a preparatory step to the assault upon Supreme Court Justice Samuel Chase, accused of partisan conduct on the bench.[78] That same day, the House voted to impeach the mercurial Justice Chase for biased conduct and an "anti-Republican" attitude.[79] A signer of the Declaration of Independence, Chase was an extreme Federalist partisan who vigorously enforced the Sedition Acts, which had been passed during the administration of John Adams to allow the prosecution of Republican editors and politicians. With pomp and circumstance, the trial began with a "ladies' gallery" and the appearance of the presiding officer, Vice President Aaron Burr, who only months earlier had dueled and killed Alexander Hamilton, and fled to avoid arrest.[80] Chase was eventually acquitted following contentious proceedings in the Senate. He effectively argued that he had not violated established judicial norms, that his actions were not criminal, and that his various rulings were justifiable, especially at a time in American history when courtroom procedures, particularly in political trials, had not been clearly spelled out and what was considered proper behavior by a judge was open to dispute.[81] The results of Chase's trial supported the views that the grounds for impeachment should be criminal rather than political.[82]

In 1868 the House impeached President Andrew Johnson, whose case revolved around the reconstruction after the Civil War. When Johnson succeeded Abraham Lincoln as president in 1865, his ideas for a mild reconstruction of the southern states and efforts to nullify the intent of Acts of Congress (e.g., the Freedmen's Bureau Act of 1865 and the Test Oath Law) clashed with the wishes of a majority of Congress, which was controlled by Radical Republicans, who believed the concessions to former Confederates undermined the very values over which the Civil War was fought.[83] Throughout the 39th Congress (1865–1867), Johnson and Republican lawmakers were locked in battle. The Tenure of Office Act, the violation of which was to be the legal basis for impeachment, was passed over Johnson's veto. The act forbade the president from relieving civil officers appointed without consulting the Senate until senators could confirm a successor, thus effectively denying the president the ability to remove and replace a federal officer without senatorial approval. Despite the certain consequences, Johnson, who deemed the law an unconstitutional limitation of his powers, decided to rid himself of Secretary of War Edwin Stanton, an ally of the radical Republicans. Johnson's suspension of Stanton set in motion a set of events that led the House to vote eleven articles of impeachment against him. For Republican lawmakers impeachment was a defensive response to a president who aggressively used his presidential powers to subvert the Constitution.[84]

By a vote of 126 to 47 the House approved a blanket resolution impeaching the president for "high crimes and misdemeanors in office." Then, in a procedural departure from previous impeachment attempts, the matter was referred to the Select Committee on the Impeachment of the President, a newly created panel to which only members who voted for the impeachment resolution were appointed.[85] The task of the committee to report articles of impeachment and not to investigate the matter was almost anticlimactic.[86] Within a week the committee presented the House with eleven articles of impeachment, two of which asserted that Johnson purposely disregarded congressional authority and brought it into "reproach, disrepute, and contempt by harangues criticizing Congress and questioning its legislative authority."[87] Johnson's impeachment trial attracted such great attention that for the first time the Senate issued tickets for admission to the public galleries.[88] The defense immediately claimed the necessity of an indictable offense for impeachment. After weeks of arguments, the Senate took a test vote on Article XI, a catch-all charge thought by the House managers most likely to produce a vote for conviction.[89] With thirty-six "guiltys" needed for conviction, the Republicans fell short by one vote. Stunned by the setback, the Radicals postponed voting for several more weeks. Then, eleven weeks after the trial began, with Johnson remaining out of view in the executive mansion, by an identical tally of 35 to 19, the Senate fell one vote short of the necessary two-thirds majority for removal of President Johnson from office.[90] Seven Republican senators defied their party's leadership and voted with the twelve Democratic senators to acquit the president. To head off further defeats for Johnson's opponents, Senator George H. Williams (R-Ore.) moved to adjourn *sine die,* and the motion was adopted 34 to 16, abruptly ending the trial.[91]

Florida District Judge Charles Swayne was impeached in 1905, accused of filing false travel vouchers, improper use of private railroad cars, unlawfully imprisoning two attorneys for contempt, and living outside of his district. Swayne's trial consumed two and a half months before it ended, when the Senate voted acquittal on each of the twelve articles, because its members did not believe his peccadilloes constituted "high crimes and misdemeanors."[92] It was during the long Swayne trial that the suggestion first surfaced that a Senate committee, rather than the Senate as a whole, should receive impeachment evidence.[93] Senator George F. Hoar (R-Mass.) proposed that the presiding officer should appoint such a committee. While Hoar's proposal would eventually be embodied in Rule XI of the Senate's impeachment rules, in 1905 the resolution was referred to the Rules Committee, which took no action.[94]

Swayne's case was followed by that of Associate Judge Robert W. Archbald of the Commerce Court in 1913, on the charge of numerous and serious acts of misconduct stretching over many years, including using his office to obtain advantageous business deals and free trips to Europe. As in the Swayne case, none of the thirteen articles charged an indictable offense. Yet, because of the seriousness and extent of his infractions, Archbald was convicted on five of thirteen articles.[95]

In 1933 Judge Harold Louderback, U.S. District Judge for the Northern District of California, had articles of impeachment brought against him by the House "for conduct prejudicial to the dignity of the judiciary in appointing incompetent receivers, for the method of selecting receivers, for allowing fees that seem excessive, and for a high degree of indifference to the interest of litigants in receiverships."[96] Louderback's Senate trial consumed nearly an entire month during FDR's "first one hundred Days" of the New Deal, one of the busiest legislative periods in congressional history. A lengthy parade of witnesses, including a faith healer who had to be brought in on a stretcher, filed through the Senate chamber to testify. Democrats charged Republicans with using the trial to delay a banking reform bill, a charge Republicans denied.[97] By all accounts, tempers in the Senate frayed as witness after witness cast doubt on the charges.[98] When the Senate finally did vote, Louderback was acquitted on all five articles. Only on the fifth and last charge, a summation of the preceding four, did the vote even reach a majority, still eight votes shy of the necessary two-thirds.[99]

Judge Louderback's trial again brought to the fore the problem of attendance at impeachment trials. A year following the proceeding, Senator Henry F. Ashurst (D-Ariz.), chairman of the Judiciary Committee, offered a resolution that eventually would be codified into Rule XI to permit the Senate to appoint a committee of senators to receive evidence and take testimony in the trial of any impeachment.

In the next impeachment trial, that of Florida District Judge Halsted Ritter in 1936, the accused was charged with a wide range of improprieties that included practicing law while a judge, filing false income tax returns, extortion, and an omnibus charge of misconduct. Ritter's counsel argued that the judge had committed no offense that merited a high crime or misdemeanor and was only at fault for exercising poor judgment. Ritter was acquitted by narrow margins on each of the first six charges. On the seventh, however, the omnibus article combining the previous six, Ritter was found guilty, by exactly the required two-thirds vote, of bringing his court into scandal and disrepute.[100]

It would be fifty years before the House would engage in another impeachment proceeding. In 1986, District Judge Harry E. Claiborne of Nevada had, in the words of Representative James F. Sensenbrenner (R-Wis.), "challenged the Congress of the United States to impeach him and to place him on trial in the U.S. Senate."[101] Judge Claiborne was imprisoned following conviction for making false statements on his income tax returns, without resigning his office as judge and continuing to receive his salary. Accordingly, his refusal to step down from the bench reminded members of Congress that the only method of removing a federal judge is through impeachment.[102] After less than a day of hearings, the Judiciary Committee reported impeachment articles to the House, which promptly forwarded them to the Senate for trial. The Senate designated a committee to hear evidence and then report to the full body for a vote. After closing arguments, the Senate swiftly voted to impeach Claiborne but rejected the charge that his conviction and imprisonment fit under the category of high crimes and misdemeanors.[103]

Claiborne's trial was the first in a series of three successive judicial impeachments. Within months of removing Claiborne from the bench, Congress proceeded against another district court judge, Judge Alcee L. Hastings of south Florida. Hastings was tried for bribery and solicitation of bribes, but was acquitted by a trial jury. Hastings was nonetheless impeached in the House of Representatives and convicted in the Senate in 1989. In 1993, he took his seat in the House of Representatives, as a duly elected Democratic member of Congress from south Florida's 23rd District, a seat he still holds. Even before the trial of Judge Hastings had begun, the House presented the Senate with articles of impeachment against Judge Walter L. Nixon. Nixon had been convicted of making false statements before a grand jury, which was later embodied within the articles of impeachment against him. The full Senate convicted Nixon on two articles, and acquitted him on a third.

Table 2.6 reports how long the congressional impeachments previous to President Clinton took from the initiation of impeachment until the committee reported its recommendation, how the House approved articles of impeachment, and how the Senate voted on the articles. Also reported is the length of time from the Senate's receipt of articles of impeachment until the end of the trial, from senators' swearing-in until votes on articles were completed, and the actual number of days the Senate considered impeachment in either the planning or trial phases. Data are also provided for the number of witnesses heard by the Senate and the number of days witnesses testified at the trial.[104]

Near Impeachments

In addition to those impeachment investigations leading to Senate trials, there have been a number of instances in which the impeachment process was initiated in the House of Representatives but did not result in articles of impeachment because of the resignation of the targeted official.[105] In 1872, for example, the House adopted a resolution authorizing the Judiciary Committee to investigate the conduct of District Judge Mark H. Delahay. The following year the committee proposed an impeachment resolution for high crimes and misdemeanors in office.[106] Although the House adopted the resolution, Judge Delahay resigned from office before articles of impeachment were prepared against him, and the House took no further action.

ble 2.6. Impeachment Data

	Mean	Media	Range
ouse			
Time from initiation of impeachment to issuance of the committee report.	166 days	66 days	2 days (Andrew Johnson, 1868) to 995 days (Halstead Ritter, 1936)
Time from initiation of impeachment inquiry until the House vote to impeach.	191 days	79 days	4 days (Andrew Johnson, 1868) to 1,006 days (Halstead Ritter, 1936)
Time from initiation of impeachment to approval of articles.	227 days	121 days	11 days (Andrew Johnson, 1868) to 1,013 days (Halstead Ritter, 1936)
nate			
Time between the Senate's notification of impeachment until the vote on the articles.	198 days	185 days	37 days (Halstead Ritter, 1933) to 439 days (Alcee Hastings, 1988–1989)
Time from when senators were sworn in at the beginning of the trial until the vote on the articles.	79 days	44 days	3 days (Alcee Hastings, 1988–1989) to 266 days (James Peck, 1830)
Actual number of days Senate considered impeachment after articles were approved in the House, in either the planning or the trial phases.	23 days	22 days	6 days (West Humphreys, 1962) to 48 days (William Belknap, 1876)
Actual number of days Senate heard testimony from witnesses (excludes four trials).	9 days	7 days	1 day (West Humphreys, 1962) to 18 days (Alcee Hastings, 1988–1989)
Actual number of witnesses Senate heard testimony from (excludes four trials).	33 witnesses	41 witnesses	5 witnesses (West Humphreys, 1862) to 55 witnesses (Alcee Hastings, 1988–1989)
Time between the beginning of the investigation in the House and the end of the Senate trial.	394 days	390 days	96 days (Andrew Johnson, 1868) to 1,052 days (Halstead Ritter, 1836)

URCE: Adapted from David C. Huckabee, *Impeachment: Days and Dates of Consideration in the House and* *nate*, CRS, Order Code RS20018 GOV, January 13, 1999, Washington, D.C., Congressional Research Service.

The most famous of these near cases was in 1974, when the House Judiciary Committee filed its report on the impeachment inquiry with regard to President Nixon's involvement in the Watergate burglary and the subsequent cover-up (1972–1974). The committee report included a resolution impeaching Nixon and setting forth three articles of impeachment against him. The first article alleged that the president delayed, impeded, and obstructed the investigation of the burglary by withholding evidence, counseling witnesses to lie under oath in court, lying about his own involvement, interfering with the Department of Justice as it sought to inquire into the burglary, paying hush money to the defendants, leaking Department of Justice information to defendants, and misusing the Central Intelligence Agency (CIA) to cover up the entire affair. The second article claimed that Nixon took part in a more far-reaching subversion of government by misusing the FBI, the Internal Revenue Service (IRS), the CIA, and the Secret Service for unauthorized, political, and oppressive purposes. A third article accused Nixon of withholding subpoenaed information from the Judiciary Committee by refusing, against law, to deliver papers and tapes to the House Judiciary Committee. Nixon resigned before the House voted on the articles of impeachment.

Cases Tabled in Committee

In some instances impeachment resolutions are introduced but no action is taken on them beyond committee referral. For example, in recent congresses impeachment resolutions have been introduced with respect to a number of executive branch officers: a resolution to impeach the ambassador to Iran in 1976 (referred to House Judiciary Committee); a resolution to impeach the U.S. ambassador to the United Nations in 1977 (referred to House Judiciary Committee); a resolution directing the House Judiciary Committee to investigate whether to impeach the U.S. attorney general in 1978 (referred to House Rules and Administration); resolutions to impeach the chairman of the board of governors of the Federal Reserve System in 1983 and 1985 (referred to Subcommittee on Monopolies and Commercial Law of the House Judiciary Committee); resolutions to impeach members of the Federal Open Market Committee in 1983 and 1985 (referred to Subcommittee on Monopolies and Commercial Law of the House Judiciary Committee); resolutions to impeach President Ronald Reagan in 1983 and 1987 (referred to House Judiciary Committee); and two resolutions to impeach President George H. W. Bush in 1991 (referred to the House Judiciary Committee).[107]

Censure

"Censure," suggests one student of Congress, is an alternative to impeachment for the punishment of "erring federal officeholders with no express constitutional basis."[108] Considered a compromise between an impeachment and
taking no congressional action, it typically expresses congressional disapproval of executive and judicial branch officials in the nature of a "sense
of the Congress," or a sense of the Senate or House resolutions developed in
congressional practice as ways for members to state opinions or facts in a
nonbinding manner. The infrequent calls for censure—primarily in the nineteenth century—most often involved financial misconduct, actions beyond
an official's legal or constitutional authority, or disagreement over policy.[109]
Unlike a congressional punishment of one of its own members, or an
impeachment and trial of the president, there is no express constitutional provision authorizing censure. In early congresses some lawmakers who
opposed resolutions that declared either an opinion of praise or disapproval of
the executive cited a lack of express constitutional authority for either chamber to pass a formal resolution of censure or disapproval stating an opinion
on the conduct or propriety of an executive officer.[110] Others argued that
impeachment was the proper, and exclusive, constitutional response for Congress to entertain when the conduct of federal civil officers is called into
question, rather than a resolution of censure.[111]

Both the House and Senate have, on infrequent occasions, expressed their
disapproval, reproof, or censure of executive officials, including the president, or certain of their actions in simple resolutions.[112] The most visible presidential censures involved the Senate censure of President Andrew Jackson,
the House censure of President John Tyler, and both houses' condemnation
of President James K. Polk as part of a resolution praising General Zachary
Taylor. In 1837, following a political clash over the Bank of the United
States, the Senate adopted a resolution broadly censuring President Andrew
Jackson for vetoing a reauthorization of the bank and subsequently redirect-
ing U.S. funds to various state banks. Senate opponents, such as Daniel Webster and Henry Clay, considered this action dictatorial and in conflict with
the Constitution. In turn, Jackson issued and sent to the Senate a strong
protestation of the censure concerning both the prerogatives of his office and
the powers of the Senate to censure.[113] Three years later, with even greater
fanfare, the resolution was reversed after Jackson's Democrats regained the
majority. Table 2.7 identifies fourteen instances of congressional attempts to
censure officers of the executive and judicial branches.

Table 2.7. Congressional Attempts to Censure Officials in Other Branches

	Official	Chamber	Disposition	Legislative Mechanism	Issue	Censure Language
1793	Secretary of the Treasury Alexander Hamilton	House	Defeated	Nine resolutions	Action beyond authority; withholding information from Congress	Statements of general principle (2); actions characterized; no judgment of individual (6); transmit resolutions to president (1)
1800	President John Adams	House	Defeated	Three resolutions	Action beyond authority; interference with judiciary	Actions characterized no judgment of individual
1834	President Andrew Jackson[a]	Senate	Adopted	Two resolutions	Action beyond authority; including removal of officers	Actions characterized; no judgment of individual
1842	President John Tyler	House	Adopted	Motion to agree to committee report	Action beyond authority; repeated vetoes	Actions characterized; no judgment of individual
1848	President James K. Polk	House	Adopted as amendment; no final action	Amendment to amendment to motion to refer joint resolution with instructions	Action beyond authority	Actions characterized; no judgment of individual
1860	Secretary of the Navy Isaac Toucey	House	Adopted	Five resolutions	Financial ethics, government contracts	Actions characterized (3); "Reproof" of president and secretary (1); "censure" of secretary (1)

Year	Official	Chamber	Disposition	Form	Grounds	Characterization
1862	Former Secretary of War Simon Cameron and Secretary of the Navy Gideon Welles	House	Adopted (Cameron); defeated (Welles)	One resolution for each	Financial ethics, government contracts	"Censure"
1862	Former President James Buchanan	Senate	Tabled	Resolution	Policy; failure to prevent secession	"Censure and condemnation"
1886	Attorney General A.H. Garland	Senate	Adopted	Four resolutions	Removal of officers	Adopting committee report (1); characterizing actions (2); "condemnation" (1)
1894	U.S. Circuit Judge J. G. Jenkins	House	Reported from committee; no floor action	Resolution	Financial ethics	"Condemnation"
1895	U.S. District Judge Augustus J. Ricks	House	Reported from committee; no floor action	Resolution	Financial ethics	"Censure"
1896	Ambassador Thomas Bayard	House	Adopted	Two resolutions	Partisan remarks in speeches abroad	Actions characterized (1); "Sense of the House . . . Condemn and censure" (1)
1973	President Richard M. Nixon	House	Referred to committee	Concurrent resolution	Removal of officers	"Sense of Congress . . . Censure and condemn"
1974	President Richard M. Nixon	House	Referred to committee	Resolution	Actions beyond authority	"Censure"

SOURCE: Adapted from Richard S. Beth, *Censure of Executive and Judicial Branch Officials: Past Congressional Proceedings*, CRS, Report No. 98-833 GOV, December 11, 1998, Washington, D.C., Congressional Research Service.

[a] In January 1837, with less than two months left in Jackson's term of office, the Senate formally expunged its censure from the record, by a vote of 24 to 19.

Censure typically takes the form of a simple resolution in either the House or Senate and is formally adopted by a vote of that body, thus indicating that censure carries no penalty, other than political embarrassment of a formal condemnation by Congress. These instances can take place without a formal trial or even allowing the president to present a defense.

Resignation

In some cases the timing of the alleged impropriety or criminal act, such as near the end of the official's term of office, avoids impeachment. For example, Vice President Aaron Burr shot and killed former Treasury secretary Alexander Hamilton in a duel. Since Burr's term was set to expire less than eight months after the duel, the House never launched impeachment proceedings against him, even though he was indicted for murder in both New York and New Jersey. Burr was never arrested and prosecuted.

CONCLUSION

Impeachment is an extraordinary mechanism, "a lawyer's solution to a statesman's problem," John Labovitz writes.[114] But, as Roger Davidson and Walter Oleszek caution, it is not always the most effective way to remove delinquent officials, especially when Congress can restrict wrongdoing by other means.[115] Among the host of less time-consuming alternatives legislators often do use are committee hearings on government scandals and oversight hearings of executive branch operations.[116] Probes into some of the nation's most notorious scandals, including Crédit Mobilier, Teapot Dome, Watergate, and Iran-Contra, while not resulting in impeachments, did implicate many who were forced to relinquish their government positions, and a number were later tried and convicted of criminal offenses.

While the Framers envisaged the occasional necessity of initiating impeachment proceedings, they put in place only a very general framework, leaving many questions open and room for change. As legal scholar Michael J. Gerhardt suggests, impeachment, as a formal legal proceeding, is not especially potent at providing for or supporting removal from office.[117] Rather, impeachment rests on a set of inherently political factors, such as how seriously lawmakers perceive any wrongdoing by an individual, as well as the nexus between that official's duties and the degree of misconduct.[118]

Members of Congress are frequently guilty of viewing impeachment as a legal affair when, to the contrary, the process is fundamentally political, part and parcel with an institution increasingly besieged by partisan and ideological differences.[119] Both presidential impeachments (Andrew Johnson, 1868; Bill Clinton, 1998–1999) were partisan by nature, proceedings wherein lawmakers disputed both the facts and the threshold for conviction along party lines.[120] While the structure of impeachment may appear judicial, a majority of members of Congress define the structural parameters: whether and how to proceed, what evidence to consider, and ultimately what is and is not impeachable.[121]

The phrase "impeachable offense" is the subject of continuing debate, one that pits broad constructionists, who view impeachment as a political weapon, against narrow constructionists, who regard impeachment as being limited to offenses indictable at common law.[122] At the turn of the twentieth century the British observer James Bryce likened impeachment to a "one-hundred-ton gun which needs complex machinery to bring it into position, an enormous charge to fire it, and a large mark to aim at."[123] Stated more pointedly by legal scholar Warren S. Grimes, impeachment is an attractive way for lawmakers to resolve uneasy questions that hold no certain answer in favor of an immediate political result that is palatable to a working majority.[124]

Over the years the gravity of the impeachment process has often dictated some "principled" basis on which to proceed, since the stress that impeachment places on a legislative institution is almost unimaginably high.[125] Yet, for all the moral posturing and legalistic rhetoric, the Clinton impeachment was just as much a political proceeding as those that had gone before. The Republicans who sought to impeach Clinton believed they had found a means for getting rid of a president intensely disliked by their core electoral constituency, and that public opinion, and even most of the Democrats, would eventually come around to their side. But the congressional Democrats also had every political incentive to rally around their party leader, who was enthusiastically supported by the Democratic core constituencies. Both sides of the aisle used the impeachment process to try to "spin" the middle ground of public opinion over to their side. The proceedings were essentially political from start to finish, in the Senate, despite its constitutional role as the "jury" in the impeachment trial, as much as in the more overtly partisan House of Representatives.

As we shall see in the chapters that follow, the Judiciary Committee of the House of Representatives, the panel charged with investigating the Clinton-Lewinsky scandal and reporting articles of impeachment, had, over time, become a bastion of each party's ideological core rather than a consensus-oriented bipartisan panel. Simply put, it was a body almost waiting for a catalyst to ignite an impeachment inquiry. In the Senate's impeachment trial members' votes were as partisan as those of their House colleagues, although the Senate's conduct of the trial was also governed by concerns for the reputation and legitimacy of the chamber, something that did not obtain in the House proceedings.[126] Senators claimed impartiality as jurors, but the trial proceeding was a finely tuned, orchestrated event.[127]

3
Ignoring Electoral Outcomes: Republican Members of the House Judiciary Committee

To think about abandoning it [the inquiry] would have been a cowardly act. We would have been surrendering in the face of conduct that we felt was wrong and damaging to the office of President. If you had considered an opinion poll—and an election is nothing but a larger opinion poll—and abandoned impeachment, we would have been saying 'Mr. President, you are above the law.' Had the election diverted us from our job I think we would have shown a lack of principle. We felt it was our duty to proceed as we did.
—Representative Henry J. Hyde (R-Ill.)

Remember you have different constituencies to consider. As far as the Republican primary constituency is concerned, a vote against impeachment signifies a potential risk.
—Representative Charles T. Canady (R-Fla.)

An age-old conflict of representation is whether legislators should govern as instructed delegates and respond directly to their constituents or govern as trustees and use their own judgment to take positions they deem responsible, even when their constituents disagree with them. Most influential works on the contemporary Congress isolate reelection as the primary force that makes other legislative goals possible, thus explaining a great deal of congressional organization, legislative output, and behavior.[1] If reelection is the essential goal, it would appear to follow that members should carefully heed the dictates of public opinion as expressed in elections and preelection public opinion polls. Moreover, the Framers of the Constitution clearly intended the House of Representatives to be the body in the new federal government that would most closely reflect and heed the popular will.

Yet the Republican House majority's decision to proceed with an impeach-ment inquiry on the Lewinsky affair in September 2002 did not reflect the view of the American public as reflected in public opinion polls. If we hold to the axiom that the imperative of reelection dictates the actions and decisions of House members, then this outcome appears to make little sense. Two months later the GOP became the first party not holding the presidency to lose seats in the second midterm election of a two-term presidency since the 1820s, and it was apparent that a large part of the reason they did so poorly at the polls (rel-atively) in 1998 was precisely because of the hard-line stance that Republicans on the Judiciary Committee had adopted on the Lewinsky matter.[2] Thus it appears that Republican lawmakers ignored the clear will of voters as expressed not only in opinion polls but also in an actual national election in their deci-sion to continue with the impeachment inquiry and ultimately vote to impeach President Bill Clinton.[3] According to conventional logic these actions theoret-ically placed at risk both Republican members' future reelection as well as their party's legislative goals. This chapter examines how Republican Judiciary Committee members came to reach the decisions they made.[4]

THE JUDICIARY COMMITTEE AND ITS REPUBLICAN MEMBERS

In their seminal work on congressional committees, Christopher J. Deering and Steven S. Smith (building on earlier work by Richard F. Fenno, Jr.) clas-sify the House Judiciary Committee as a "policy" body, one that attracts members motivated by a desire to make good public policy.[5] This contrasts sharply to "constituency" committees (e.g., Agriculture) in which the moti-vation to join is based largely on district or reelection concerns, or to "pres-tige" committees (e.g., Ways and Means or Appropriations) for which power within the House and a lengthy House career are the primary motives behind membership. In short, there is little to be gained in terms of electoral inter-est or prestige by serving on the Judiciary Committee. Members gravitate to the Judiciary panel because of their enjoyment of the law or their keen inter-est in policy making in the many sensitive and divisive issues over which the committee has jurisdiction, such as abortion, civil rights, and tort reform.

Interviews with several Republican Judiciary members who voted to impeach President Clinton in December 1998 corroborate this. Representa-tives Charles T. Canady (Fla.) and Howard Coble (N.C.) indicated that their interest in the law and legal issues was a critical factor in determining their membership of the committee. Canady explained:

I was interested in Judiciary because of my background as a lawyer, and I had served in the Criminal Justice Committee of the Florida state House. The Judiciary Committee in the U.S. House deals with a range of issues that are interesting from my perspective as a lawyer. It also deals with several "hot button" issues that are important to me. I'm glad that I served on Judiciary. I wouldn't trade the opportunity for anything. In terms of political benefit, it's not that great. The issues we deal with tend to be controversial and make one group of people happy and the other group upset. In some districts there's probably a net advantage, but it's not like Appropriations or Commerce. It's not hard to get an assignment on Judiciary. When I got to the House some people wanted me there. It's not sought after much but there aren't seats going begging as there are on some committees.[6]

Coble had this to say:

I was a lawyer by trade and I had served on the Judiciary Committee in the state legislature, so it seemed like a nice fit. I looked at other committees, especially the Commerce Committee, but it was almost impossible to get on the Commerce Committee as a freshman in those days. Two terms later after [former North Carolina Representative] Jim Broyhill had been appointed to the Senate, my good friend Tom Bliley—we were old tennis buddies—said he could get me Broyhill's seat on the Commerce Committee. We met with Alex Macmillan, who had a district in the Charlotte area. I said I didn't want to give up Judiciary, but Alex said he was willing to give up everything to be on Commerce, and he got the seat. Bliley said, "You may want to take him [Coble] to see the House psychiatrist!" He meant that on high-profile committees like Ways and Means, Appropriations, and Commerce, fund raising comes easier. On the other hand, if you give up a seat on a committee you give up your seniority, and I would have started at the bottom on Commerce.[7]

Policy committees by their very nature are more polarized and partisan, because members seek to change public policy in a certain direction, which is likely to be bitterly resisted. Given that ideology and partisanship now largely overlap in the House, these divisions invariably fall along party lines, particularly on issues about which the parties have strongly polarized views. The Judiciary Committee is more polarized than most committees because it has jurisdiction over the high-profile issues that define the so-called "culture war" between the core electoral constituencies of the two major parties:

abortion, religious freedom, the death penalty, minimum mandated sentences, bankruptcy, school busing, and flag burning. For this reason the committee tends to attract socially conservative Republicans and socially liberal Democrats rather than moderates of either party. No Republican "moderate," for instance, sat on the Judiciary Committee in the 105th Congress (1997–1999). The mean ADA (Americans for Democratic Action) score of the twenty GOP members was 5.5 percent, and no member had a higher score than fifteen.[8] In terms of *Congressional Quarterly*'s Conservative Coalition score the committee's Republicans had a score of ninety-three, two points higher than the Republican chamber mean of ninety-one, while committee Democrats' score of twenty-one was seventeen points below the Democratic chamber mean of thirty-eight.[9]

Table 3.1 reflects just how polarized Republicans on the Judiciary Committee have become since the Nixon impeachment. Where the median ACA (Americans for Constitutional Action) score for Republicans who sat on the 1974 Rodino Committee was seventy-three, with a range of twenty-seven to ninety-six, during the Clinton impeachment, on the Hyde Committee, Republicans averaged twenty-two ACA points higher (ninety-five), with a minimal range of eighty-four to one hundred. (These increased differences are strong and statistically significant, $t = -4.214$, $p = 0.001$.)

Committee members' comments further paint a picture of polarization. Representative Henry J. Hyde (Ill.), the committee's chairman and the longest-serving Republican member (elected 1974), saw the preponderance of lawyers on the committee as a contribution to its frequently polarized debates. "You have 'verbalizers' on the Judiciary Committee," he said: "Lawyers who think they are intellectuals and are contentious and opinionated. Many of the issues that we deal with—abortion, religious freedom, the death penalty, minimum mandated sentences, bankruptcy reform—are issues where you are going to have polarizing views heard and expressed by members or interests before the committee. It's stimulating and never boring."[10]

Comments by Representatives Coble and Lindsey Graham (S.C.), however, indicate that the day-to-day work of the committee is not nearly as polarized as the public rhetoric might make it appear. On many of the more technical or legal questions that the committee deals with there is, apparently, a fair amount of cooperation and bipartisanship: "It's a very partisan, highly polarized, committee," declared Representative Coble. "My subcommittee is not, because intellectual property issues—copyrights, trademarks, and patents—do not come with partisan colors. But crime bills, abortion, and prayer bills tend to define Republicans on one side and Democrats on the other, and the debate is very volatile, polarized, and partisan. Henry Hyde

Table 3.1. Ideological Leanings of House Judiciary Republican Committee Members, 1974 and 1998

1974 (Nixon Impeachment)	ACA[a] Rating	1998 (Clinton Impeachment)	ACU Rating
Hutchinson, Edward (Mich.)	93	Hyde, Henry J. (Ill.)	92
McClory, Robert (Ill.)	40	Sensenbrenner, F. James (Wis.)	92
Smith, Henry P., III, (N.Y.)[b]	57	McCollum, Bill (Fla.)	84
Sandman, Charles W. (N.J.)[c]	86	Gekas, George W. (Pa.)	84
Railsback, Thomas F. (Ill.)	46	Coble, Howard (N.C.)	96
Wiggins, Charles E. (Calif.)	73	Smith, Lamar S. (Texas)	92
Dennis, David W. (Ind.)[b]	96	Gallegly, Elton (Calif.)	76
Fish, Hamilton, Jr. (N.Y.)	50	Canady, Charles T. (Fla.)	88
Mayne, Wisley (Iowa)[b]	61	Inglis, Bob (S.C.)[c]	100
Hogan, Lawrence J. (Md.)[b]	61	Goodlatte, Bob (Va.)	100
Butler, M. Caldwell (Va.) .	87	Buyer, Stephen E. (Ind.)	88
Cohen, William S. (Maine)	27	Bryant, Ed (Tenn.)	100
Lott, Trent (Miss.)	85	Chabot, Steve (Ohio)	96
Froehlich, Harold (Wis.)[b]	—	Barr, Bob (Ga.)	100
Moorhead, Carlos J. (Calif.)	87	Jenkins, William L. (Tenn.)	100
Maraziti, Joseph J. (N.J.)[b]	—	Hutchinson, Asa (Ark.)	92
Latta, Delbert L. (Ohio)	86	Pease, Edward A. (Ind.)	100
		Cannon, Christopher (Utah)	95
		Rogan, James E. (Calif.)	100
		Graham, Lindsey (S.C.)	88
		Bono, Mary (Calif.)	98
Median	73		95
Range	69		24
Mean[d]	69.00		93.38

SOURCE: Adapted from Philip D. Duncan and Christine C. Lawrence, eds., *Politics in America 1998, 105th Congress* (Washington, D.C.: CQ Press, 1997); Philip D. Duncan and Brian Nutting, eds., *Politics in America 2000, 106th Congress* (Washington, D.C.: CQ Press, 1999); and Michael Barone, Grant Ujifusa and Douglas Matthews, *The Almanac of American Politics 1974* (Boston: Gambit, 1973) and *The Almanac of American Politics 1976* (New York: Dutton, 1975).

[a]Americans for Constitutional Action (ACA) was a precursor of the ACU.

[b]Members who either were defeated or retired in the 1974 congressional elections. Rating is for 1972. In the cases of Representatives Froehlich and Maraziti data is unobtainable.

[c]ACU scores for Representative Inglis are from 1996.

[d]Difference of means: t = -4.214; d.f. = 15.96; p = 0.001. Corrected t-test due to unequal variances in the two groups.

has needed the patience of the biblical character Job on several occasions, but he has been a good chairman."[11] According to Representative Graham:

On certain issues the committee is very partisan and polarized. Guns, abortion, burning the flag are extremely high-profile issues. But on our day-to-day work there is a lot of crossover while crafting legislation on the courts system, legal reform, property rights, access to the Internet, or asbestos, which we are working on today. A lot of our work is on these "nondesigner" issues. Where you see us divided is where you see the country divided, and that's why you have conservative Republicans and liberal Democrats on the committee. Personally, I get along with the guys on the other side, especially Bill Delahunt (Mass.). We have philosophical disagreements on the major issues, but day-to-day we do a good job.[12]

THE STARR REPORT AND THE OPENING OF
THE IMPEACHMENT INQUIRY

While the Judiciary Committee might not be polarized on all issues, it was immediately apparent in the summer of 1998 that any impeachment inquiry into President Clinton's conduct would arouse members' most partisan passions. Even before the inquiry opened, the Clinton administration had, with considerable success, attempted to undermine the character and the allegations of Independent Counsel Kenneth Starr.[13] Many Democrats on the committee—such as the second-most-senior Democrat, Representative Barney Frank of Massachusetts—were already among the president's staunchest defenders in the House, while some Republican members (most notably former Representative Bob Barr of Georgia) were among his most vocal critics.

When it became apparent in early September 1998 that Independent Counsel Starr would submit a report on the Lewinsky affair that might provide evidence for the possible impeachment of the president, there was speculation in the news media that precisely because of the Judiciary panel's reputation for partisanship and ideological polarization, the House might revert to earlier practice and establish a select or special committee to examine the evidence and conduct an impeachment inquiry. According to the Republican members interviewed, however, this was never a serious option. In fact, most believed that taking the inquiry away from the Judiciary Committee would only intensify committee partisanship. "It was better that the inquiry stayed in Judiciary even with its partisan flavor," said Representative Coble. "If you had started farming it out to a special committee it would have been an admission that the committee of jurisdiction couldn't handle it."[14] Representative Canady added:

A special committee would have been worse. When it was clear that we needed to consider whether to impeach the president, the leadership gave consideration to a select committee. I wrote to the Speaker that I thought it was a bad idea. I thought that then and I think that now. A select committee would have been subject to the accusation that the Speaker had "stacked" the process against the president. It would only have dragged Newt Gingrich into the middle of the controversy, and his "hand-picked" committee would have focused the process on the Speaker and undermined the credibility of the process. Bad as it was in the Judiciary Committee, it would have been qualitatively worse in a select committee.[15]

Less certainty existed among committee Republicans over the next significant decision they had to take: how much of the vast amount of information and testimony contained in the Starr Report should be released to the public, particularly the more salacious material relating to the president's encounters with Ms. Lewinsky and the video of the president's testimony before the federal grand jury investigating the Lewinsky matter. The decision to release much of this evidence and the showing of the videotape on national television appeared to backfire with the public and actually increased sympathy for President Clinton and his family. Representatives Christopher B. Cannon (Utah), Asa Hutchinson (Ark.), and Lindsey O. Graham (S.C.) all believed that the Republicans mishandled this issue, which ultimately impeded their case against the president. "It was a mistake and it certainly hurt us," Cannon noted. "What is sometimes missed is the context of the times. A great deal of money and effort had been spent on this, and when it reached the time that we got the report we just used a scanner to convert it to text and released it on the internet before anybody had had a chance to see what it said. It was clear that the Democrats had better access to information than we had. We didn't know about the sex in the report. If we had, we could have taken the latitude of removing some of the more salacious bits."[16] According to Representative Hutchinson: "With hindsight it might have been wiser to keep more of the report confidential, until it was needed during the proceedings. The video should not have been released in the manner that it was, because it was not good public relations. Evidence in a court proceeding is normally only released when it's being used. It would have been better to have released the evidence when we needed it, and also more meaningful to the public."[17] Representative Graham stated:

> We made two mistakes early on. First, the motion to release everything was originally a Democratic motion, sponsored by John Dingell (D-Mich.) and Gene Taylor (D-Miss.). When this thing broke the Democrats in the House were really leery of Clinton. I thought we should have accepted their motion, because then it would have been their request not ours. Of

course, the White House did a good job of spinning the videotape by raising media expectations. I know that a lot of reporters felt used, but the
video certainly generated sympathy for the president. When Whitewater,
Filegate, and campaign finance reform never got legs, it was easier to say
that this one was "all about sex," and an overreaction to a general misdeed.
The second thing was [Representative Howard] Berman's (D-Calif.) idea
of a time limit on the investigation. That would have made our efforts
more bipartisan.[18]

By contrast Chairman Hyde and Representative Canady believed they
were in a "no-win" situation regarding the release of the material. Democrats
insisted on it for fear that Republicans might conceal material exonerating
the president, and, as Hyde reports, the Republican majority did not want to
expose themselves to a charge of concealing information:

> We could have been more selective in the portions of the Starr Report that
> were released, but the story that has not been told is that the Democrats
> wanted it all released. Mr. Gephardt and Mr. Dingell were so fearful that
> we would withhold material that would be exculpatory for the president
> and then selectively leak harmful material, that the idea of guarding
> against that perception forced us to release everything, although we did
> redact names and phone numbers to protect innocent people. On the sala-
> cious material, I would add that at no time did we get any cooperation
> from the White House admitting the nature and extent of the relationship
> between the president and Ms. Lewinsky. We had denial after denial after
> denial and then convoluted definitions of certain acts. All the salacious
> matter might have been avoided if the president had been forthright.[19]

Representative Canady had this to say:

> As far as the video is concerned, I felt sorry for the man as I watched the
> president take out a little piece of paper and read it. It was a sad thing to
> see the leader of our country in such a jam. But if we hadn't released the
> tape we would have been attacked for not releasing it. As a matter of pol-
> icy we leaned in favor of the public having access to information. And
> while some of the information on some of the sexual conduct could have
> been withheld, we thought there was an overall public interest in letting
> the public have access to the information. We might have been better off
> to take the heat for withholding some information, but would the public
> have reacted more favorably? I don't know.[20]

With public opinion overwhelmingly against impeachment after the release of the Starr Report, and with the midterm elections only a month away, the full House passed a resolution 258 to 176, directing the Judiciary Committee to open an impeachment inquiry on October 8, 1998.[21] Although not a matter of high principle, unlike the actual impeachment votes to follow, the vote became a partisan showdown.[22] All 227 House Republicans and thirty-one House Democrats (none of whom sat on the Judiciary Committee) voted in favor. In such a context it was inevitable that the inquiry would be thoroughly partisan, with both sides of the aisle aiming to score political points among the wider public, with an eye on the imminent November poll that had already more or less turned into a referendum on impeachment.

The Republicans had hoped that the Clinton inquiry would follow a course similar to the 1974 Watergate inquiry and that a bipartisan consensus would eventually emerge over the president's misdeeds.[23] But with President Clinton enjoying high poll ratings in a booming economy, and given the controversial nature of the charges against him, there was little incentive for committee Democrats to desert their chief. From the outset it thus seemed highly unlikely that the Republican majority on the Judiciary Committee would have any support from committee Democrats, and the thirty-one Democratic votes for the inquiry on the House floor was far lower than the figure Republicans required in order to give an impression of bipartisan support to the media and the public. Chairman Hyde voiced his frustration: "We had the precedent of the Nixon impeachment, when congressional Republicans went to Nixon and suggested he resign. I thought that there might be some courageous Democrats who would emulate the Republican record and I was wrong. I thought, naively, that once the total story was told in a coherent, comprehensive way, the public would move closer to our position and the support that the president had would evaporate once the details were related coherently rather than in sound bites. But when the whole story was told it did not move the public."[24]

Representative Canady's retrospective view was that Republicans made a tactical error in adhering too closely to the Nixon precedent of an open-ended inquiry, and that they should have accepted Democratic demands for a time limit on the investigation. Yet he too admitted that in the absence of a shift in public opinion, there was never much prospect of significant bipartisan support for impeachment:

> There were maybe a couple of things that we didn't handle well and might have helped increase our credibility. Our first mistake was to insist on following the model of the Nixon inquiry: that is, an open-ended investigation

into the misdeeds of the president. It would probably have been wiser to limit the scope of the inquiry to the matters related in the Independent Counsel's referral. If we had done that we would have gotten significantly more than thirty Democratic votes for the resolution of inquiry on the House floor. Another bogus issue was the length of the inquiry. The resolution of inquiry adopted by the last Congress could not outlive the last Congress, which ended on January 3rd, 1999, according to the natural operation of the rules of the House. It would have served our interests well to state that the inquiry would end not later than January 3rd, and deflected one of the Democrats' lines of attack. Even if we did not give them everything they wished, more Democrats would have voted for a narrower resolution, so that was a mistake on our part.

I don't know if this would have affected the ultimate outcome, which was maybe determined before the referral was even sent to us. It was difficult to get more Democratic support because in most Democratic districts there would have been a big political price to pay for going against the president, so we never had much hope of great Democratic support. Of course, if public opinion had shifted it would have been a different story, more importantly among the Democrats in the Senate.[25]

Democratic support was even less likely to be forthcoming after the party defied the usual midterm trend and gained House seats. According to the civics-book view of the American political process, the people had spoken and they evidently did not wish to see the president impeached. Yet, in defiance of this logic, Republicans persisted with their inquiry and the Judiciary Committee Republicans almost unanimously (with only one defector on one of the four articles) voted to impeach the president in December 1998. This occurred because Republican Judiciary Committee members and virtually all the Republicans in the House as a whole came to understand that in accordance with the real electoral logic of the contemporary House, a vote in favor of impeachment was actually the much safer option.

THE IMPACT OF THE 1998 ELECTION AND THE VOTE TO IMPEACH

Immediate media reaction to the November election results assumed that the unexpected Republican losses in the House would ensure that the impeachment inquiry would be quickly terminated by the party leadership before it did further damage to the party's standing. Continuing with the inquiry and a possible impeachment vote before the end of the year also meant that a lame-duck Congress would carry out the second impeachment of a president in U.S. history. Moreover, by this point it also appeared inconceivable that there would be anything like the sixty-seven votes required for conviction in a Senate impeachment trial. There was much speculation, therefore, that the House Republicans would find a way to quietly drop the inquiry and settle for a face-saving compromise with the Democratic minority involving a resolution "censuring" the president for his conduct in the Lewinsky affair. According to interviews with Republican Judiciary Committee members, however, the option of dropping the inquiry was never seriously considered. Representatives Hutchinson and Canady were adamant on this point, as were all the other members interviewed. "The media treated the 1998 election as a referendum on impeachment and they assumed that we would back down," noted Hutchinson. "I always say that the election had nothing to do with the decision to proceed. After the election we Republicans had a conference of all the Republican members of the committee. Henry Hyde said that in the election our party got a shellacking but the election had nothing to do with our responsibility so let's do our duty! So we shocked the world when we decided to go ahead with it."[26] According to Representative Canady:

Some people were thinking about that [calling off the inquiry] after the election, but I wasn't, and no Republican on the Judiciary Committee voiced that sort of sentiment, although we did get it from some of our constituents. It wasn't about the election, and remember that although we didn't do as well as we had hoped, we did win! Our problems in the election were not attributable to impeachment. I was disappointed but I left here [Florida] the day after the election to get ready for a hearing the following Tuesday. The election did not affect our planning and didn't slow me down in my desire to move fast if the facts were as presented by the independent counsel. I will say that the Democrats were stunned that we moved forward. After the election they thought that we would just tuck our tails and slink away. They were taken aback by the fact that we were serious about it and were going to pursue it even if it was not the politically smart thing to do.[27]

The argument that an election has little more validity than a poll is interesting and raises fundamental questions about the role or value of elections in contemporary politics. Arguments based on "duty" as opposed to those based on electoral/rational calculation give pause to those who would explain all congressional behavior according to the latter motives, unless we assume that members are frequently conscious or subconscious liars. Yet even if we adhere to the electoral/rational calculus alone in explicating lawmakers' votes, most of the House Judiciary Committee Republicans' votes were, in fact, quite "rational" considering various facts about the current electoral environment and the kind of districts most of these members represented.

Tables 3.2 and 3.3 illustrate this point. Most of the Judiciary Committee Republicans represented such solidly Republican and conservative districts that any vote to continue with impeachment carried little or no electoral risk. Even in the 1998 elections, only three of the twenty committee members running for reelection were returned with less than 60 percent of the vote, and most increased their winning margins from 1996 to 1998. The overwhelming majority of members also represented districts that were carried by Robert J. "Bob" Dole, the losing Republican presidential nominee with the second worst

Table 3.2. General Election Winning Margins of GOP House Judiciary Committee Members, 1996 and 1998 (by percentage)

	1996	1998	+/–%
Hyde, Henry J. (Ill.), chairman	64.3	67.3	+3.0
Sensenbrenner, F. James, Jr. (Wis.)	74.4	91.4	+17
McCollum, Bill (Fla.)	67.5	65.8	–1.7
Gekas, George W. (Pa.)	72.2	unopposed	—
Coble, Howard (N.C.)	73.4	88.6	+15.2
Smith, Lamar (Texas)	76.4	91.4	+15.0
Gallegly, Elton (Calif.)	59.6	60.1	+0.5
Canady, Charles T. (Fla.)	61.6	unopposed	—
Inglis, Bob (S.C.)[a]	71	—	—
Goodlatte, Robert (W.Va.)	67.0	69.3	+2.3
Buyer, Steve (Ind.)	64.6	62.5	–2.1
Bryant, Ed (Tenn.)	64.1	unopposed	—
Chabot, Steve (Ohio)	54.2	53.0	–1.2
Barr, Bob (Ga.)	57.8	55.4	–2.4
Jenkins, Bill (Tenn.)	63.9	69.1	+5.2
Hutchinson, Asa (Ark.)	55.7	80.7	+25.0
Peace, Ed (Ind.)	62.0	68.9	+6.9
Cannon, Christopher B. (Utah)	51.1	76.9	+25.8
Rogan, James E. (Calif.)	49.9	50.7	+0.8
Graham, Lindsey (S.C.)	60.3	unopposed	—
Bono, Mary (Calif.)[b]	64.1	60.1	–4.0

SOURCE: Authors' calculations from *Politics in America 2000: The 106th Congress* (Washington, D.C.: CQ Press, 2000).

[a]Representative Bob Inglis (S.C.) gave up his seat in 1998 to run for the Senate.

[b]1998 General election percentages for Rep. Mary Bono are for 1998 special and general elections.

national GOP percentage (41 percent) since the 1964 Goldwater landslide. For most of these members a vote against either the inquiry or impeachment might have entailed a serious primary challenge that would have posed more of a threat than any potential Democratic windfall from impeachment in those districts in a general election. The apparent unlikelihood of a Clinton conviction in the Senate would also likely minimize further any negative electoral fallout from a pro-impeachment vote. Finally, the fact that eleven of the twenty-one Republican committee members came from the South—the most conservative and most anti-Clinton region of the country—was also significant. (During the Judiciary Committee's 1974 impeachment inquiry against President Nixon there was only one southerner in the Republican ranks—then Republican Representative Trent Lott of Mississippi.) Most House districts are "safe" for one party or the other, and the seats of Judiciary Committee

Table 3.3. 1996 Presidential Election Results in GOP House Judiciary Committee Members' Districts (by percentage)

	District	Clinton	Dole	Margin
Hyde, Henry J. (Ill.), chairman	6th	43	48	−5
Sensenbrenner, F. James, Jr. (Wis.)	9th	37	52	−15
McCollum, Bill (Fla.)	8th	43	48	−5
Gekas, George W. (Pa.)	17th	37	54	−17
Coble, Howard (N.C.)	6th	42	50	−8
Smith, Lamar (Texas)	21st	30	63	−33
Gallegly, Elton (Calif.)	23rd	46	42	+4
Canady, Charles T. (Fla.)	12th	43	46	−2
Inglis, Bob (S.C.)	4th	37	56	−19
Goodlatte, Robert (Va.)	6th	41	50	−9
Buyer, Steve (Ind.)	5th	37	50	−13
Bryant, Ed (Tenn.)	7th	41	54	−13
Chabot, Steve (Ohio)	1st	50	43	+7
Barr, Bob (Ga.)	7th	40	51	−11
Jenkins, Bill (Tenn.)	1st	37	55	−18
Hutchinson, Asa (Ark.)	3rd	44	45	−1
Pease, Ed (Ind.)	7th	35	52	−17
Cannon, Christopher B. (Utah)	3rd	29	58	−29
Rogan, James E. (Calif.)	27th	49	41	+8
Graham, Lindsey (S.C.)	3rd	39	54	−15
Bono, Mary (Calif.)	44th	44	45	−1
National Margin		49	41	+8

SOURCE: Authors' calculations from *Politics in America 2000: The 106th Congress* (Washington, D.C.: CQ Press, 2000).

members are even "safer" than most because this committee tends to attract committed partisan members from committed partisan districts.

Thus, while rationality may not be the complete story, the makeup of members' districts made a stand on "duty" and "principle" much easier. That members were aware of this is exemplified in their comments on constituent reaction during the impeachment inquiry. "I have a very anti-Clinton district," Representative Graham commented, "and the only time I got complaints was when I voted against the second impeachment article! Every time I asked the president to just reconcile himself with the law, set this right, and avoid impeachment, I got criticism. It was pretty intense there for a while!"[28] Representative Canady declared: "The district was strong for impeachment by way of what we were getting in the office in terms of phone calls and mail. The local paper (owned by the *New York Times* Company) called for Clinton's resignation but did not want him impeached. The *Tampa Tribune*—the second paper in circulation in the district—supported impeachment."[29] Representative Coble explained it this way: "My district is a conservative district and most folks were fed up with the president but were not very comfortable about impeaching him even though they thought he was a scoundrel. One time, though, a woman I formerly dated came marching across the room at an event, and I was scared that she was going to come over and chew my face off but, instead, she said, 'Howard, impeach the son-of-a-bitch!' Bill Clinton had violated the sanctity of her womanhood vicariously."[30]

Although the Republicans did not abandon impeachment in the wake of the November election they did oust their controversial leader, Speaker Newt Gingrich. Ever since the unpopular 1995 government shutdown the Democrats had used the Speaker as the perfect foil, tracing all Republican congressional activity, including impeachment, to Gingrich's "Dinosaur Room" in the Capitol building.[31] They did the same with impeachment, and the idea that Gingrich was ultimately behind the moves to impeach Clinton had a powerful resonance with Democratic voters. In point of fact, Chairman Hyde argued that the Speaker played little to no role in the impeachment deliberations. "That is another mistake that many of the writers have made," he declared. "There was absolutely NO, ZERO, intervention from the leadership during impeachment. They kept their hands off. They didn't call me and they didn't direct me to do anything. Some pundits alleged that Newt Gingrich did this and Tom Delay did that—that is also untrue. They stayed as far away from this as they could, by design."[32]

Despite the decision to continue with the inquiry, there were indications that some Republican committee members were willing to entertain something short of impeachment in the weeks after the election. In an effort to get the White House to acknowledge that potentially criminal offenses had been committed, the committee sent the president a list of eighty-one specific questions on the Lewinsky affair (see the appendixes). With some admission by the president, a few Republican committee members might have been ready to compromise and resolve the issue. Representative Lindsey Graham, the Republican committee member who appeared least comfortable with impeachment, was certainly looking for the president to use this opportunity to explore a deal. That door closed when President Clinton did not provide the answers Representative Graham sought:

We overplayed our hand before the election, when we missed an opportunity for bipartisanship on the Berman motion [on a time limit for the inquiry] and releasing the information from the Starr Report. After the election it was the president who overplayed his hand by refusing to answer our written questions and using a defense that was all process and Starr bashing. As a result a lot of moderate Republicans became convinced that the president did abuse the legal system. The president could have gotten a deal on censure by admitting that his testimony was not the truth. At that point I would have supported an agreement to put it behind the country, but it was important for me as a lawyer that he admit that his testimony to the grand jury was not legally correct. If he had admitted to some wrongdoing there would have been a concentrated effort on everybody's part to avoid impeachment because the votes were not there after the election. But the behavior of House Democrats and the fact that his defense was so technical and over-stretched turned off the moderate Republicans. To this day 80 percent of the public agree that he lied and obstructed justice.[33]

Representative Asa Hutchinson was part of efforts within the committee to find a bipartisan solution to the impeachment question, but these efforts foundered on Republicans' unease with various censure proposals that formed the core of any possible compromise: "There were a lot of discussions about what our options were. Because of the partisanship on the Judiciary Committee I was part of a bipartisan group of members that met for breakfast to try and come to some agreement. We looked at the options and whether to go down the different path of censure. We Republicans ultimately reached the conclusion that since censure was not a constitutional option, we could not go down that path."[34]

Most committee Republicans objected to censure, fearing such a precedent would make it all too easy for future congresses to invoke similar actions when they were displeased with a president and, thus, might ultimately weaken the institution of the presidency. There were also concerns that such a motion would violate the constitutional prohibition on bills of attainder. "The suggested alternative of a motion of censure runs the risk of being a bill of attainder and being too facile. Something the next dissident Congress might turn to too frequently," said Representative Hyde.[35] "We thought that the president needed to be impeached and removed or exonerated. The country should get the whole thing over with and then put it behind us. Censure would just have weakened the presidency, and we need a strong presidency," added Representative Cannon.[36]

On December 16, 1998, following weeks of witness testimony on the history of impeachment as well as presentations by the president's attorneys, counsel to the committee, and Independent Prosecutor Starr, the Judiciary Committee voted to impeach President Clinton on four counts: perjury before the federal grand jury, perjury in the Paula Jones case, obstruction of justice, and abuse of power. All but one Judiciary Committee Republican voted in favor of the four articles (Representative Graham rejected Article II—the possible perjury in the Jones case). Committee Democrats unanimously opposed all four articles. Despite general public displeasure, Judiciary Committee Republicans remained convinced that the president committed offenses meriting impeachment, and that the rule of law had to be upheld. "We viewed what the president did as trying to fix a case—the Paula Jones case," declared Chairman Hyde. "Whether you liked her or not, she had her litigation, and the president by not telling the truth and encouraging others not to tell the truth was putting the fix in. When the American people said a collective 'so what?' it didn't make it any more palatable. The White House spin was that 'everybody does it,' 'it's all about sex,' and that we were 'puritanical' supporters of the religious right. We were focusing on perjury and obstruction of justice, which were public acts not private acts, but their spin was wonderfully effective and made good copy."[37] "It wasn't primarily about sex," declared Representative Coble. "First, everybody is not doing it [having sex with interns]. Second, he was a married man. Third, he didn't tell the truth about it to his constituents, and fourth, he violated the oath of office. Together, these four factors took him beyond the 'threshold of immunity,' and were grounds for impeachment in my view."[38] According to Representative Cannon:

I made up my mind that the president had acknowledged perjury and committed obstruction of justice. I never had an explanation of how the gifts were under Betty Currie's bed, and the phone bills supported Monica Lewinsky's claim that she had been talking to Betty Currie on a cell phone. That call vindicated Lewinsky's story and was very fundamental for me. I thought the obstruction of justice was the more serious charge, and that was not dealt with [by the president's defense]. I came to the conclusion that I should vote for impeachment because the president had committed perjury and obstruction of justice and there was never any proof to explain away the facts of obstruction of justice.[39]

Representative Canady vehemently rejected the argument that the president's offenses, even if proven, were ultimately too trivial to justify such a momentous step as impeachment:

I think that's a silly argument. The principle that "no one is above the law" is something that sets the United States apart from many other countries in the world. Like everybody else in this country the president is subject to the law, and it is the president's responsibility to protect the rule of law. Clinton failed to do that. He showed contempt for the rule of law and he is a disgrace to the institution of the presidency. He set out to derail a civil rights lawsuit and set out to do everything he could to thwart the rights of the plaintiffs in that lawsuit. He flat-out lied when he went into his deposition. For someone to lie is not unusual, but for the president of the United States to take an oath and then lie in his deposition, and compound it all by lying again before the grand jury is serious, and he did lie! To say that because the offenses related to sex that they don't count is to impose a standard on the law that isn't in the law.[40]

Representative Lindsey Graham eventually came to the conclusion that impeachment was merited on three of the articles, primarily on obstruction of justice grounds. Referring to the negative information that the president provided to his aide Sidney Blumenthal on Monica Lewinsky, he noted:

I voted against Article II because the case had been settled, and no prosecutor would have brought a prosecution for lying in the deposition, so I gave him the legal benefit of the doubt. The standard I applied was that an ordinary person would not likely be sent to jail for these offenses, and Clinton also paid $90,000 for lying in the deposition. But anyone who lied in front of a federal grand jury and tried to manipulate the testimony of potential witnesses would be in serious jeopardy of going to jail. It all turned for me because of the forces that the president unleashed to destroy Monica

Lewinsky. . . . If it had stayed at the level of lying about a relationship it was embarrassing, but everything he did then to obstruct justice was more calculated and more abusive of the legal system. . . . Mr. Blumenthal's testimony was particularly helpful, because by talking to an aide who was media savvy, Clinton knew that the negative stuff about Lewinsky was bound to get out.[41]

And so the president was impeached in a largely partisan vote in committee and on the floor, with both sides of the aisle secure in their conviction that they were doing the right thing, but also secure that most of them would pay no electoral penalty for doing so.

CONCLUSION

As a group, Republican members of the Judiciary Committee were not predisposed to look too kindly on President Clinton. In an increasingly partisan House, the Judiciary Committee is one of the most partisan and polarized. Its Republican members were almost all social conservatives who represented very conservative and Republican districts, most of which Clinton did not carry in a comfortable reelection in 1996. As the impeachment issue emerged, and the inquiry opened, it became apparent to most observers versed in contemporary congressional politics that a vote against impeaching Clinton would be politically risky, even after an election in which the Republican Party lost seats nationally. To do so would expose Republicans to a primary challenge, and on the basis of the feedback that these members were getting from constituents, the more politically aware and aroused voters in their districts favored impeachment. Voting against articles of impeachment could carry other penalties in terms of forfeiting support from PACs and interest groups vehemently opposed to the Clinton administration. Dissidents might have found themselves subject to ostracism and loss of influence both within the committee and in the House as a whole at a time when party loyalty offers enhanced value to members in terms of career advancement.

For contemporary lawmakers there are simply more electoral incentives to be partisan than was the case over twenty years ago during the Nixon impeachment. Yet while the Republican Judiciary Committee members interviewed admitted to the electoral incentives if pressed, in their own words and recollections they were generally unwilling to concede that this was the principal justification for defying the expressed will of the general electorate and proceeding with impeachment. Members' comments seem to reveal more of a "trustee" than a "delegate" conceptualization of representation.[42] They were willing to vote for articles of impeachment against President Clinton on the merits even after the election. They were convinced of his guilt, and the alternative of censure was deemed unsatisfactory, although they were well aware that the country did not want it. In this case they seem to have made the rare admission in democratic America, that their own judgment was superior to that of the electorate as a whole.

Even with the cushion of time, Republican committee members held little doubt that their actions were right even at the cost of some personal pain. "The whole process was like military service," Chairman Hyde reflected. "I didn't like it while I was doing it but looking back I'm pleased that I had the opportunity to do something very useful. To be candid, the whole thing was a personally debilitating experience for me. The personal attacks reduced the joy and pleasure with which I served in Congress by some measure. On the other hand, I must say that I received over 300,000 letters and calls, 90 percent favorable, and some were very touching. That makes it all worthwhile."[43]

Only one Republican member of the Judiciary Committee who voted to impeach Clinton, Representative James E. Rogan of California (who also served as a manager in the Senate trial), lost his bid for reelection in 2000. After the election, the conservative California lawmaker chalked up his loss as part of the price of impeaching the president, saying he knew at the time that his impeachment actions would be "unhealthy for my political longevity."[44] This race galvanized both Republican and Democratic donors across the nation, but the district was already highly marginal and its demographics were becoming decreasingly favorable to the GOP.[45] While impeachment likely played some role in Representative Rogan's defeat, the fact that the remaining Judiciary Republicans were home free is perhaps the more interesting and unusual circumstance, especially given the volume of commentary on how much impeachment "damaged" the GOP at the time of the inquiry and subsequent Senate trial. Again, this is testimony to the uncompetitive nature of most House districts and the power of incumbency in House elections.

Even if Judiciary Committee Republicans were unrepentant about impeaching President Clinton, they learned that when it comes to removing a president, a narrowly and somewhat naive legalistic viewpoint is unlikely to prevail unless the public can be convinced that the removal of the president is something worth doing. Up until his Senate trial the president lost almost all the legal battles but routed his opponents in the court of public opinion. For Judiciary Committee Republicans, the whole experience was another lesson that impeachment (at least in the case of presidents) is ultimately a political not a legal process. Perhaps the last word from the House Republican members of the Judiciary Committee should go to Representative Lindsey Graham, who acknowledged the following lesson about any congressional impeachment: "One part is legal and two parts are political. I'd never found myself making a case to a jury and then debating them at night on television!"[46]

4
Standing by Their Man: Democratic Members of the House Judiciary Committee

There's always a tension between the White House and the president's party in Congress. They thought that we were unreasonable, and the liberals were frustrated that Clinton had moved further to the right than was necessary. But Democrats recognized that Clinton was an enormously potent political force—the Democrats' best political figure since FDR—and they will be eternally grateful to him for that.
—Representative Barney Frank (D-Mass.)

At the beginning everybody was mad at the president, but the Republicans really hated Bill Clinton and were looking for any reason to hate him more. Democrats were angry that he would do such a stupid thing. What he did was repulsive but it was not a threat to the system of government, and my constituents responded on that basis. They would have liked for Hillary [Clinton] to belt him on the chops, but they didn't want the government to be turned upside down.
—Representative Zoe Lofgren (D-Calif.)

Equally as conspicuous as the united Republican vote on the House Judiciary Committee was the solid show of party unity on the part of congressional Democrats in opposition to the impeachment inquiry and the subsequent articles. This solid support is somewhat ironic considering that Clinton's foibles partly contributed to the Democrats' losing control of the House for the first time in forty years; his controversial 1996 reelection strategy ("triangulation") had undermined Democratic efforts to win back Congress, and many of his administration's policy positions conflicted with the prevailing ideological position of most House Democrats. Differing electoral cycles and constituencies also contributed to a level of tension. While President Clinton had to appeal to the entire country (and particularly the 1992 Perot voters) for his 1996 bid for reelection, congressional Democrats were largely beholden to their (in this case overwhelmingly liberal) activist voter base in solidly Democratic states and districts. But Clinton was the only president congressional Democrats had, and he remained the most formidable figure in the party and the last line of resistance against Newt Gingrich's "Republican Revolution" that challenged the policies and programs that most Capitol Hill Democrats and their clienteles held dear. The House Democratic leadership thus, recalls Representative Martin Frost (D-Tex.), "set the tone for the Democratic position, which was that President Clinton had done wrong, but it didn't rise to the level of an impeachable offense."[1]

CLINTON AND CONGRESSIONAL DEMOCRATS

Congressional Democrats were overjoyed to win control of the White House and solidify their control of the American national government for the first time in twelve years in 1992. Frustrated by over a decade of Republican presidents who blocked their policy objectives, Democratic lawmakers looked forward to working with one of their own to overcome "gridlock" in Washington and initiate an ambitious legislative agenda reminiscent of the New Deal and the Great Society. Democrats were mindful that Clinton won office, in part, on his promises to rejuvenate a stagnant economy with government action and to deal with the "crisis" in national health care policy by coming up with a comprehensive scheme to make sure that all Americans, regardless of income or employment status, were provided with coverage.[2] Moreover, Democrats enjoyed comfortable majorities in both houses of Congress, providing the likely votes for such programs, whereas Republicans appeared in disarray following an election in which incumbent George Bush secured only 38 percent of the popular vote.

With the benefit of hindsight, however, there were clear reasons to expect from the outset that Clinton's relations with congressional Democrats would prove somewhat problematic. The president secured a fairly narrow plurality of the vote in a three-way contest, with a small winning total, just 43 percent, lower than the popular vote (46 percent) of losing Democratic presidential candidate Massachusetts Governor Michael Dukakis in the two-party 1988 presidential race. And the third candidate in the election, Texan billionaire Ross Perot, was able to garner 19 percent of the popular vote on the basis of a campaign directed against the massive federal budget deficits that had been endemic to American government since the early 1980s. Clinton felt impelled for reasons of political survival to address the deficit, but the latter constrained his ability to launch ambitious new government programs, particularly entitlement programs, typical of previous Democratic administrations. Third, in an age of ephemeral party loyalties among voters, coupled by widespread ticket splitting, the relationship between presidents and members of Congress of the same party is inherently problematic. The presidential election cycle almost ensures that a president's party will lose seats in the subsequent midterm election, especially in the House (see Table 4.1). Subsequently, members in marginal districts generally have some interest in distancing themselves from the president. Moreover, the majority of congressional Democrats representing safe districts and states had generally run well ahead of President Clinton in their respective bailiwicks in 1992, and felt that they owed him little electorally.[3]

After running as a "new kind of Democrat" in terms of fiscal policy, Clinton gave deficit reduction priority over his other major 1992 campaign issue, health care policy, in the first year of his presidency.[4] Despite the unease of the more liberal wing of the Democratic party, Clinton's deficit reduction package, including tax and spending reductions, eventually passed both chambers by a single vote, with Vice President Al Gore casting the deciding vote in the Senate. Congressional Democrats exposed their own weaknesses two years later, however, when they failed to muster enough votes to pass the president's 1994 health care package. The White House's failure to "sell" the measure effectively to the public was compounded by apparently ineffectual Democratic leadership in Congress, as the measure fell victim to turf battles among no less than four House committees.[5] Later in the summer, an omnibus crime measure containing the president's popular assault weapons ban was also delayed and nearly derailed by rebellious congressional Democrats.[6]

Neglecting the Party?

The 1994 elections took place at the nadir of Bill Clinton's presidential fortunes, with a Democratic Congress under the twin clouds of "ineffectiveness" and numerous "corruption" scandals. Few were prepared for the upset that followed the 1994 midterm elections, however, as the Republicans gained not only eleven seats to regain the Senate, but over fifty House seats, providing them the first GOP majority in that body since 1954. In essence congressional Democrats were victims of the election cycle, punished for the mistakes of President Clinton, who survived to fight another day.[7]

The shock of minority status left an indelible mark on congressional

Table 4.1. Losses by the President's Party in Midterm Elections, 1862–1998

	Party Holding Presidency	President's Party Gain/ Loss Seats in House		Party Holding Presidency	President's Party Gain/ Loss Seats in House
1862	R	–3	1934	D	9
1866	R	–2	1938	D	–71
1870	R	–31	1942	D	–55
1874	R	–96	1946	D	–45
1878	R	–9	1950	D	–29
1882	R	–33	1954	R	–18
1886	D	–12	1958	R	–48
1890	R	–85	1962	D	–4
1894	D	–116	1966	D	–47
1898	R	–21	1970	R	–12
1902	R	9	1974	R	–48
1906	R	–28	1978	D	–15
1910	R	–57	1982	R	–26
1914	D	–59	1986	R	–5
1918	D	–19	1990	R	–8
1922	R	–75	1994	D	–52
1926	R	–10	1998	D	5
1930	R	–49			

SOURCE: Adapted from Norman J. Ornstein, Thomas E. Mann, and Michael J. Malbin, *Vital Statistics on Congress, 1999–2000* (Washington, D.C.: AEI Press, 2000).

Democrats used to untrammeled power. The defeat of many incumbent members in marginal and conservative districts also left the Democratic caucus, particularly in the House, much more dominated by minority or liberal members at odds with the president's "New Democratic" agenda. This, along with bitterness over the 1994 debacle, initially served to widen the rift between the president and his fellow partisans now in the minority on Capitol Hill.[8] Congressional Democrats learned the value of controlling the White House, however, as the new Republican majority proceeded to pass almost the entire "Contract with America" through the House.[9] In the battle over the Republican budget package, which included tax cuts with "reductions in the rate of increase" in Medicare and Medicaid, the White House and congressional Democrats made political hay by denouncing the Republicans for "balancing the budget on the backs of the poor" and "cutting Medicare to pay for tax cuts for the wealthy."[10] As the Republicans sank in the polls, Clinton was emboldened to veto the Republican reconciliation bill and several appropriations bills, thereby effectively shutting down much of the federal government in November–December 1995. Again congressional Democrats who loathed Republican Speaker Newt Gingrich and his attacks on their cherished programs rallied behind their embattled president and precluded the Republicans from contemplating a successful override of Clinton's vetoes.[11]

Clinton's ultimate victory in the budget battle with the Republican Congress emboldened the hitherto despondent congressional Democrats to believe that they could regain control of one or possibly both houses of Congress in 1996. Democratic leaders Richard A. Gephardt (D-Mo.) in the House and Tom Daschle (D-S.D.) in the Senate launched an all-out assault on the Republicans and their agenda in the hope of provoking a backlash victory on the likely winning coattails of Clinton in the fall.[12] Senator Daschle was particularly effective. Taking advantage of solid Democratic unity and the Senate's lax rules, the minority leader created major headaches for Republican Majority Leader and presidential candidate Bob Dole. In the spring of 1996 the Democrats held back legislation badly wanted by the Republicans, specifically their version of welfare reform, which was held hostage to Democratic demands for a minimum wage increase and health insurance "portability."

This strategy was somewhat undermined, however, by the countervailing strategy of "triangulation" pursued by President Clinton and his political advisor Dick Morris.[13] The essence of "triangulation" was that the administration should do enough to keep the Democratic base in line (particularly on issues most dear to Democratic activists like choice on abortion and affirmative action), while simultaneously co-opting Republican positions on several carefully selected issues such as welfare and immigration reform, crime, and same-sex marriage. Clinton's willingness to accommodate the Republicans on these issues for the sake of his reelection campaign led to a flurry of legislative activity in the summer of 1996, and the new Senate majority leader, Trent Lott (R-Miss.) struck a series of bipartisan deals to pass welfare reform, immigration reform, and the so-called Defense of Marriage Act (DOMA), in exchange for giving the Democrats what they wanted on the minimum wage and health insurance. Unfortunately for the electoral prospects of many congressional Democrats, however, this undermined the case they were trying to make against a "do-nothing" and ineffectual Republican Congress, because it showed substantial legislative achievement on the Republicans' part. Clinton's lack of enthusiasm for the congressional party was evident when he kept his distance from them for most of the fall campaign, while trumpeting the issues that he had co-opted from the Republicans like welfare reform. The fund-raising excesses of the Clinton campaign that came to light in the final week also hindered congressional Democrats' campaigns, and the Republicans recognized the opportunity Clinton had given them by running ads on television arguing for a Republican Congress to "rein in" a reelected Clinton.[14]

Congressional Democrats felt somewhat bitter about an easy Clinton reelection that left Republicans with slim control of the House and Senate, but the more politically astute among the liberals, such as Representative Barney Frank (D-Mass.), realized that any president in Clinton's position might do the same: "Clinton did not cost us the House in 1996," he declared. "Presidents always concentrate on themselves and congressional candidates always complain about it. It was the campaign finance scandals at the end that stopped us from getting the House back in 1996."[15]

Clinton's reelection and continuing Republican control of Congress led to something of a lull in partisanship in 1997, as Barbara Sinclair notes.[16] Large bipartisan majorities put through a compromise budget deal early in the year, and congressional Democratic misgivings about the president's backbone were further demonstrated by the votes on the "Fast Track" trade procedure to expedite the conclusion of free trade agreements enthusiastically endorsed by the pro-business Clinton White House. Majorities of Democrats in each chamber, including the party leadership, voted against the president's position.

In the first five years of Clinton's presidency, then, congressional Democrats had enjoyed a somewhat uneasy relationship with the president. The differing election cycles and constituencies of each virtually guaranteed a certain level of tension between them. Clinton had to appeal to the entire country and the 1992 Perot voters to get reelected; congressional Democrats were largely beholden to the liberal activist base in solidly Democratic states and districts. Congressional Democrats held Clinton's ineptitude largely responsible for the loss of Congress in 1994, while the White House held the ineptitude of congressional Democrats responsible for the failure of their sweeping health care reform proposal. Yet while they had their differences with Clinton, congressional Democrats had no interest in eliminating their most effective defense against a conservative Republican congressional policy agenda that most of them abhorred. Thus throughout the series of Republican-inspired investigations into the "scandals" of the Clinton White House the Democrats were to be solidly loyal to the president.

Congressional Democrats and the Clinton Scandals

In addition to the Paula Jones sexual harassment lawsuit that served as the catalyst for the Lewinsky investigation, the Clinton administration was plagued by a series of House and Senate investigations into the Whitewater land deal, the firing of White House Travel Office employees, the collection of FBI files, and the campaign fund raising "excesses" of the president and vice president during the 1996 reelection effort. Although Attorney General Janet Reno had appointed a special prosecutor under the independent counsel statute in 1994 to investigate most of these matters (plus the death in suspicious circumstances of White House Counsel Vincent Foster), she found insufficient grounds to do so regarding the campaign finance excesses of 1996, much to the annoyance of congressional Republicans.

Most congressional Democrats, however, believed that these investigations were largely driven by a specific right-wing Republican animus against the president, and they rallied solidly behind Clinton. Ranking minority member Representative Henry A. Waxman (D-Calif.) was particularly effective in undermining various efforts to investigate the White House by House Government Operations Committee chair Dan Burton (R-Ind.), and the aura of partisanship around these investigations undermined their credibility with the news media and the wider public. Although frequently exasperated with Clinton, liberal Democrats defended him against conservative accusers whom they regarded as a far more serious threat to the integrity of the political system than the president. Representative Jerrold Nadler's (D-N.Y.) reaction to Clinton's nemeses was typical of the mainstream of the House caucus:

> I can also tell you that there was unparalleled enmity against Clinton that I have never seen against any other president. If he thought he would get a honeymoon he was mistaken, because they [conservative Republicans] had that venom and animus from the very beginning. What did he do to get such hostility? I know that they lost the election but, hey, that happens! I didn't see it with the Republicans and Jimmy Carter, and I didn't see it with either Bush, but with Clinton it never ceased: not just investigations by congressional committees and independent counsels, but also by conservative groups like Judicial Watch. People laughed at Hillary when she spoke about the "vast right wing conspiracy" but she was right on the money, although I don't know how "vast" it was. They were the targets of beyond normal, venomous attacks.[17]

Representative Frank, who also served on the House Banking Committee that investigated Whitewater in 1995 and was later to be the effective leader of the Democrats on the Judiciary Committee during the impeachment inquiry, found equally little substance in the pre-Lewinsky "scandals": "I was peculiarly well suited to deal with this [the Lewinsky matter] because the

Banking Committee had dealt with the Whitewater affair in 1995. [Iowa Republican Jim] Leach's Banking Committee never issued a report because the rule seemed to be—'if you've nothing bad to say then don't say anything.' We had Whitewater, Vince Foster, the Travel Office, and the FBI files, and nothing was ever found, and except for the 'arithmetic of the media,' nothing equals nothing!"[18]

Democrats were particularly incensed that David Sentelle, a conservative judge close to archconservative North Carolina Republican Senator Jesse Helms, headed the requisite panel of three federal judges that refused to reappoint Whitewater Independent Counsel Robert Fiske and appointed Kenneth Starr in his place.[19] From the outset congressional Democrats saw Starr's investigation as tainted by partisanship, and he did little in the course of spending three years and $40 million to disabuse them of that notion. From Whitewater, Starr's probe expanded to cover all the Clinton scandals: the Travel Office, the Foster suicide, the FBI files; but while he obtained indictments against some lesser figures in the drama, Starr never came close to finding anything substantial against the president and first lady.

Democrats were singularly unimpressed. For the pugilistic Nadler only the FBI files affair of all the Clinton scandals aroused some temporary concern: "If it was true that they [the White House] took various people's FBI files and used them for intimidation or punishment and the president countenanced it, then that was impeachable. Thank God that turned out to be bullshit and just a lower-level staffer screwing up."[20]

By the time the Lewinsky affair broke in early 1998, congressional Democrats were accustomed to defending Clinton against what they saw as utterly partisan attacks, whether in Congress or from the Office of Independent Counsel. It was clear that any new scandals arising from Starr's investigations would be regarded with a high degree of skepticism in the ranks of the congressional minority. For all Clinton's shortcomings, congressional Democrats still admired him and feared and despised his principal accusers, and this reinforced unity in their ranks. Nadler, the unrepentant Manhattan liberal, summed up the general perception of Clinton from his fellow partisans in Congress prior to the Lewinsky affair:

A lot of us were very angry with the president because of triangulation. We felt he was playing off the congressional Democrats for his own political purposes: selling out issues important to us and playing political games with the Republicans, regardless of our interest in getting back the House. On civil liberties issues, such as privacy and habeas corpus, he wasn't sensitive at all. But he was far better than any Republican would be, and after 1996 he tried to undo a lot of the crap we [Congress] did on the immigration bill and the welfare act, and we got a lot back. He also tried to do the right thing on gay issues.[21]

The Inquiry

When Attorney General Reno allowed Independent Counsel Kenneth Starr to extend his investigation to cover the Lewinsky matter, and the story broke in the press in late January 1998, Democrats, albeit nervous, were highly skeptical of any alleged criminal behavior. On the basis of previous scandals they doubted if there would be much more substance to this inquiry than the fact that Clinton had an affair with a White House intern, and might have lied about it in his testimony in the Jones case. Representative Frank was unimpressed: "On Lewinsky, I was agnostic, as there seemed to be nothing more than fooling around."[22]

As the year proceeded, a succession of witnesses were paraded before the grand jury by Independent Counsel Starr to demonstrate that Clinton had had a sexual relationship with Lewinsky and therefore had lied in his testimony in the Jones case; and that he had attempted to obstruct justice by "coaching" Lewinsky and other witnesses in the Jones case and urging his friend Washington lawyer Vernon Jordan to find Lewinsky a job. Clinton's grand jury testimony in August and the confirmation that sexual encounters had taken place between himself and the intern made it appear that he was evasive at best in his videotaped answers to Starr's prosecutors, and the independent counsel felt that he had enough evidence to submit a report to the Judiciary Committee of the House of Representatives recommending impeachment of the president. This turn of events made several Democrats edgy, and in the Senate, hinted toward cracks in an otherwise solid defense and support of the president. On September 3, 1998, Senator Joseph I. Lieberman (D-Conn.) walked on to the Senate floor to denounce President Clinton's "immoral" behavior, and his remarks were endorsed by two other senior and respected Democrats, Senators Daniel Patrick Moynihan (N.Y.) and Bob Kerrey (Neb.).[23]

Meanwhile the House had to decide how to deal with the Starr Report and the independent counsel's thirty-six boxes of evidence, including the videotape of the president's testimony. The first concern for House Democrats was to ensure a fair hearing for the president by setting strict standards for what constituted an impeachable offense, setting a reasonable timetable for reaching a decision, and minimizing the release of embarrassing details of sexual encounters from the Starr Report. Many referred to the procedures of the House Judiciary Committee under Chairman Peter Rodino (D-N.J.) that had conducted the 1974 impeachment inquiry on the Watergate scandal, which they felt had been characterized by a fair measure of bipartisanship.[24] The final Rodino Committee votes on the articles of impeachment against Nixon certainly provided some evidence for this assertion, at least on the part of the Republican minority. Six of the seventeen Republicans on the 1974 Judiciary panel had joined all twenty-one Democrats in voting for the first article of impeachment against President Nixon. The second article, which did not rest on criminal charges, nonetheless received one more vote than the first, with seven Republicans joining the twenty-one Democrats. On the last article against Nixon, nineteen Democrats and two Republicans voted in favor, while two Democrats, both southerners, bolted the majority of their party and joined fifteen Republicans to vote nay.

With regard to the Starr Report Minority Leader Gephardt did not want to appear to be covering up for the White House but felt that it was appropriate that the president be given an opportunity to respond prior to the release of the material. Following much debate over whether the details of the president's intimate contacts with Monica Lewinsky should have been kept private, on Friday, September 11, 1998, the full House voted (with only sixty-three Democrats in opposition) to release the Starr Report on the Internet. In the following weeks the Judiciary Committee voted to release more of the evidence collected by Starr, including the videotape of the president's Grand Jury testimony. These committee votes were strictly along partisan lines, with the committee Democrats wanting to make the unanimous point that they did not favor releasing "salacious" material to the public. It was also smart politics, because the public reaction was disgust at the details of the released material and sympathy for the president after his grand jury appearance.

Pleasantly surprised by the public and constituent reaction, Representative Frank recalled:

> I steeled myself after it became clear that the president had lied and then gave a more bellicose speech than was wise. He seemed to be in trouble. But the grand jury testimony turned the tide. I was pleasantly surprised that people sympathized after the grand jury testimony. [Most people thought that was enough humiliation and the president did a better job of seeming human.] After that the constituent reaction got better and better. In fact it's rarely been stronger. I've rarely had a period in my political career where strangers stopped me [to talk about this issue].[25]

Committee Democrats concurred with Representative Nadler, believing that releasing most of the evidence was a partisan attempt to embarrass the president, with little regard to due process:

> When the Starr Report was given to Congress, the first thing we do is release it to the public with Henry Hyde leading the way. The traditional practice had been when a critical report came out about someone, that you always gave the target a copy a few days in advance, so that if and when you do release it to the public you do so with the target's response. The Democrats demanded that the president be given one day, even one hour, to look at the Starr Report. Newt Gingrich was given a week in advance of the [House Ethics Committee] report being made public, and we felt that the president should be given the same courtesy. They said no and Henry [Hyde] defended it on the floor. "The president was due *due process*," he said, "not a PR advantage."[26]

As we saw in the last chapter, in retrospect, most Judiciary Committee Republicans admitted that releasing so much material had been a tactical mistake. Representative Frank expressed little sympathy for them: "They only think it was a mistake because it backfired. It was also illogical. They said it was their constitutional duty to impeach Clinton regardless of what the public thought, but in that case why release the material publicly? That undercut their own argument that it was the Constitution that mattered not public opinion. They thought this would move public opinion, but they made a terrible mistake about how it would be perceived."[27]

"YOU DON'T CHOOSE THE JUDICIARY COMMITTEE, THE COMMITTEE CHOOSES YOU"

The Judiciary Committee's reputation for partisanship and polarization results from the fact that the two major parties in Congress have been so bitterly divided in recent decades on social and cultural issues. Thus the Democratic leadership has consistently encouraged more liberal members to serve on Judiciary to counteract the legislation emanating from the culturally conservative Republicans who had gravitated toward the panel for similar reasons.[28] As a consequence the Democratic membership of the committee is now almost unanimously composed of liberal Democrats—almost all representing especially safe districts—appointed by the party leadership for the primary task of blocking Republican-sponsored measures that deal with highly charged issues, such as abortion and flag burning, from reaching the House floor. "I didn't choose the Judiciary Committee," recalled Representative Frank. The Massachusetts lawmaker added: "The committee chose me. The Democrats put people on the committee who were more likely to be immune to right-wing pressure, because they had liberal districts. Moderate Democrats didn't want to be on it, and the Republicans decided to put only anti-abortion people on the committee."[29] Representative Zoe Lofgren (D-Calif.) echoed this point: "Your centrist Democrat or Republican from a marginal district doesn't want to get anywhere near the [Judiciary] committee."[30]

Table 4.2 reflects just how polarized Democrats on the committee have become since the Nixon impeachment. Where the median ADA score for Democrats who sat on the 1974 Rodino Committee was 76.7, with a range of ten to one hundred, during the Clinton impeachment, on the Hyde committee, Democrats averaged 15 ADA points higher (91.3), with a minimal range of eighty to one hundred. (These increased differences are strong and statistically significant: $t = -2.22$, $p = 0.02$.)

Thus, in the highly polarized Hyde Judiciary Committee, with a significantly higher level of party unity among the minority Democrats, the prospects for a similar pattern of behavior to that of the Republican minority on the Rodino committee were slim. As it became evident to the Democrats that Republican members of the Hyde committee would likely vote to open an impeachment inquiry into the Lewinsky affair, the House Democratic leadership faced the problem of how to finesse the issue. There was clearly considerable disgust with Clinton's behavior and potential support for an inquiry among moderate and conservative Democratic members in the House Democratic caucus, while the more liberal majority followed the Judiciary Committee Democrats in seeking to defend the president at all costs against what they saw as a right-wing conservative assault. The fact that congressional elections were looming and that the president's party could traditionally expect to lose seats in the second midterm election of a two-term administration was an additional complicating factor. (See Table 4.1.) Despite continuing strong public support for the president, Minority Leader Gephardt believed that the House Democrats could not appear to be condoning or exonerating Clinton. The ideal solution was for the Democrats to draft their own impeachment inquiry resolution in such a manner that the Republicans would find it impossible to accept, and thus taint any subsequent impeachment inquiry conducted according to Republican specifications as partisan.[31] Gephardt worked with committee Democrats to draft a resolution behind which the party could unite, their central aim being to establish a definition of

Table 4.2. Ideological Leanings of House Judiciary Democratic Committee Members, 1974 and 1998

1974 (Nixon Impeachment)	ADA[a] Rating	1998 (Clinton Impeachment)	ADA Rating
Rodino, Peter W., Jr. (N.J.)	91	Conyers, John, Jr. (Mich.)	95
Donohue, Harold D. (Mass.)[a]	81	Frank, Barney (Mass.)	100
Brooks, Jack (Tex.)	45	Schumer, Charles (N.Y.)	85
Kastenmeier, Robert W. (Wis.)	95	Berman, Howard L. (Calif.)	80
Edwards, William D. (Calif.)	100	Boucher, Rick (Va.)	85
Hungate, William L. (Mo.)	68	Nadler, Jerrold (N.Y.)	100
Conyers, John, Jr. (Mich.)	95	Scott, Robert C. (Va.)	90
Eilberg, Joshua (Pa.)	73	Watt, Melvin (N.C.)	100
Waldie, Jerome R. (Calif.)[a]	81	Lofgren, Zoe (Calif.)	95
Flowers, Walter (Ala.)	10	Jackson-Lee, Shelia (Tex.)	80
Mann, James R. (S.C.)	10	Waters, Maxine (Calif.)	95
Sarbanes, Paul S. (Md.)	91	Meehan, Martin T. (Mass.)	90
Seilberling, John F. (Ohio)	96	Delahunt, William (Mass.)	95
Danielson, George E. (Calif.)	77	Wexler, Robert (Fla.)	90
Drinan, Robert F. (Mass.)	100	Rothman, Steven R. (N.J.)	90
Rangel, Charles B. (N.Y.)	95		
Jordan, Barbara (Tex.)	91		
Thornton, Ray (Ark.)	39		
Holtzman, Elizabeth (N.Y.)	100		
Owens, Wayne D. (Utah)[b]	—		
Mezvinsky, Edward (Iowa)	96		
Median	91		90
Range	10–100		80–100
Mean[c]	76.7		91.3

Sources: Adapted from Michael Barone, Grant Ujifusa, and Douglas Matthews, *The Almanac of American Politics, 1974* (Boston: Gambit, Inc., 1973); Michael Barone and Grant Ujifusa, *The Almanac of American Politics, 2000* (Washington, D.C.: National Journal, 1999).

[a]ADA scores for Representatives Donohue and Waldie are from 1972; neither lawmaker returned to the House following the 93rd Congress.

[b]Representative Owens was newly elected to the House in 1972, then unsuccessfully ran for the Senate in 1974.

[c]Difference of Means: $t = -2.22$; d.f. = 21.72; $p = 0.02$. Corrected t–test due to unequal variances in the two groups.

an impeachable offense before moving on to consider the evidence, and secondly, to establish a definite timetable and concluding date for the inquiry. "There was an initial meeting of the Judiciary Committee Democrats with Gephardt about what to do if this thing came down," declared Representative Nadler. "We had to take any hearing seriously because the Republicans were playing games and we shouldn't. We also needed to be prepared for a media assault like you've never seen in you lives. It was holy writ for us to try and narrow down the issue to the definition of an impeachable offense."[32]

Such concern for definition, which highlighted the basic argument of the president's defenders that his misconduct did not rise to the level of an offense that merited possible removal from office, formed the basis of the eventual Democratic resolution drafted by Judiciary Committee Minority Counsel and Staff Director Julian Epstein and Representative Rick Boucher of Virginia, the only Democratic member of the panel who could accurately be described as "moderate."[33] Preventing the defection of the normally low-key Boucher had been a central preoccupation of Judiciary Democrats. According to Representative Lofgren:

> Rick Boucher is a more conservative Democrat. Telecommunications pol-
> icy is the man's whole life, and that is why he is on the Judiciary Commit-
> tee. Early on, with the help of my chief of staff, John Flannery, I wrote a
> "Fairness Document." We were sitting there and I presented it and asked
> all the committee Democrats to sign it as a group. Rick was reluctant, so I
> gave him the basis of the document: the executive summary report of the
> 1974 [Judiciary] committee, which was a tightly argued analysis of the con-
> stitutional standards for impeachment. Rick read it, told me that he found it
> very useful, and then signed the statement.[34]

The eventual Democratic resolution called for a definition of an impeach-able offense before examining evidence, along with a specific timetable that would conclude the impeachment inquiry by November 25, 1998. Chairman Hyde and the Republicans, by contrast, copied the wording of the 1974 res-olution to open an inquiry into President Nixon's actions in the Watergate scandal, which contained no such definition and no time limit. By a party-line vote, the House Judiciary Committee voted 21 to 16 recommending that the House begin formal impeachment proceedings. Three days later the issue reached the House floor in the form of H. Res. 581, a Republican-sponsored resolution directing the Judiciary Committee to undertake an open-ended inquiry into whether grounds existed to impeach President Clinton. In curi-ously undramatic fashion, despite frequent references to history, the resolu-tion passed, 258 to 176. The thirty-one Democrats who joined all the Republicans in voting for the resolution were mostly southern white conser-vatives and moderates.

With the gauntlet thrown down, committee Democrats, while taking their duties seriously, prepared for a pitched partisan battle, which they wanted to spin favorably for their side, not only to further reduce the number of potential Democratic defectors if any impeachment articles should reach the House floor, but also perhaps to secure Democratic control of the House in the elections just one month away. Although Chairman Hyde had been hitherto generally respected by committee Democrats, during the impeachment inquiry few Democrats maintained faith in his ability to conduct a fair process or in the committee counsel hired for the inquiry, an old Hyde friend and Chicago lawyer, David Schippers. Representative Lofgren, herself a Rodino Committee staffer during the 1974 impeachment inquiry, shared the reaction of her Democratic committee colleagues:

> Henry Hyde and I had a positive professional relationship. I probably held the record for the number of Democratic amendments agreed to on the committee, and he helped me on a number of things. Well before March, I went over to the Republican side of the House floor to ask him for help, and he started musing about impeachment! I thought that it was so strange that they were already planning how to get the president impeached, and that he was telling me that! Every process was calculated to get Clinton. There was one standard about what to do here. In 1974 we had a bipartisan process and we never did things like changing what we were going after. In 1998 the Republicans didn't care about the Constitution, they just wanted to get him.[35]

Representative Frank commended Chairman Hyde's actual conduct of committee sessions but argued that the broader context of the inquiry had been stacked against the president: "Once the gavel started, Henry was a very fair, thoughtful, and sensible presiding officer. What was unfair were the basic decisions that shaped the proceedings: how to handle materials, how to structure the questioning for witnesses, whom to call. The broader strategic questions were done to get an impeachment, but the actual proceedings were done fairly."[36]

Given that the Republicans had rejected their own preferred form of inquiry, the role of the Judiciary Committee Democrats and their minority counsel, Washington, D.C., lawyer Abbie Lowell, was to try to ensure that the president's position got as fair a hearing as possible, and take every opportunity presented by the Republicans to demonstrate the partisan nature of the proceedings.[37] Judiciary Committee Democrats also worked in tandem with Minority Leader Gephardt and the White House legal team led by the president's counsel Greg Craig. The overall objective was to make sure that there was maximum Democratic unity in the ultimate showdown floor votes on impeachment. Because of the constitutional sensitivities, however, even the largely pro-Clinton Judiciary Committee Democrats had to maintain a respectful distance from the White House. Representative Lofgren described how the Democratic committee members worked during impeachment and their relationship with Clinton's attorneys:

> The committee staff was camped out at the Ford Building going through boxes of stuff. John [Flannery, Lofgren's chief of staff] and I helped pull the committee together, and every time we redrafted things they got better. We had an inclusionary approach and Rick Boucher [Va.], Maxine Waters [Calif.], and Bobby Scott [Va.] helped. We had good work-product and also "buy-in" from committee members. We did our own thing and I told the White House that if we did find that Clinton violated the constitution that I was out of there—I would vote to impeach, and they had to understand that. [Greg] Craig on two occasions wanted to give me a legal brief but I said I was in a different constitutional role and that private meetings with the president's attorneys would undercut the public's faith that we were doing a fair job.[38]

Well aware that the Republicans did not want to risk the embarrassment of calling witnesses, the Democrats argued that such a serious business as impeaching a president demanded cross-examination, and were thus able to put the Republicans in a bind. Representative Lofgren commented:

> We should have had witnesses. They said we were just a grand jury, but it's a poor analogy. We are not a grand jury and that seemed to be hypocritical. To impeach a president is a hell of a thing to do and you have to have a real basis for it. In fact nobody wanted to be blamed for calling witnesses because it came down to perjury about what was and wasn't "sex." It would have come down to "Okay, Monica, what did he do next?" and Henry Hyde and the Republicans didn't want to be blamed for putting that on TV. But if you're not willing to do that, then you have no business impeaching the president. If you don't have the stomach for that, you should drop impeachment and end the hearing. Their position assumed the truthfulness of the witnesses.[39]

The greatest political vindication of the Democrats' tactics on impeachment came in the middle of the inquiry, when they made a net gain of five seats in the midterm congressional elections. No president's party had actually gained seats in the second midterm election of a presidential term since the 1820s, and the election corroborated the evidence of the opinion polls that the pursuit of impeachment was damaging the GOP. The resignation of the Democrats' bête noire, Speaker Gingrich, appeared to further vindicate their resolution in standing by the president. Indeed, several Democrats now wished that they had made a bigger issue of impeachment in the election campaign. "If we had discussed impeachment more in our campaigns in 1998," declared Lofgren, "the House would have turned over. I knew how people were talking and I have the emails to prove what I was thinking, that the Democrats could win the House. Candidates who did use it like Rush Holt [D-N.J.] and Jay Inslee [D-Wash.] won."[40]

While the news media and public might have been surprised, the House Democrats, having witnessed the degree of Republican animosity toward the Clintons, were hardly amazed when the Republicans decided to proceed with the impeachment inquiry in a lame-duck Congress. Representative Frank expressed his conviction that the Republicans' zeal superseded their political judgment:

> The right wing was appalled to see the deterioration of moral America. It's like they fell asleep in a Norman Rockwell painting and woke up in a work by Hieronymus Bosch. They couldn't understand how a majority of the people could be wrong. Unlike European conservatives, American conservatives are more majoritarian-type social conservatives. When it seemed that Bill and Hillary Clinton had bewitched the people, they were determined to drive a stake through their hearts. It was *The Bridge on the River Kwai* syndrome with Henry [Hyde] as Alec Guinness. Otherwise how can you explain why they would not go to censure or even allow censure as an option?[41]

POLITICAL ENDGAME

The endgame in the House impeachment drama concerned the issue of censorship of the president as opposed to impeachment. Minority Leader Gephardt saw censorship as a means by which Democrats could appear responsible in condemning Clinton, yet also avoid the trauma of impeachment and a Senate trial over perjury concerning a sexual affair. Like Representative Frank, the Democrats never seriously believed the Republicans would accept censure, particularly Majority Whip Tom Delay (R-Tex.), who they now perceived, accurately, as the driving force behind impeachment after Gingrich's departure to the sidelines. While there were some bipartisan discussions within the committee about a deal on censure, a strongly worded proposal offered by Democrats Rick Boucher of Virginia, Bill Delahunt of Massachusetts, and Thomas M. Barrett of Wisconsin (see boxed text on p. 93), never really got off the ground. Moreover, within Democratic ranks there was reluctance even to censure the president, first because there were serious doubts (ironically shared by conservative Republicans) about its constitutionality; and second, because many liberal Democrats felt that President Clinton had done nothing wrong. Representative Nadler summarized this view:

> The Democrats were pushing the censure resolution to avoid an impeachment vote, but the Republicans refused to allow that. Tom Delay wanted impeachment and he didn't want to give people an "out." I was ambivalent about censure. I thought it was constitutionally okay for Congress to express an opinion, for example censuring McCarthy or Saddam Hussein. Whether we should do so is another question. When [Rick] Boucher and a few other people, I think Bill Delahunt [D-Mass.] was one, were involved in drafting a censure resolution, I was concerned that the "whereas" clauses were appearing like statements of fact. They said in effect that the president had done things, crimes, like perjury. I said that was improper and Congress had no business passing a resolution accusing someone of being guilty of a crime. It's almost a bill of attainder. But if you don't accuse him of a crime, why censure him? Clinton was being censured for: having an affair with a young intern and lying to the American people. On the first it was not Congress's business to censure the president for his private actions. Why single him out? And on the second, who's the last president who didn't lie to the American people? And his lies were less damaging to the public interest than lying about Iran-Contra, for example. Why him? So I voted for the censure resolution in committee only to bring it to the floor. It was less evil than impeachment would be, and I said I would vote against it.[42]

There was never any prospect that a censure resolution would reach the floor, since the Democrats on Judiciary had accurately read the Republican determination to impeach Clinton. From a political perspective, the strategy of cautious criticism of Clinton, combined with distaste for impeachment, served Democrats well. While cleverly maneuvering for their own advantage they succeeded in making the Republicans appear shrill and partisan and gradually solidified their own ranks in opposition to impeachment. Representative Frank recalled: "On the first vote to release all the material the numbers were 365 to 65 in favor." On opening the inquiry it was 240 to 180, and then the final impeachment vote was almost a tie, so the Republicans lost

Draft of Democratic Censure Proposal

It is the Sense of the Congress that—
On January 20, 1993, William Jefferson Clinton took the oath, prescribed by the Constitution of the United States, faithfully to execute the Office of President; implicit in that oath is the obligation that the President set an example of high moral standards and conduct himself in a manner that fosters respect for the truth; and William Jefferson Clinton has egregiously failed in this obligation, and through his actions has violated the trust of the American people, lessened their esteem for the office of President and dishonored the office which they have entrusted to him.

Be it resolved that:
(1) The President made false statements concerning his reprehensible conduct with a subordinate;
(2) The President wrongly took steps to delay discovery of the truth;
(3) No person is above the law, and the President remains subject to criminal and civil penalties;
(4) William Jefferson Clinton, President of the United States, by his conduct has brought upon himself and fully deserves the censure and condemnation of the American people and the Congress; and by his signature on this Joint Resolution, the President acknowledges this censure.

(Source: Congressional Record)

votes every time. The Judiciary Committee Democratic members were more pro-Clinton than the caucus as a whole, but we always worked with Dick Gephardt and eventually he did a good job of rallying members."[43]

Additionally, Democrats were able to pick up seats in the House, and effectively remove a Republican Speaker they loathed, and his designated successor. Given the partisan nature of the contemporary House, it was inevitable that if the move to impeach Clinton were seen as a partisan effort, the Democrats would rally solidly in his defense. Like their Republican counterparts, whose impeachment votes were in large part a response to conservative activists and donors in their districts, House Democrats were responding to an electoral and donor base that adored the president. These committed activists and associated interest groups are the primary mobilizing agents in contemporary congressional elections, and the Democrats' base constituency of minorities, feminists, gays, teachers, and labor unions had no desire to see the president impeached.[44] Thus it is hardly surprising that the Democratic Party in the House of Representatives did everything possible to assist the president in the travails of the Lewinsky affair.

CONCLUSION

Partisanship and partisan maneuvering for advantage are the defining characteristics of the contemporary Congress, particularly in the House of Representatives. The mobilization of single-issue and ideological activists behind one or other of the major parties and the transformation of low-turnout primary (and increasingly general) elections into exercises in mobilizing the committed, plus the concomitant increase in the power of the party leadership on Capitol Hill, have increased the incentives of members to rally behind the party unless a clear constituent interest is directly at stake.[45] The deliberations of the Rodino Judiciary Committee over Watergate in 1974 occurred during a period of transition from the period of congressional domination by interparty coalitions (especially the "conservative coalition") and strong committee barons, and those proceedings were conducted in a far less partisan context. This was reflected in the far less partisan voting patterns on the Rodino Committee votes on the impeachment articles, and of course led to the committee's impeachment articles being taken all the more seriously by the press and the public—so seriously in fact that in the face of public and political pressure, President Nixon resigned before the whole House had voted on the articles.

The less satisfying legacy of Watergate was that in the increasingly partisan context of Washington politics since the late 1970s, both parties in control of Congress frequently resorted to congressional investigations of the executive for partisan benefit.[46] During the 1980s congressional Democrats harassed the Reagan and Bush administrations in an effort to undermine them politically, and the Republicans adopted similar tactics against the Clinton administration when they gained complete control of Congress for the first time in forty years in 1994. In each case the accusers were aided by an independent counsel statute (since discarded) that gave virtually unlimited investigative authority and budgets to prosecutors who had every incentive to justify their investigations with an indictment of some kind—regardless of the scale of the "illegality" in question or its implications for national government.

In this atmosphere it is hardly surprising that the zeal of Independent Counsel Starr and the partisan atmosphere within Congress that helped sustain Republican animosity toward President Clinton ultimately found a pretext for the possible impeachment of the president. Once this appeared as a possibility, the dynamics of contemporary House politics impelled the Republicans toward impeachment regardless of the scale of the alleged crime. The core Republican primary constituency, and the cadre of activists and fund-raisers necessary for reelection, was howling for the head of the president, and the key committee that would conduct the impeachment inquiry—Judiciary— had, because of the primacy of cultural cleavages in the contemporary American partisan alignment, become the most polarized and partisan in the House.

But while impeachment was almost inevitable once a pretext had emerged, the likelihood that it would ultimately fail because of the perception of partisanship was equally likely. To succeed, the Clinton impeachment, like the near impeachment of President Nixon, would have required substantial bipartisan support from the president's party both on the Judiciary Committee and the House floor. But failing proof of egregiously criminal conduct on the part of the president, this was always extremely unlikely. The Democratic core electoral constituency strongly supported President Clinton and loathed his Republican accusers from Kenneth Starr on downward, and thus there was every incentive—except for the dwindling minority of House Democrats in southern or western, predominantly white, conservative districts—for the president's co-partisans in the House to rally behind him, and do everything they could to convince the public that the investigation was, as Representative Lofgren contended, a "partisan witch-hunt."[47] Being perceived as such by the press and the middle ground of public opinion (as reflected in the opinion polls) meant the effort to remove Clinton on grounds of his conduct during the Lewinsky affair was always doomed to failure, but of course the congressional Democrats' own actions contributed to that perception. Their ingenuity was to succeed in making the Republicans look "partisan" to the general public, while they themselves were equally so.

The irony remains that House Democrats helped save a president whose errors had contributed to their loss of congressional power for the first time in four decades, and who had undermined them electorally and ideologically with his "triangulation" strategy for reelection in 1996. Of course, the imperatives of modern presidential politics left Clinton with little choice in the latter regard, and the more politically astute of his co-partisans in the House by and large understood that he had to sell them out to some extent to prevent the Republican "enemy" from taking complete control of the federal government. That partisan imperative made it inevitable that they would attempt to save him if the threat of impeachment and removal from office loomed. Aside from the more direct electoral and career motivation, the near impeachment of Nixon arguably set the Republican Party back twenty years in congressional elections—a fact that was not lost on the House Democratic leadership during 1998. (On the other hand, sticking by Clinton through thick and thin may not have been such a wise long-term strategy, given poor

Democratic election results in culturally conservative states that lost Vice President Gore the White House in 2000, and contributed to the loss of the Senate and failure to recapture the House in 2002.)

One final interesting aspect of the Clinton impeachment proceedings in the House was the fact that while the minority party could not prevent impeachment, they succeeded in undermining the proceedings to such a degree with the press and the public and that there was never a serious prospect of the president's conviction and removal in the Senate trial. In contemporary congressional scholarship we have gotten used to regarding the minority party in the House as ineffectual by comparison with its counterpart in the nonmajoritarian Senate. At least as far as impeachment is concerned, the Clinton example demonstrates that this need not necessarily be the case.

5

House Floor Debate

Tom Delay understood that while the American people were overwhelmingly against impeachment, if you went to a typical Republican congressional district you'd find that the party activists—the people who vote in primaries—were overwhelmingly for impeachment. So if it came to a vote most Republicans would not vote "for Bill Clinton."
—Representative Peter King (R-N.Y.)

The Clinton impeachment was the epitome of over-the-top partisanship and polarization.
—Representative David E. Price (D-N.C.)

After the House Judiciary Committee (in yet another straight partisan vote) approved the fourth and final article of impeachment ("abuse of power") on December 13, 1998, it became apparent that the prospect of William Jefferson Clinton's becoming only the second president of the United States to be impeached by the full House of Representatives was very real. Regardless of the public opinion polls and the Republicans' losses in the November elections, it was clear that, like their Judiciary Committee colleagues, an overwhelming majority of the House Republicans would vote to impeach the president, while the highly partisan deliberations in the Judiciary Committee had reinforced the loyalty of the House Democrats to Clinton. The impeachment of President Clinton thus hinged on the relatively small group of moderate Republicans and Democrats who remained uncommitted at the close of the Judiciary Committee proceedings.

While opinion polls and the November elections demonstrated disapproval of impeachment and a desire to drop the entire matter, which had now preoccupied American politics for almost a year, opinion in the House—which according to the Framers of the Constitution is the body that is supposed to most closely represent the views of the American people—still remained more inclined toward impeachment. According to James Madison's comments in

97

reference to the proposed House of Representatives in *Federalist* No. 52: "As it is essential to liberty that the government in general should have a common interest with the people, so it is particularly essential that the branch of it under consideration [the House of Representatives] should have an immediate dependence on and an intimate sympathy with, the people."[1] But in the final calculus that determined the individual votes of House members on impeachment in December 1998, the views of the general public apparently mattered relatively little, at least by comparison with those of members' "primary" and "reelection" constituencies.[2] The outcome of the House floor vote was decided by the same factors that had driven the impeachment process from the outset and would also determine the outcome in the Senate trial: partisanship engendered by a congressional electoral environment that magnifies the influence of cultural cleavages and ideological party activists in American politics.

LEADERSHIP SHUFFLE

While the initial media reaction to the election results on November 3 had been to blame impeachment for the Republican failure, the reaction among Republicans was to blame their long-controversial Speaker. Newt Gingrich had been the mastermind of the Republican electoral strategy since he became de facto minority leader and then Speaker in 1992–1994. Although he had been seen as an electoral liability since the government shutdown of 1995–1996, he had succeeded in weathering an ethics investigation later that year and an effort to oust him as Speaker in 1997. He had survived because of his undoubted political skills and the continuing loyalty of many Republican members who still revered him as the architect of the 1994 electoral triumph.[3] Yet Gingrich became a lightning rod for criticism not just from congressional Democrats but the wider public, and no matter how strenuously Henry Hyde and the Judiciary Committee Republicans denied it, it was considered that his hand and that of the Republican leadership was behind the entire impeachment enterprise. Representative David E. Price's (D-N.C.) reaction was not untypical of Democrats and supporters of the president on Capitol Hill and in the country: "Impeachment was unleashed by the Gingrich revolution and the factors fueling it were a heavy mix of the 'anti-this, anti-that' passions stirred up by the 1994 Republican revolution. If you look back at the polls before the 1994 election, you can see the portends of the gathering storm that peaked in 1993–1994. The talk-show political culture had become almost mainstream and was tied into extreme animosity toward Clinton and the Clinton presidency. We had also gotten into the habit of moral accusation and scandal-mongering: 'gotcha' politics."[4]

Despite the animosity he aroused from Democrats, however, it was Gingrich's own Republican Party that ended his political career following the palpable failure of his strategy for the 1998 midterm elections. Parties not holding the White House traditionally make heavy gains in midterm elections and particularly in the second midterm of a two-term presidency (see Table 4.1). Republicans assumed that this factor plus the scandals hovering over the Clinton White House would deliver them an increased House majority in November 1998.[5] During the campaign Gingrich's strategy had been to play safe by reaching accommodations with the Democrats and the Clinton White House on the budget, to avoid having Republicans appear irresponsible and extreme as in 1995–1996.[6] Yet the Republican capitulation to the White House on the Fiscal Year (FY) 1999 budget in October angered many congressional and grassroots Republicans while bringing no obvious credit to the party among Democrats and Independents, who were upset by the impeachment proceedings. As it became clear that the election was not swinging the way of the Republicans in the closing weeks, Gingrich argued that Republicans should raise the impeachment issue in selected marginal districts. The subsequent television advertisements received free national airplay through news media coverage, but the effects seemed to be exactly the opposite of that intended.[7] Representative Martin Frost (D-Tex.), who was the chairman of the Democratic Congressional Campaign Committee (DCCC), described how the impeachment issue evolved during the campaign:

After the president's speech in August, there was some short-term negative fallout, especially among older women voters and older women party volunteers, some of whom said they were ashamed to be working at Democratic campaigns' headquarters. As the elections got closer that kind of wore off, and when Newt Gingrich forced the Republicans to make this into a campaign issue in the closing weeks of the campaign, the entire thing turned and the public reacted in entirely the opposite way. When the Republicans tried to capitalize on the scandal it was exactly the wrong thing for them to do. They miscalculated when they thought they could use this as an election issue. I was on the Sunday morning news shows two weeks before the election with my Republican counterpart, John Linder (R-Ga.), and two weeks out he was saying that the Republicans would not make impeachment a campaign issue. Then Newt Gingrich intervened and tried to make it into an issue. When Linder and I were back on the same shows a week later, he had to eat his words.[8]

The poor election results were the absolute last straw for many conservative House Republicans, who had become increasingly exasperated with Gingrich. (They were to be even more embarrassed after his ouster by revelations of an extramarital affair with a House staffer during Gingrich's divorce from his second wife Marianne.) Judiciary Committee Republican Charles T. Canady (R-Fla.) was typical of these conservative Republican critics who felt let down by their erstwhile leader: "I think it was a good thing that Gingrich stepped down. I thought he should have gone after the 1996 election, but I was part of a small minority then. I ended up voting for him as Speaker, but I wish I hadn't. It would have been better for the House Republicans if he had made his exit at that point, because his leadership style was no longer effective. I knew nothing about his personal life then, but knowing what we know now, it was even more reason for him to go." Veteran Republican Florida Representative E. Clay Shaw, Jr., was even more blunt: "The last couple of months have been a giant screw-up!"[9]

Reflecting this discontent within Republican ranks, Appropriations Committee Chairman Robert L. "Bob" Livingston announced on November 6, 1998 (three days after the election) that he was going to challenge Gingrich for the Speakership.[10] A standard Republican economic and social conservative, Livingston had demonstrated a pragmatic approach to the job of Appropriations chair and was an experienced and nonthreatening television performer. Apparently Livingston had been quietly rounding up commitments from Republican members for over a year, and had tacitly built up a considerable base of support among House Republicans, should Gingrich vacate the Speakership.[11] Later that day Gingrich announced his resignation, and it became clear that Livingston's quiet legwork in lining up commitments from members and his willingness to challenge Gingrich openly had precluded any rivals for the Speakership in the newly elected 106th Congress (1999–2001).

The new Speaker-in-waiting was not particularly keen to be closely associated with the impeachment drive that had contributed so heavily to the downfall of the old regime.[12] Trying to reorganize House Republicans for a fresh start under his leadership, Livingston adopted an "above the fray" position toward impeachment (until he was ignominiously dragged into the center of events at the bitter end of the drama in the House). With most Republicans still back in their districts after the election, the heavy lifting on the impeachment proceedings was left to Henry Hyde and the Judiciary Committee Republicans, who had decided without much hesitation to proceed with their inquiry after the elections. It was also at this point, however, that House Majority Whip and chief Republican vote-counter Tom Delay of Texas began to play a decisive role in the process. Ostensibly only the third-ranking Republican in the House, Delay had been in the ascendant within the House GOP after Gingrich's ostensible number two, Majority Leader Dick Armey (R-Tex.) had been effectively neutralized by his part in the 1997 abortive coup against Gingrich.[13] The leadership vacuum between Gingrich's resignation and Livingston's assumption of the full powers of the Speakership when the new Congress convened in January enabled the Texan to play a critical role in mobilizing House Republicans behind the eventual impeachment of the president: an event that seemed all but impossible in the days following the 1998 election.

THE PARTIES MOBILIZE

If there was ever a serious prospect that the impeachment inquiry would be abandoned in favor of a compromise acceptable to a broad majority of members in both parties, it should have occurred in the weeks immediately following the November 3 elections. The public had expressed a distaste for the continuation of the impeachment proceedings at the ballot box and in opinion polls. The most polarizing figure in the House—Speaker Gingrich—was gone. Finally, even if impeachment could be rammed through the House floor on a party-line vote, the prospects of twelve Democratic senators joining with all fifty-five Republicans to provide the required sixty-seven Senate votes to convict the president and remove him from office appeared to be minimal. Any face-saving formula appeared to involve an admission of "guilt" by President Clinton and the passage of a resolution of censure in the House, perhaps accompanied by some financial penalty. The Democratic House leadership had been suggesting censure as a possible way out of the partisan impeachment impasse since late September, and the White House had indicated interest in the idea.

Henry Hyde and several of the Judiciary Committee Republicans appeared open to the idea of compromise at this stage, but Independent Counsel Kenneth Starr had still to testify before the committee and they felt that Starr deserved the chance to make his case and respond to his detractors.[14] On November 5 Chairman Hyde announced that Starr would testify before the committee and at the same time sent the White House eighty-one very specific questions about the case in an effort to elicit some admission of guilt or wrongdoing by the president (see the appendixes).[15] The problem for President Clinton and his attorneys was that any admission of guilt in response to the committee's questions might risk a stampede toward impeachment or a possible criminal prosecution when President Clinton left office. This meant that any responses to the committee's interrogatories were likely to be vague, cautious, and lawyerly, and probably not providing the kind of admission that the Judiciary Committee Republicans were looking for.[16]

Independent Counsel Starr finally appeared before the committee on November 19, providing a two-hour statement and being cross-examined by committee counsel, the president's attorneys, and committee members.[17] The hearing resolved nothing, however. Starr's presentation of the case for impeaching President Clinton impressed the Republican majority, while Democrats, the president's attorneys, and minority counsel Abbie Lowell believed that their questions had demonstrated the highly partisan nature of his inquiry. Chairman Hyde opined that "Judge Starr has set forth a clear, documented, compelling case against the president," while the ever-voluble Representative Frank for the Democrats was less impressed: "What we learned today was that Starr reads well and speaks slowly."[18] The Democrats felt their case was reinforced when Starr's "ethics advisor," the former Senate Watergate Committee Majority Counsel Sam Dash, resigned the following day on the grounds that Starr had impugned his neutrality as an independent counsel by even accepting the committee's invitation to appear.[19]

At this juncture it appeared that the impeachment vote on the floor was going nowhere, with Democrats almost unanimously against impeachment and some thirty to forty Republican members unlikely to support it on the floor, according to the president's closest ally among House Republicans, Representative Peter King of New York.[20] (As it happened, Representative King, the Democrats, and the press probably underestimated the degree to which Starr's testimony, while it changed few minds in the country according to the pollsters, served to reinforce support for impeachment of the president within Republican ranks.) The committee was anxious to adhere to its self-imposed deadline of concluding the proceedings by year's end, placing impeachment behind them, and making a fresh start with a new Congress and new leadership in January. Unsurprisingly, it seems to have been at this point that the censure option was most seriously considered. Veteran Democratic Washington, D.C., lawyer Lloyd Cutler offered his services as a middle man and approached Chairman Hyde and several other leading Republicans about a censure deal. Representatives Lindsey Graham and Asa Hutchison were also involved in discussions about censure with Judiciary Committee Democrats such as Representative Howard Berman (Calif.), and White House counsel Greg Craig approached Representative Graham.[21] Some kind of compromise involving censure was the way the political process in Washington is supposed to work: reasonable members on both sides arrive at a deal that satisfies Washington and public opinion, and the country moves on. It did not happen in the case of the Clinton impeachment because contemporary observers and some of the participants in the drama failed to understand the factors that really drove partisan dynamics in the late 1990s House of Representatives, and also because any kind of censure deal was premised on an admission of "guilt" by the White House sufficient to satisfy a substantial number of House Republicans. For political and legal reasons mentioned above, such an admission would not be forthcoming. When added together these elements would lead to the impeachment of the president on the House floor.

One person who was acutely aware of channels of partisan influence—at least on the Republican side—and who was absolutely determined to impeach President Clinton was Majority Whip Tom Delay. Delay's head count of members after Starr's appearance before the committee surprisingly demonstrated that impeachment was still a real possibility, particularly on the grand jury perjury charge.[22] The Majority Whip's problem was the thirty or so moderate House Republicans, mainly from districts and states that had supported Clinton for president in 1996 and where impeachment appeared to be extremely unpopular.

An entire school of academic scholarship on Congress has been premised on David R. Mayhew's simple proposition that most of what goes on in Congress can be explained by the need of members to be reelected.[23] Richard F. Fenno, Jr., and others have demonstrated, of course, that there is not just one reelection constituency and that members also have to respond to primary electorates, and an even smaller subset within that electorate for financial and physical campaign support.[24] These constituencies are invariably far more partisan and ideological than the district's general electorate.[25] (And the tendency of the redistricting process to create districts overwhelmingly safe for one or the other party reduces even further any moderating influence.) Both political parties also rely heavily on national political action committees (PACs) and single-issue or ideological networks for funding and grassroots support in both primary and general elections.[26] In short, as election turnouts remain generally low, American politics has increasingly become what Steven E. Schier refers to as a politics of "mobilization," and that game places a great premium on party loyalty and the ideological networks that support the contemporary parties.[27] On Capitol Hill since 1980, advancement requires loyalty to party leaders, who as Barbara Sinclair observes, can provide the requisite committee assignments, and help with reelection through their links with sympathetic PACs and conservative or liberal single-issue and ideological networks.[28]

For these reasons a vote against the mainstream of conservative Republican (as opposed to national) opinion on impeachment was no easy matter for Republican members, and no Republican was more aware of this factor than Majority Whip Tom Delay, who had built intimate relationships with national conservative networks in the course of his political career.[29] Members on both sides of the aisle unhesitatingly point to Delay as the key figure in determining the eventual outcome of the impeachment vote. He had entered politics in Texas after building a successful pest control business in the greater Houston area. From the beginning of his congressional career in 1984, he had proven to be a prodigious fund-raiser and political operator, but he first came to public attention when he surprisingly won the position of majority whip in the wake of the 1994 Republican takeover by defeating Newt Gingrich's closest confidant, former Representative Robert S. Walker (R-Pa.) at the zenith of Gingrich's political power. In the course of campaigning for this position, the Texan contributed more than $2 million to Republican candidates, and his fund-raising skills were highlighted again when he set out to build stronger ties between the new Republican majority and Washington lobbyists by bringing the latter into the drafting of legislation.[30] Outside the House, Delay had also channeled millions of dollars to Republican candidates and party committees through his own political action committee and groups he founded. In 1999 alone he raised $15 million in campaign funds for the House Republican campaign committee.

Delay had also acquired a reputation as the best vote counter in the House, and delighted in the nickname of "The Hammer," bestowed on him for his hard-headed view of his job as Whip.[31] Yet this was no cynical political operator, for all of Delay's vote counting and fund-raising was done with a purpose: to advance his hard-core of conservative ideological convictions, and Bill Clinton as president was the most formidable obstacle to the advancement of those convictions. Moreover, Clinton's conduct offended Delay's deeply ingrained social and religious conservatism. Thus while other Republican leaders might have been ready to wriggle off the hook of impeachment after the election, Delay welcomed the challenge, and the leadership vacuum after Gingrich's resignation gave him the opportunity to direct events, and almost single-handedly bring impeachment back to life. The minority whip also had the advantage of being in Washington while the Judiciary Committee hearings were winding down after the election, while most members were still home in their districts. Impeachment opponent Representative King remembers the shift toward impeachment in late 1998:

> We had a party conference down here [Washington D.C.] to elect the leadership about ten days after the election, and I didn't hear one person mention impeachment. As far as I was concerned it was dead. Then Starr testified because the Judiciary Committee Republicans felt that they owed Starr. He made the case and that was it. Newt Gingrich was finished and Bob Livingston was Speaker elect, and I'm certain that Livingston wanted no part of going ahead (we didn't know that Bob Livingston had his own problem), and that explains why Delay took this over. Then Clinton gave his answers to the Judiciary Committee's eighty-one interrogatories. Those were basically bullshit answers and they gave some impetus to the impeachment case. . . . I came back to Washington the Saturday after Thanksgiving and the world had turned upside down. Republican members were against impeachment when they were coming back two to three days a week, but while we were isolated out in the district, Delay was calling the shots here in Washington. We didn't come back to D.C. from mid-November until the day of the final vote.[32]

Representative King's remarks also indicate another factor that revived impeachment from the doldrums after the elections: Clinton's responses to the Judiciary Committee's eighty-one questions, which arrived on Friday, November 27. The highly legalistic and evasive responses to the questions infuriated Republicans, and set back the hopes of those who were looking for some acknowledgment of wrongdoing that might serve as the basis for a censure deal. The answer to the first question was characteristic:

Question: Do you admit or deny that you are the chief law enforcement officer of the United States of America?

Answer: The President is frequently referred to as the chief law enforcement officer, although nothing in the Constitution specifically designates the president as such. Article II, Section 1 of the United States Constitution states that "'the executive power shall be vested in a president of the United States of America," and the law enforcement function is a component of the executive power.[33]

The president's attorneys were determined to give the committee nothing that might lend any credence to Starr's case for perjury and obstruction of justice or set up the president for possible criminal prosecution upon leaving office.[34]

But the responses they provided actually played right into Delay's hands and reinvigorated the waning impetus toward impeachment among Republicans, by reminding them of the "slickness" and "slipperiness" that stoked their dislike of the president. According to *Washington Post* journalist Peter Baker, "The answers landed like an unguided missile on Capitol Hill. Hyde and the other committee members saw the president's response as flagrant disrespect for them and the House as a whole. The momentum Delay had begun to detect among Republicans only accelerated. Any inclination to give the president a break, to extend the hand of forgiveness, or even to cut their own losses following the election debacle died at this point."[35] Baker's view is corroborated by the response of Representative Lindsey Graham, the Judiciary Committee Republican most predisposed to finding a way out of the impeachment impasse, who felt his efforts had been totally undermined by the president's evasiveness (see Chapter 3).

In the meantime Tom Delay had been hard at work utilizing his connections to the conservative media, fund-raising, and activist networks to orchestrate a single message on the importance of impeaching the president to wavering Republicans. Again, according to Baker:

> In addition to constantly distributing anti-Clinton information to House Republicans and keeping up a steady drumbeat of public criticism of the president, Delay was using a network of conservative talk shows and party fund-raisers to generate pressure within the GOP. He would go on as many as ten radio talk shows a day, and his staff would blast-fax talking points and tip sheets to perhaps two hundred such programs at a time, revving up the conservative audience that would then turn up the heat on their local congressmen. Similarly major campaign contributors and local party officials were encouraged to talk with members about impeachment.[36]

After the Judiciary Committee had voted four articles of impeachment from December 1 through 12, and it became clear that a floor vote on impeachment was imminent, the pressure really began to build on undecided Republican members, coming from Delay and the Republican base.

Representative Mark Souder of Indiana was one of those members. A very socially conservative member of the large Republican freshman class of 1994, Souder came to Congress after working for his conservative Republican predecessors in Indiana's fourth congressional district, Senator Dan Coates and Vice President Dan Quayle. Since entering the House he had consistently clashed with the Clinton administration on almost every issue and had been one of the diehard Republicans during the 1995–1996 government shutdown.[37] Moreover, Representative Souder had actually supported a 1997 resolution from hard-line Judiciary Committee Republican Bob Barr calling for the Judiciary Committee to open an impeachment inquiry into the 1996 Clinton fund-raising scandals. Yet as the Lewinsky affair unfolded Representative Souder had serious doubts about whether the president's conduct really merited the drastic remedy of impeachment:

> My district is conservative, and everyone knew that I was on Bill Clinton's case before. I was one of the hard-core nineteen who signed the Barr resolution, and I am a conservative Christian. I was outraged at Clinton's behavior, but the more I study the Founding Fathers, I do not recognize them as the type of people who would be elected as elders in my church. Their behavior was not always so open and honest. They also never used the impeachment clause, which wasn't used until Andrew Johnson, and although there may have been good intentions behind it, the Johnson impeachment was a pretty political business. All that leads me to believe that the impeachment clause was intended for traitors and abuse of public office. Would there have been a serious effort to impeach Clinton if he had lied about something other than sex?[38]

Majority Whip Delay was far too subtle a political operator to lean overtly on such an independent-minded legislator as Souder, but the Indiana Republican had no doubts that there was a great deal of pressure being generated from his political base:

> They [the leadership] didn't lean on me, but if Tom Delay had not done the research and put out his briefing books, impeachment would not have occurred. The leadership, however, respected that it was a conscience vote. Some Republicans went on TV and embarrassed the leadership, but I was pretty silent and never publicly criticized my fellow Republicans for being overzealous. I know that quite a few members of the Judiciary Committee had doubts. Lindsey Graham had lots of doubts, and Asa Hutchinson had doubts too, but was not as forthcoming about them. Some were seriously thinking about voting "no" right up to the vote. Lots were wavering up to the tail end, but I don't recall a single person saying they voted for impeachment because the leadership hammered them. The leadership worked with the conservative groups, though, and those groups may have threatened members. All the leadership did was provide the information. People who hated Bill Clinton didn't need to be organized by Tom Delay.[39]

Most of the other Republican waverers were northeastern moderates far closer to the political center than Representative Souder, and the Clinton White House had reasonable expectations that they might be able to reach out to them, given the apparent strong opposition to impeaching the president in their home regions. Clinton's main ambassador to the moderates was Republican Representative King. A populist social conservative and economic moderate, the Irish American King grew close to Clinton during the president's Northern Ireland peace trips (he twice traveled with the president to Ireland) and had been the first Republican to come out against impeachment:

> I first heard about it when my wife came running into the bedroom and told me "you won't believe what your friend's done!" The atmosphere was hysterical with people like Sam Donaldson saying "if it's proven true, he must resign." Legally I never saw it as being impeachable. I had followed the Nixon impeachment carefully and I was an historical opponent of independent counsels. I felt that the Iran-Contra Special Prosecutor Lawrence Walsh had gone too far, and after what happened to Clarence Thomas and John Tower, I thought this town was destroying itself by investigations. Still I couldn't believe that Bill Clinton had been so crazy, but I didn't think it was impeachable.[40]

In trying to broker some kind of censure deal with the moderates, Representative King found himself caught between the pressure on the moderates coming from the Republican base and the president's fear of admitting too much:

> In the first week of December I was talking with [Republican Representative] Mike Castle [Del.] and we spoke about alternatives to impeachment that would involve Clinton making some statement and paying a large fine. The White House was basically in agreement, and Mike thought that a number of moderates would go along with that. I floated the idea on CNN that Republican moderates were close to a deal on impeachment, but before the day was out they were backing away from it. A number who told me they were against impeachment started coming out for it that week. I think a lot of moderates were scared off because they were getting flak from Republican women who were particularly offended at what Clinton had done. The following week I met with Clinton in a hotel room. He was speaking at a dinner and he asked me to be there. I told him I still felt that a lot of Republican moderates were waiting for a way to get out, and that some contrition and admitting of what he had done would be enough. But the problem became insurmountable because he feared that

if he dealt with them, they would grandstand and accuse him of jury tampering. That's how tense things had gotten. He had to deal with them but as far as I know, he never spoke to any of them.[41]

On the Democratic side, the leadership concentrated on trying to get a censure resolution onto the floor. Such a resolution, they believed, would attract a large number of Republican votes and come much closer to reflecting the true consensus of the House (and the nation) than any impeachment resolution that might be passed on a largely party-line vote. It would also allow Democrats in more conservative parts of the country to condemn the president's conduct while supporting their party leadership. But of course these were exactly the reasons why Tom Delay was determined to keep such a resolution off the floor. And in this effort he secured the support of both Henry Hyde and Speaker-elect Livingston by convincing them that allowing a censure vote might spark a revolt by conservatives in the Republican conference.[42] If the censure option were denied to the wavering Republican members, then a vote in favor of impeachment would be their only opportunity to go on the record in condemnation of Clinton's conduct and thereby conciliate their Republican electoral base. The likelihood, moreover, that Clinton would be acquitted by the Senate meant that a vote for impeachment would have little long-term negative political impact among more moderate general election voters. Representative David E. Price, a moderate Democrat from North Carolina and one-time professor of political science at Duke University, would have welcomed a chance to vote for a censure resolution but also perfectly understood the partisan dynamics of the contemporary House that denied him that opportunity:

> There was uncertainty until very late and I had predicted censure as a matter of course. But the Republican electoral setback made it [impeachment] more likely because of the ascendancy of Tom Delay, and Delay found ways of pushing the issue that made it hard for Republican moderates to oppose impeachment, and jerked the rug out from under centrist alternatives. He defined impeachment down like it was censure, and the activation of the Republican base had assumed such intensity that the moderate members felt they had to throw some red meat to the base. Delay was very skillful at shutting off all the censure options, so that the final vote on impeachment was a vote on approval or disapproval of the president's conduct. Had the leadership been there to create alternatives [censuring the president without impeachment], they would have attracted a good number of Republicans and a large majority of Democrats.[43]

The Democrats rallied behind Representative Rick Boucher's resolution that had been turned down earlier by the Judiciary Committee, but they knew by now that their chances of forcing a floor vote were minimal.[44] To do so they would have to defeat the rule for debate on the impeachment articles, and significant party defections on a rules vote are extremely rare in the contemporary House.

One final element was thrown into the mix during the tumultuous week between the Judiciary Committee vote and the floor vote on impeachment. There still remained a considerable amount of "redacted" material from the Starr Report that had been thought to be too unsavory or irrelevant to be released to the press and public. Some of this material involved the so-called "Jane Does," women who had given testimony to Starr on their relationships with the president. The most sensational material was in the testimony of "Jane Doe, No. 5"—an Arkansas nursing home operator named Juanita Broaddrick—who claimed that President Clinton had raped her twenty years previously. Undecided Republican members in the final days before impeachment were encouraged by Delay and his whip organization to visit the room in the Ford House Office Building where the redacted material was stored. Representatives Souder and Christopher H. Shays (R-Conn.) were two of those undecided members who read Broaddrick's testimony. Representative Souder recalled:

> Starr didn't pursue Juanita Broaddrick's allegations because he already thought he had enough. Chris Shays and I felt he didn't have enough, but we were told that the Judiciary Committee members couldn't talk about the "Jane Does" until after the release of the report, but we were told to "watch tomorrow." Steve Buyer [R-Ind.] and Ed Pease [R-Ind.] from Judiciary told us to go in and look at the unreleased material, and Chris Shays and I were the first to go in. In fairness, Clinton's lawyers had had no opportunity to cross-examine Broaddrick, but her testimony was compelling stuff.[45]

Thus as the impeachment vote loomed on December 16, 1998, it increasingly appeared likely that at least one of the four articles of impeachment passed by the House Judiciary Committee would also pass on the House floor, despite almost unanimous opposition from the minority party and some two-thirds of the American public as measured by public opinion polls. This outcome, which seemed inconceivable six weeks earlier in the wake of the Republican election debacle, came about because none of the major parties could extricate themselves from a partisan conflict in a manner that would satisfy them all and the American public. White House and Democratic arrogance in the wake of November 3 led them to ignore the potential power of partisanship, ideology, and culture over the Republican House members, no matter how uneasy the latter were about impeaching the president in defiance of public opinion. As we have seen, Majority Whip Delay, who had moved into the temporary Republican leadership vacuum, exploited that potential. Delay also succeeded in closing off the censure option, although he was abetted in this regard by the White House's inability to provide some kind of acknowledgment of wrongdoing that might have allowed Chairman Hyde and other wavering Republicans to get off the impeachment hook. As has been apparent at every stage of this process, however, the determining factor in the outcome of impeachment was partisanship pure and simple, and from the very beginning of congressional involvement in the Lewinsky affair, it had been partisanship that had driven the course of events. Clinton was impeached because those Republicans and conservatives who vote regularly in primary and general elections for the House strongly believed that his conduct was impeachable. Almost all House Democrats opposed impeachment because their electoral, activist, and fund-raising bases were equally vehement in defense of the president. Representative Souder neatly summarized the situation:

> There were thirty or so Republicans who told me that they had doubts about impeachment but that they didn't want a primary. There were also some Democratic colleagues who wouldn't even look at the redacted material in the Starr Report because they feared they would feel pressure to vote to impeach and they didn't want a primary. Neither side wanted to look at the other side's stuff. Many Democrats were appalled at Clinton but could not vote to impeach him. It was the same thing that drove the Republicans, and they were just as bad. Among the third that hated Clinton were the traditional Republicans, the primary voters, the givers, and the precinct committeemen. It was the same story in the other direction on the Democratic side. Where were the middle people?[46]

"DELIBERATION" IN THE CONTEMPORARY HOUSE

The Framers were purposeful with their intent to design Congress to promote deliberation, and throughout much of its history the institution has maintained a rich tradition of debate and deliberation.[47] Celebrated orations in the tradition

of Webster, Clay, and Calhoun—hallmarks of compelling debate that combined eloquence with argument, and sentiment with evidence—influenced the
way people perceived and took sides on the great issues of the day. Legislators fought over words, as Robert T. Oliver suggests, because they believed
that words mattered.[48] Politics was a central topic of the age and formal oratory the preeminent mode of political expression.[49] On a matter as grave as
the impeachment of a president, one would expect that the standard of debate
and deliberation on the House floor would be particularly high. Yet aside
from dramatic moments such as Speaker-elect Livingston's unexpected resignation, there was little that was memorable in terms of rhetoric in the House
floor debate on the Clinton impeachment: an indication of the diminished
role of debate and deliberation in the contemporary House.

The concept of deliberation has been defined in varying ways. Barbara
Sinclair defines deliberation as the process "by which a group of people get
together and talk through a complex problem, mapping the problem's con-
tours, defining the alternatives, and figuring out where they stand."[50] George E.
Connor and Bruce I. Oppenheimer separate the concept of deliberation into
two components: "*inter*-institutional" (that is, between institutions) and
"*intra*-institutional" (or "rational discussion tempered by reasoned debate"
within a particular institution).[51] Deliberation is inevitably associated in most
people's minds with formal debate occurring on the House and Senate
floors.[52] It is the part of the lawmaking process that is most observable to the
outsider. In congressional parlance, debate refers to speeches delivered during floor consideration of a measure, motion, or other matter, different from
speeches in nondeliberative situations—for example, one-minute or special
order speeches.[53] Thus Steven S. Smith distinguishes between debate, "a verbal contest between people of opposing views," and deliberation, "reasoning
together about the nature of a problem and solutions to it."[54]

Debate and deliberation work to clarify national issues, to provide a forum
for members of Congress to discuss pros and cons. Together they provide an
opportunity for the instruction of lawmakers who have not considered the
problem at hand and as a source of new information that those with previous
convictions on the matter may not have considered.[55] According to political
communications scholar Giraud Chester, debate reconciles diverging positions of conflicting groups and policies by establishing a basis for compromise.[56] For most of the nineteenth century debate and floor behavior provoked
noisy response and, occasionally, fierce physical violence.[57] In the heat of
deliberation, members were known to assail one another with fists, pistols,
knives, canes, even fire tongs, as well as freely indulge in such epithets as

"liar," "scoundrel," "moral traitor," and "puppy."[58] The often unmanageable size of the House chamber further conspired to produce commotion, chaos, and irritation, as the acoustics and ventilation of the old Hall were crude by modern standards. Before the construction of the first office building—Cannon Office Building—for representatives, lawmakers were forced to transact their business from their desks on the floor. There they read the daily record of proceedings, answered letters from home, and would confer with their colleagues over the day's agenda. As one congressional observer noted, "The clatter from the slamming desk drawers, the rustling [sic] of paper, the hurly-burly of pages scampering about the Hall, and the hum of many voices raised a din through which only an exceptional voice could penetrate."[59]

In the contemporary Congress, especially the House, debate and deliberation have been relegated to a necessary ritual in the formal legislative process, only rarely conforming to what the Framers had in mind: legislators persuading their colleagues with apt phrases, emotional appeals, or concise explications of the problems at hand.[60] Pure oratory is increasingly uncommon and unfashionable, and generally replaced by partisan posturing.[61] Speechmaking on the floor is often tolerated rather than being used to inform, much less persuade other members.[62]

While their task of getting themselves elected depends largely upon their ability to verbally appeal to the sentiments as well as to the reason of constituents, today's lawmakers place greater emphasis on tactical position-taking and lobbying activities than on significant public statements.[63] Moreover, representatives are generally obligated by the chamber's size and complexity to shorten the time frame for floor debate and drastically limit individuals' participation. In most instances lawmakers decide on how they will vote well before stepping foot on the floor. Floor deliberations are thus often too "foreshortened to facilitate persuasion and allow serious examination of the questions at hand."[64] Instead, members of the House fill the *Congressional Record* with speeches for constituents or engage in prearranged formal dialogues with other members. A new school of speakers has developed, one in which practitioners are trained in "brevity" and "telling the phrase" or "sound bites."[65] It is a style emblematic of an era of heightened partisanship, centralized legislative influence, and a work load that has grown in size and complexity. Communications scholar Kathleen Hall Jamieson observes that some elements of the House impeachment debate were handled with decorum and thoughtful exchanges, but in general the impeachment resolution generated low levels of cooperation and substantial increases in vulgarity and name-calling.[66]

Still, despite the reduced importance of debate in Congress, no legislative strategist dares to ignore formal debate on one of the largest and oldest of congressional arenas, the House floor; neither camp in any floor fight could risk yielding debate by default to the opposition, for to do so would hazard the very outcome of the vote.[67] On the contrary, on every contested question both sides of the aisle try to bring forward their ablest and most articulate speakers to argue their cause on the floor.[68] And as with any other lawmaking activity, there are legislators of wit and humor, who attract attention almost every time they rise to speak. For both parties, during the two-day House floor deliberation, various members were called upon to sum up the debate, rally the troops, and to shape the public's understanding of the impeachment process.[69]

THE HOUSE IMPEACHMENT DEBATE

The House votes on impeachment occurred amid an out of the ordinary and dizzying juxtaposition of historic events, with the nation watching as television networks preempted regular programming. Less than seven weeks after Democrats picked up a net of five House seats in the midterm elections, representatives were summoned back to the Capitol for a special impeachment session. The debate was due to open on Thursday, December 17, 1998, but was delayed for twenty-four hours because of the president's announcement of American bombing raids over Iraq in retaliation for its expulsion of United Nations arms inspectors. Of course this only heightened tensions even further, as Republicans suspected that Clinton had planned a national security crisis to distract attention from his impeachment troubles along the lines of the current Hollywood movie *Wag the Dog,* while Democrats were outraged that the Republicans would attempt to undercut the Commander-in-Chief while the nation was engaged in hostilities abroad.[70] The drama was heightened even further on impeachment eve when the press began to run stories (originally emanating from pornographer Larry Flynt) that Speaker-elect Livingston had had extramarital affairs.

As mentioned above, the rule for the debate, written by the House Republican leadership, allowed merely a straight up and down vote on the four articles with no provision for debate of the Democratic censure resolution. In order to force a vote on censure the Democrats would have to win a vote changing the rule, an almost impossible task given the House norm of not deserting one's party on a procedural vote.

Throughout the two-day floor deliberation on impeachment, which opened on Friday, December 18, 1998, both sides held firm to familiar arguments but did not respond to the other side's points.[71] Republicans framed their arguments on moral grounds, deriding the president for what they regarded as clear felonies and crimes of perjury and obstruction of justice, misdeeds that in their view unequivocally merited impeachment in order to preserve the rule of law. Democrats insisted, equally persistently, that the president's lies about an illicit affair, often described as "private wrongs," posed no threat to the state, and did not rise to the standard of "high crimes and misdemeanors" established for impeachment in the U.S. Constitution.

The tone of the debate was set right at the beginning, with Democrats pressing Republican leaders to delay, arguing in the words of Representative David E. Bonior (D-Mich.) that "this is not the proper time to debate the removal of the commander-in-chief while our troops are fighting abroad."[72] Democrats did engage in minor and hopeless parliamentary skirmishing, motioning first to adjourn even before debate started. The motion was easily shot down on a party-line vote, but served a purpose. "We wanted the Republicans on record as moving forward to remove the commander-in-chief in wartime," a Democratic aide commented of "the context" of the historic debate, coming as the United States was taking military action against Iraq.[73]

Procedural wrangling failed to halt the debate, which started with House Judiciary Committee Chairman Henry Hyde of Illinois outlining the case against the president and declaring: "No man or woman, no matter how high placed, no matter how effective a communicator, no matter how gifted a manipulator of opinion or winner of votes, can be above the law in a democracy."[74] From then on, Republicans tried to keep the focus on the issue of the rule of law, arguing that no other facts mattered than that Clinton had perjured himself and obstructed justice to cover up his relationship with former White House intern Monica Lewinsky. Much of the substance of the debate had been heard earlier in the House Judiciary Committee's hearings and, before that, in the immediate aftermath of the Starr Report.

Democrats by and large continued to adhere to the position earlier outlined by their leadership, and restated succinctly by their then Campaign Committee Chair Martin Frost three and a half years after the event: "President Clinton had done wrong but it didn't rise to the level of an impeachable offense."[75] "Perjury on a private matter—perjury regarding sex—is not a 'great and dangerous offense against the Nation,'" charged Representative Jerrold Nadler (D-N.Y.) on the House floor. "It is not an abuse of uniquely presidential power. It does not threaten our form of government. It is not an impeachable offense."[76] Nadler continued: "Is the president above the law?

Certainly not. . . . But impeachment is intended as a remedy to protect the nation, not as a punishment for a president. The case is not there—there is far from sufficient evidence to support the allegations, and the allegations, even if proven, do not rise to the level of impeachable offenses. We should not dignify these articles of impeachment by sending them to the Senate. To do so would be an affront to the Constitution and would consign this House to the condemnation of history for generations to come."[77] Nadler concluded by commenting that Republican charges were clearly a "partisan railroad job," in which the same people who advocated impeaching the president for lying under oath had previously voted to reelect Speaker Gingrich, who had acknowledged lying to Congress in an official proceeding about abuse of the tax laws for particular purposes.

Democrats also took Republicans to task for questioning the president's motives in deciding to bomb Iraq the night before impeachment, maintaining Republicans had been out to get Clinton since his election to the White House in 1992. They talked about Independent Counsel Starr's vengefulness, emphasized the role of Linda Tripp in the Lewinsky affair, and contended that only division could come of impeaching the president.[78]

Judiciary Committee Republicans kicked off the impeachment debate with short speeches summarizing the charges against the president. "The president was obliged, under his sacred oath, to faithfully execute our nation's laws," charged Representative James E. Rogan (R-Calif.). "Yet he repeatedly perjured himself and obstructed justice."[79] Resigned to defeat even before the debate began, Democrats objected vainly but vociferously to what they deemed a "partisan coup d'état."[80] Representative Ken Bentsen (D-Tex.) stated: "It is truly a shame that the leadership of the Republican majority is effectively forcing the hands of members in a process that is very unfair and undemocratic. Is it the American way to stifle debate? Is this just another procedure by the House leadership not to trust the members to make up their own minds? Presenting the Congress with a vote on impeachment only is like saying to a jury, you can vote for either the death penalty or acquittal."[81]

What appeared as a normal legislative session on the House floor was anything but off the floor and in the ornate Speaker's lobby and in the corridors around the chamber, where it was much more tense, loud, and, at times, aggressive. There was little respect, trust, fairness, or forgiveness. At one point, red-faced and fuming, Massachusetts Democrat Patrick J. Kennedy launched into a tirade about Georgia Republican Bob Barr, who had cited in his floor speech an address by President John F. Kennedy concerning the importance of the rule of law.[82] The thirty-one-year-old nephew of the former president lambasted Barr and all the Republicans for pursuing a partisan vote.[83] Later, spotting Barr talking to journalists, Kennedy walked up and denounced the sight of "a racist quoting my uncle, a racist like Bob Barr," in reference to an earlier speech the Georgia legislator had made to a southern conservative organization.[84] Representative Barr, a former federal prosecutor, reminded Kennedy of House rules that require lawmakers to maintain civility in the corridors of the Capitol.

The most dramatic and emotional moment of the entire proceedings came when Speaker-elect Livingston came to the podium at 9:30 A.M. on Saturday, December 19. Livingston's demand that the president should resign to prevent further damage to the country was greeted by howls of outrage from the Democrats who shouted that he himself should also resign because of his admission of adulterous conduct. The Speaker-elect proceeded to announce that he would do exactly that to set an example to the president. In fact, since the revelations about his private life had surfaced Livingston had faced pressure from some elements of the Republican conference to withdraw, although the other top Republican leaders in the House, including Delay, had stood by him. Later Minority Leader Gephardt took to the floor and in a rousing and impassioned address implored Livingston to reconsider his decision, but it was to no avail.[85]

As the overwhelming majority of moderate Republicans had announced that they would vote to impeach President Clinton on at least one of the articles during the last few days prior to the debate, the outcome was never seriously in doubt. The only question was which and how many of the four articles would be approved. Before the votes on the articles, the Democratic leadership and a handful of moderate Republicans who felt Clinton's actions were reprehensible but not impeachable attempted a parliamentary maneuver to substitute censure language for the impeachment articles. The Democrats proposed censure language that harshly condemned the president for making "false statements" concerning his culpable conduct and charging that he "violated the trust of the American people, lessened their esteem for the office of the president, and dishonored the presidency" (see box on p. 118). The move was ruled out of order by the presiding officer, Representative Ray H. LaHood (R-Ill.), as nongermane, based on long-standing precedents from the House parliamentarian's office. An attempt to overturn the ruling was beaten back 230 to 204 on a near-party-line procedural vote, with just two Republicans siding with the Democrats and four Democrats voting with the Republican majority.

House members approved Article I (see Table 5.1), which charged President Clinton with lying before a federal grand jury, in a 228 to 206 vote, and

H. Res. 614

In the House of Representatives, U.S., December 19, 1998.
Resolved, That Mr. Hyde of Illinois, Mr. Sensenbrenner of Wisconsin,
Mr. McCollum of Florida, Mr. Gekas of Pennsylvania, Mr. Canady of Florida,
Mr. Buyer of Indiana, Mr. Bryant of Tennessee, Mr. Chabot of Ohio, Mr. Barr of
Georgia, Mr. Hutchinson of Arkansas, Mr. Cannon of Utah, Mr. Rogan of
California, and Mr. Graham of South Carolina are appointed managers to conduct
the impeachment trial against William Jefferson Clinton, President of the United
States, that a message be sent to the Senate to inform the Senate of these
appointments, and that the managers so appointed may, in connection with the
preparation and the conduct of the trial, exhibit the articles of impeachment to
the Senate and take all other actions necessary, which may include the following:

(1) Employing legal, clerical, and other necessary assistants and incurring such
    other expenses as may be necessary, to be paid from amounts available to
    the Committee on the Judiciary under applicable expense resolutions or from
    the applicable accounts of the House of Representatives.
(2) Sending for persons and papers, and filing with the Secretary of the Senate,
    on the part of the House of Representatives, any pleadings, in conjunction
    with or subsequent to, the exhibition of the articles of impeachment that the
    managers consider necessary.

Speaker of the House of Representatives.

Attest: *Clerk.*

(Source: *Congressional Record*)

Article III, which accused the president of obstructing justice, passed 221 to
212. Only five Republicans broke ranks with their party in the vote on the
first article, with twelve more breaking ranks to oppose Article III.[86] Alternatively, only five Democrats broke ranks to vote for all of the first three articles.[87] Article II, alleging perjury in the Jones case deposition, failed 205 to
229 (with 28 Republicans voting against), while Article IV—"abuse of
power"—was easily defeated by 204 votes to 147, with only one Democrat
voting in favor and eighty-one Republicans voting against.

CONCLUSION

The House floor debate on the Clinton impeachment and the maneuvering
that preceded it confirms that the House impeachment of President Clinton
was an essentially partisan, political proceeding. While censure remained a

Table 5.1. House Vote on Articles of Impeachment Against President Clinton

Article		DEMOCRATS		REPUBLICANS		ALL	
		For	Against	For	Against	For	Against
I	Alleged that the president perjured himself in federal grand jury testimony in August 1998	5	201	223	5	228	206
II	Alleged that the president perjured himself in his January 1998 civil deposition in the Paula Jones sexual harassment lawsuit.	5	201	200	23	205	229
III	Alleged that the president obstructed justice by attempting to persuade witnesses to testify falsely on the question of whether or not he had had a sexual relationship with a White House intern, Monica Lewinsky.	5	200	216	12	221	212
IV	(As amended by the Judiciary Committee) Alleged that the president had abused his power and misled the Committee through his responses to eighty-one questions submitted to him in November, 1998.	1	204	147	81	148	285

SOURCE: *Congressional Record*

viable nonpartisan alternative to impeachment right up to the last days before the vote, neither side felt it could make the compromises necessary to accomplish this without inflicting long-term political damage on themselves and their party. To satisfy Henry Hyde, a censure resolution would have required an admission by the president to crimes that might have left him liable to criminal prosecution upon leaving office. Anything less than that would have been an effective concession that the Starr Report and the entire Judiciary Committee proceedings had been a complete waste of time, something that could not be sold to the Republican core electoral constituency back in the districts, after a year of Lewinsky-related revelations. In such a fervid partisan and media atmosphere both sides came to believe that the costs of proceeding outweighed the costs of appearing to back down. The members in the middle who might have been the key players in cutting a deal to avoid impeachment were simply too few and too beholden to their district electoral bases and the party leadership to exercise any real influence.

The resignation of Gingrich and the tentative approach of Livingston meant that the director of events for the Republicans was Majority Whip Delay, the member of the Republican leadership most determined to impeach the president. Without Delay's subtle direction of the shell-shocked and uncertain House Republicans after their unexpected election setback, some way out of the impeachment process might have been found. But the fact that the majority whip was able to pass two impeachment articles on the floor of the House with only five GOP defectors, after an electoral setback and the destruction of the political careers of a Speaker and a Speaker elect, is testimony to the ease with which a partisan response can be provoked in the contemporary House even in the unlikeliest situation. After the November election, a significant number of House Republicans—not all moderates— were willing to set impeachment aside. Delay then provided them with what they saw as solid reasons to impeach President Clinton, or at least reasons that satisfied most of their core supporters back home. The majority whip's success in sidetracking the censure option (and the virtual certainty of a subsequent Senate acquittal) left the impeachment articles in the House as the only opportunity to condemn Clinton for his conduct, and thus facilitated a pro-impeachment vote on the part of ambivalent Republican members.

The Democratic House minority was in a "win-win" situation and had no apparent political reason to forfeit any ground in search of a bipartisan compromise. The November 1998 election results and the opinion poll numbers demonstrated that the Democrats had already successfully made their case to their core supporters and much of the undecided public on impeachment, namely that the entire proceeding had been a partisan course of action on the part of Kenneth Starr and the House GOP leadership. If the Republicans backed down on impeachment, the Democrats could take political credit and appear statesmanlike. If, by contrast, impeachment proceeded, the Democratic minority might lose on the House floor but feel vindicated before the court of public opinion. Apart from a few scattered members in very conservative districts, House Democrats could also feel very secure that their core voters were wholly behind their defense of the president (although the events of 1998 may have had a more subtle and largely detrimental effect on Democratic performance among swing voters in the 2000 presidential race and the 2002 congressional elections).

Those who had been bitterly disappointed, even shocked, by the partisan manner in which the House conducted the impeachment proceedings might have hoped that the Senate, the body that is constitutionally empowered to temper the House's impetuosity, might arrive at a solution to the impeachment crisis and finally satisfy the public and all the parties to the conflict. As we shall see, the "other body" did go some way toward accomplishing this task, but hardly in a manner untainted by partisanship and not before the entire constitutional impeachment process had run its course.

6
Herding Cats to Trial

The Senate demonstrated a capacity to carry out its constitutional responsibilities in a partisan atmosphere and during a national emotional debate with sharp partisan divisions. It was important for the Senate to do so in a way that would satisfy the desires of the American people for fairness and that we would carry out our duties in a thoughtful, serious-minded way, that would reflect credit on the constitution and encourage the notion that the government had done well. I think the Senate rose to the occasion and the American people appreciated it. They respected the fact that we had resolved the matter with a process and procedure and tone that reflected credit on the American people and government.
—Senator Thad Cochran (R-Miss.) on the Senate trial of President Clinton

The Senate had stumbled through a pseudo trial, a sham trial, really no trial at all. In the end, letting the House managers put on their case with a full White House defense would have taken less time than the helter-skelter procedures adopted by the Senate. The president had dodged perjury by calculated evasion and poor interrogation. Obstruction of justice had failed by gaps in the proofs. The case had not been proved.
—Senator Arlen Specter (R-Pa.) on the Senate trial of President Clinton

In contrast to the House of Representatives, the individualistic features of the Senate generally ensure senators a greater degree of independence, help-ing to dilute partisanship and to limit party control. But while the delibera-tions and rhetoric of the Senate's impeachment trial of President Clinton was far less partisan than the rancorous impeachment proceedings in the House, and while senators employed various themes to justify their deci-sions, their votes at the end of the trial were ultimately as partisan as those of their House colleagues, with their party affiliations closely tied to their concluding explanations.[1]

Publicly, the opening of the trial looked decorous. In a slight touch of "geopolitical bipartisanship," the Senate even situated the thirteen House impeachment managers at a table on the Democratic side of the Senate chamber, while the White House defense team sat on the Republican side.[2] (The managers commented sarcastically about this arrangement, because of the opposing side's distinct proximity to the Senate's "candy desk.")[3] But, as political journalist Peter Baker observed, despite the deliberate pretrial choreography, the proceedings quickly became partisan in nature.[4] Senators protested that the chamber's "vaunted bonds of collegiality" endured, but the votes on the two articles of impeachment offered vivid evidence that the contemporary Senate's "decorum" is often a matter of "surface comity, a triumph of style masking division."[5]

In the aftermath of the impeachment imbroglio, some observed that while both houses of Congress felt the pressure to descend into bitter partisan acrimony, the matter was much harsher in the House than in the Senate, where a smoke screen of civility and harmony often clouded partisan divisions.[6] Such comity is generally attributed to the culture of the body, shaped by its overall prestige, which has historically inculcated in members a sense of institutional loyalty over party allegiance.[7] So while the popularly elected House of Representatives is liable to succumb to partisan public passions, the Senate is designed to provide a brake, a second look, a longer-run view, and a well-deliberated decision; in short, it is intended as a body where cooler heads prevail. This design has been institutionalized over the years by precedents and rules specific to the chamber—unlimited debate, the absence of a "germaneness" rule for amendments to most bills—that require "supermajorities" of sixty votes (or sixty-seven votes for rules changes) for the passage of key legislation.

Yet the contemporary Senate has become a partisan and ideological body, despite the apparent norms of courtesy and civility between senators.[8] "I was not so much surprised that President Clinton was impeached," recalled Senator Thad Cochran (R-Miss.), "but I was surprised by how vigorously the Democrats defended him, and how they defended him unanimously in the Senate."[9] As evident from both voting patterns and the testimony of individual senators, the advent of heightened partisanship (see Figure 6.1) and ideology has had a profound effect upon the Senate, most notably the erosion of the decorum traditionally associated with the institution.[10] One cause behind the changing nature of the Senate is the members themselves. Members known for compromise, moderation, and institutional loyalty seemingly have been replaced with more ideological and partisan senators who, like their House counterparts, look for opportunities to promote their parties'

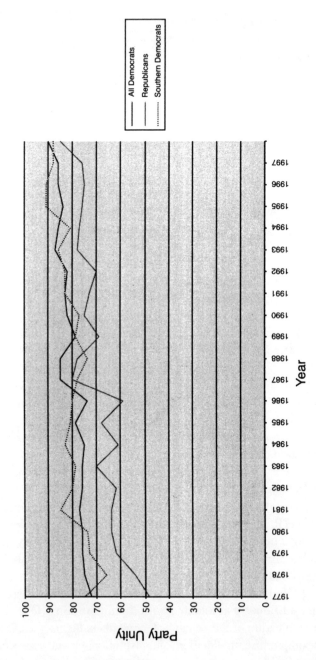

Figure 6.1. Party unity and polarization in Senate voting, 1977–1998. (Data derived from Norman J. Ornstein, Thomas E. Mann, and Michael J. Malbin, *Vital Statistics on Congress, 1999–2000* [Washington, D.C.: AEI Press, 2000])

agendas.[11] As a consequence, life on the Senate side of Capitol Hill has become less harmonious, with the Senate almost morphing itself into the House in recent years, at least in terms of the relations between committee leaders, party leaders, and the party caucuses.[12]

The increased ideological homogeneity of the two parties and the concomitant decline in the number of "centrists" in the chamber has been, in part, due to electoral realignment in the South since the mid-1960s.[13] Southern Democrats in the Senate now vote more like national Democrats, and conservative southern states and districts now elect Republicans more often than Democrats.[14] The main ideological cleavage in the contemporary Senate now parallels the division between the two parties rather than bisecting each party, as was the situation during the 1950s. In the 1980s and early 1990s, moreover, the budget deficit was the major issue of domestic policy making, provoking sharp debates between the parties over taxation and reducing the size of government. Partisan stakes were raised by the tendency to address the budget crisis through periodic deficit-reduction packages that effected major policy change while bypassing the regular authorizing process.[15]

During the 1990s it became increasingly obvious that partisan repositioning had washed out the ideological center by drawing the two parties apart.[16] So as the two parties became more cohesive internally, they simultaneously grew further apart externally. Or, as centrist Senator John B. Breaux (D-La.) anecdotally observes: "The parties have increasingly taken the position that it's my way or no way—so what we end up with is no way."[17] Party votes that began expanding under Presidents Carter and Reagan, for example, soared to 67 and then to 69 percent under President Clinton.[18]

With the decline of the old "conservative coalition" in the Senate during the 1970s and 1980s, the growing assertiveness of the news media and the multitude of new policy-oriented interest groups interacted with the rise of candidate-centered campaigns to turn the chamber into an assembly of what Barbara Sinclair calls self-promoting "policy entrepreneurs," who were often in collective disarray.[19] When in the minority, senators of both parties increasingly exploited floor amendments and dilatory devices—filibusters, nongermane floor amendments, and holds—to bring the chamber to a standstill. In response to this "new Senate," party leaders on both sides of the aisle were only occasionally able or willing to assert themselves in an "untidy chamber."[20]

In the 1990s, however, some of the same trends that had become evident in House elections and internal proceedings seeped into the Senate, albeit in a somewhat more attenuated form. Senators, too, found themselves becoming more reliant on ideological and single-issue groups for activist support and fund-raising. Some members also found that in order to fulfill the policy demands of these groups they had to work in more coordinated fashion with the party leadership.[21] This first became evident when the Republicans took control of the Senate in 1980 and used that control to help implement President Ronald Reagan's program under Majority Leaders Howard H. Baker Jr. (R-Tenn.) and his successor Robert J. "Bob" Dole of Kansas. The pattern continued when the Democrats regained control under Majority Leader Robert C. Byrd (W.Va.) and particularly during the leadership of his successor George Mitchell (Maine), who successfully thwarted much of the domestic legislative agenda of Republican President George H. W. Bush. Bitter and highly ideological confirmation battles over the Supreme Court nominations of Robert Bork (1987) and Clarence Thomas (1991) also raised the partisan tenor in the Senate. But during the 1990s it became apparent that greater partisanship under the Senate's loose debating rules and "supermajority" requirements was more effective at blocking agendas than advancing them. Senator Bob Dole, leading a cohesive Senate Republican minority, created headaches for Democratic President Bill Clinton in 1993, and Senate Minority Leader Tom Daschle (D-S.D.) was highly effective in derailing the House Republicans' "Contract with America" in 1995–1996.

PRETRIAL WRANGLING

At the outset of the Clinton impeachment trial, senators wished to shield themselves from the partisan rancor that had permeated the House. Following a closed-door speech to his colleagues in the days preceding the trial, Senator Byrd, the courtly guardian of Senate tradition, admonished his colleagues that "the House has fallen into the black pit of partisan self-indulgence," adding, "the Senate is teetering on the brink of that same black pit."[22] In fact, many senators hoped that the impeachment problem would steer well clear of the Senate altogether and that the House would find a way to halt the process.[23] "I expected the president would resign to prevent a House vote for impeachment," remembers Senator Cochran, who was first elected to Congress in 1972 as a Nixon supporter.[24] Nonetheless, Senate Majority Leader Trent Lott (R-Miss.) and other Republican members contemplated possible compromises between an impeachment trial and taking no congressional action, especially alternatives that might be accomplished without waiting for the House.[25] Such a course of action might have been attractive to those Democrats looking for a way to protect their president from an impeachment trial, and Minority Leader Daschle also called Democratic senators individually to discuss the impeachment process.

A Slow-Moving Locomotive

When the House managers appeared at the Senate's doorsteps with their articles of impeachment, the initial order of business was the burden of deciding how to deal with a president accused of committing "high crimes and misdemeanors," something not seen by the chamber in over a hundred years. Initially, comity and bipartisanship looked likely to resolve the impeachment mess.[26] The leader of the Republican majority, Trent Lott, "wanted to escape the tar of partisanship."[27] "We could have rolled [Minority Leader Tom] Daschle," the majority leader said, but because both leaders wanted to protect the Senate from becoming rancorous, they decided to maintain a cordial atmosphere as far as possible.[28] Nevertheless, securing bipartisan support for the trial procedure would not prove to be an easy task, considering the few resources Senate party leaders have to promote party unity.[29] Leading the Senate, as former majority leader Howard Baker (R-Tenn.) theorized, is like herding cats: "It is trying to make ninety-nine independent souls act in concert under rules that encourage polite anarchy and embolden people who find majority rule a dubious proposition at best."[30] Senate Minority Leader Daschle proposed a more respectful approach for the White House legal team, one aimed at keeping three influential and free-thinking Democrats (who had already been openly critical of the president's conduct in the Lewinsky affair) within the party fold: Joseph I. Lieberman of Connecticut, Daniel Patrick Moynihan of New York, and Byrd of West Virginia.[31]

Censuring the president was one disciplinary substitute floated around the halls of the Senate. But the conclusive decision to hold a trial, instead of pursuing alternative forms of discipline, was made with some attention to precedent, upon which the Senate relies to clarify and preserve its legislative practices, and according to Senator Cochran, with the desire to "preserve the decorum of the Senate."[32] Or as Donald R. Mathews identified it some forty years ago, and as revisited a generation later by Ross K. Baker, *institutional patriotism*—the upholding and safeguarding of the reputation of the Senate—played an important role in the decision of the Senate to conduct a formal trial rather than opt for censure or an abbreviated inquiry.[33] Such strictures of institutional loyalty are not nearly as significant for House members, where Richard Fenno, Jr., observed little adherence to the belief that "members are supposed to value the House as an institution and do nothing to diminish its prestige or demean its members"; such allegiance is often dismissed as "a pleasant Capitol Hill hypocrisy."[34]

This sort of devotion on the part of senators is hardly surprising in an institution so steeped in tradition that members' desks still have inkwells and goose-quill pens along with crystal sand shakers for blotting ink, as well as the names of previous occupants etched on the inside. Several institutionally minded, senior senators—most notably Senators Byrd, Edward M. Kennedy (D-Mass.), Orrin G. Hatch (R-Utah), Pete V. Domenici (R-N.M.), and Richard G. Lugar (R-Ind.)—viewed themselves as keepers of Senate tradition.[35] These members expressed concern for preserving legislative practices as well as attention to historical perspective on the potential legacy of impeachment. Despite the immediate drama, several understood, as anthropologist J. McIver Weatherford observes, that on Capitol Hill long-range institutional effects can be akin to a tsunami wave at sea: the initial earth tremor is impressive in itself, but the real impact is a rippling wave that crests near shore, and eventually crashes down far from the epicenter.[36]

Modeling his conduct on that of the kind of senator he believed the Founders had in mind when they devised the body, Senator Byrd, known for a style of "oratory and loquaciousness that evokes the Senate's 'Gilded Age,'" opposed any process that might halt a trial before senators could hear a full presentation of evidence and witnesses as well as cast up-or-down votes on the articles of impeachment.[37] "This is not an agricultural appropriations bill we're talking about," he declared. "This is not minimum wage. This is not the environment. They are all important, and we all, to some extent, play politics when it comes to legislation. But this is the Constitution! This approach will leave a blotch upon the political escutcheon of any individual who thinks first of politics and second of the institution."[38] The West Virginian's comments did not go unheeded. Weekly meetings for Senate Democratic legislative directors were strategic in their quest to locate a judicious nexus point: to dispense with the proceedings as swiftly as possible while simultaneously providing enough semblance of a trial to placate Senator Byrd and other institutionally minded senators.[39]

The Gorton-Lieberman Plan

Even before the House had taken its vote on impeachment, during the 1998–1999 Christmas break, Senators Slade Gorton (R-Wash.) and Lieberman met regularly to broker a bipartisan way to move the Senate quickly and without acrimony through an impeachment trial. The two political moderates had become close while working on other legislative matters. Theirs was the kind of personal relationship, Ross K. Baker explains, that "grows up readily in the more intimate confines of the Senate and often crosses party lines."[40] Respected for his independence, civility, and devotion to causes in which he believes, Lieberman "was dismayed by Clinton's August 17, 1998, speech in which he grudgingly admitted lying about the Lewinsky affair for seven months."[41] When the Senate resumed in September after its recess, he took the floor and strongly criticized the president for having extramarital relations with an employee "half his age" and doing so "in the workplace, in the vicinity of the Oval Office":

> I was personally angry because President Clinton had, by his disgraceful behavior, jeopardized his administration's historic record of accomplishment, much of which grew out of the principles and programs that he and I and many others had worked on together in the new Democratic movement. I was also angry because I was one of the many people who had said over the preceding 7 months that if the President clearly and explicitly denies the allegations against him, that of course I believe him. . . . I am afraid that the misconduct the President has admitted may be reinforcing one of the worst messages being delivered by our popular culture, which is that values are fungible. And I am concerned that his misconduct may help to blur some of the most bright lines of right and wrong in our society.[42]

The junior senator from Connecticut concluded his remarks by saying the president's behavior was "wrong and unacceptable and should be followed by some measure of public rebuke and accountability."[43]

Both Lieberman and Gorton believed Republicans would fail to muster the higher Senate threshold of sixty-seven votes for conviction. Under the basic plan, prosecutors from the House of Representatives would have a day to make their case for conviction and removal from office. The following day the White House would present its defense. On the third day, senators would forward questions to the two sides. And on the fourth day, the chamber would take a "test vote" on whether the articles of impeachment for perjury and obstruction of justice, if proven, rose to a level that demanded the president's removal from office. If, as expected, the test did not produce the necessary two-thirds votes to remove President Clinton from office, the trial would stop and the Senate could move on to consider censure.

Underlying the plan was a fear of what would happen in the Senate if the impeachment trial dragged on for weeks or months. With the State of the

Union Message impending, Lieberman said that the Senate had a "very short window here to try to work out a procedure for this trial," adding, "If we don't, we are going to descend, I fear, to the kind of partisan rancor that characterized the House proceeding."[44]

By most accounts, the Gorton-Lieberman proposal, or some variation, had strong majority support in the Senate, starting with nearly all the Democrats. But among the Republicans it became readily apparent that the plan would not reach consensus-level support. It was strenuously opposed by the House impeachment managers, who wanted to include evidence from Juanita Broaddrick's deposition that the managers had informally shared with several House colleagues as they lobbied for votes on the articles of impeachment in December 1998. "They're acting like this is a high school exam," Senator Patrick J. Leahy (D-Vt.) said of the House managers. "They flunked the exam in their body. They hope to do a makeup exam in the Senate, and that's not going to happen."[45] Majority Leader Lott decided to leave the decision to a caucus of his Republican colleagues, where opposition to proceeding without witnesses was evident.

When it did become clear that Republicans would not embrace the Gorton-Lieberman proposal, an assortment of options arose, most divided sharply along the partisan fault line of whether or not to allow the testimony of live witnesses, creating the prospect of a protracted partisan battle in the Senate, or to rely on the voluminous House impeachment record and grand jury testimony. "If the Republicans really want witnesses," noted one leadership aide during a Senate Democratic legislative director's meeting, "our strategy is to let them produce the votes to depose witnesses and drag this [impeachment] out."[46] Several Democrats in the Senate, for example, feared the possibility that salacious material would find its way to the floor of the Senate, despite a pledge by prosecutors to avoid questioning Lewinsky about the details of her sexual relationship with President Clinton.[47]

Judicial Inquiry or Ritual Convention?

In any ordinary trial a potential juror who is related to the prosecutor would be immediately disqualified, as would one who had stood before reporters and expressed an opinion about the guilt or innocence of the defendant. Some newly elected senators who had previously held seats in the House and had already cast votes for or against the articles of impeachment there would serve as "jurors" during the Senate trial. As Senator Richard J. Durbin (D-Ill.) commented on the senators' solemn oath to do impartial justice in the impeachment trial, "If you wanted 100 impartial Americans, would you start with the United States Senate?"[48]

Senators may request to be excused from an impeachment trial, and in some cases members have disqualified themselves when possible conflicts of interest arouse. Prior to the Clinton impeachment trial there had been two trials in which attempts were made to disqualify certain senators. In the trial of Judge John Pickering, three senators, Samuel Smith (R-Md.), Israel Smith (R-Vt.), and John Smith (R-N.Y.), who had been members of the House of Representatives and who had voted on the question of impeaching Pickering, were members of the Senate during the trial.[49] A resolution was introduced to provide that any senator, having previously acted and voted, as a member of the House on the question of impeachment, be disqualified, but this resolution was simply ordered to lie over for consideration, and all three senators voted during the trial.[50] During the trial of President Andrew Johnson, the issue of disqualification arose prior to the administration of the oath to Senator Benjamin F. Wade (Whig-Ohio).[51] The argument was raised that since Wade, the president pro tempore of the Senate, had an interest in the outcome of the trial, inasmuch as he would succeed to the office of the president if conviction had been obtained, that he was not qualified to sit as a member of the high court.[52] Senator Oliver Hazard P. T. Morton (R-Ind.) pointed out that under the Constitution the Senate has the sole power to try all impeachments and that Senator Wade, as a member of that body, had a constitutional right to sit there.[53] After discussion of the issue, Senator Thomas Andrews Hendricks (D-Ind.) withdrew his objection, stating that he thought the question might more properly be raised when the Senate would be fully organized for a trial and when the accused party was present.[54] Ultimately the oath was administered to Senator Wade.[55]

As the Clinton trial prepared to open, partisan, political interests haunted the unusual pool of jurors. As journalist Terry M. Neal discovered, three newly elected senators, Charles E. Schumer (D-N.Y.), Jim Bunning (R-Ky.), and Michael D. Crapo (R-Idaho), participated as lame duck members in the House impeachment vote, raising the question of how they could fulfill the impartiality oath they took as Senate jurors. Senators Tim Hutchinson (R-Ark.) and Carl M. Levin (D-Mich.)—whose brothers, Representatives Asa Hutchinson (R-Ark.) and Sander Levin (D-Mich.), served in the House— were questioned about familial conflicts; and Representative Asa Hutchinson was also one of the thirteen House managers presenting the case against Clinton to the Senate. Senator Barbara Boxer's (D-Calif.) daughter was, at the time, married to First Lady Hillary Rodham Clinton's brother. Some

Democrats publicly hinted that they were predisposed to vote on the two articles of impeachment before the trial even began. And six senators had voted on Chief Justice Rehnquist's nomination to the high court, with two—Democrats Daniel K. Inouye of Hawaii and Kennedy of Massachusetts—having opposed him. Rehnquist himself was indirectly involved in offstage events that led to Independent Counsel Starr's investigation of President Clinton. He wrote the Supreme Court's 1988 decision in *Morrison v. Olson* upholding the Independent Counsel Act, which allows a three-judge panel to appoint a prosecutor to investigate charges of government misconduct. As chief justice, he also appointed the panel that named Kenneth Starr to replace Robert Fiske as Whitewater Independent Counsel in 1994. In 1996, Rehnquist had joined the other eight Supreme Court justices in the unanimous *Jones v. Clinton* ruling that permitted Paula Jones's sexual harassment lawsuit to go forward while Clinton was still president. Finally, many senators openly acted against juror sequestration. Senator Jon Kyl (R-Ariz.) offered the largest newspaper in his state regular excerpts from his personal diary on the trial, while former Senator Frank Lautenberg (D-N.J.) allowed a crew from *Court TV* to follow him around during the trial.[56]

THE TRIAL

The trial began the day after the 106th Congress (1999–2001) convened. Sworn in by Senate Pro Tem Strom Thurmond (R-S.C.), who was born only thirty-four years after Andrew Johnson's impeachment, Chief Justice Rehnquist's role as the constitutionally mandated presiding officer was to keep order in the chamber, rule on questions of evidence and burdens of proof, and control the pace and flow of the trial. Before the proceedings, Rehnquist emphasized that impeachment was not "a referendum on the public official's performance in office," but rather a form of judicial inquiry in which the House makes specific charges and the Senate decides whether the charges have been proven.[57] Once having taken his seat at the dais in the front of the chamber, however, the highest-ranking judicial officer, who had written a book on impeachment that many senators read throughout the trial (the Chief Justice autographed copies during breaks in the proceedings), had little say over a jury of individuals unaccustomed to showing deference to someone not an elected member to the world's most exclusive club. At times Chief Justice Rehnquist appeared perplexed by Senate culture, unfamiliar with the pronunciation of various senators' names, and frequently looking to the chamber's parliamentarian for advice.[58] "I underwent the sort of culture shock that naturally occurs when one moves from the very structured environment of the Supreme Court to what I shall call, for want of a better phrase, the more free-form environment of the Senate," Rehnquist admitted in reference to the Senate's irregular rules of jurisprudence.[59] Such minimalist authority was particularly unfamiliar for a "stern taskmaster" known for presiding over the high bench with his "signature brusqueness."[60]

One by one, in alphabetical order, senators signed a registry in the well of the Senate, affirming their pledge with black-ink pens inscribed with an unfortunate typographical error: "*Untied* States Senate," they read. Members were a picture of conviviality as they took their seats: Senator Byrd threw his arm around the shoulder of Republican Arlen Specter of Pennsylvania, while Republicans Strom Thurmond and John Warner of Virginia chatted amiably with David Kendall, the president's attorney. Yet three paragraphs shy of finishing his opening presentation, House prosecutor Representative Bob Barr (R-Ga.) was interrupted by the first objection of the Senate impeachment trial. From the back of the ornate Senate chamber, Democratic Senator Tom Harkin (D-Iowa) rose to object to Barr's repeated references to the senators as "jurors," which he believed did not fully describe the Senate's duty; senators were empowered to take into account other factors, such as the good of the nation. The objection violated the rules, which barred any senator, on pain of imprisonment, from speaking during the trial, and it exposed the raw partisan nerves that had been simmering all along. Juries are expected to hear from witnesses, Senator Harkin declared. Not so with "triers of fact" or judges, necessarily. "It sort of pulls the rug out from the argument that we are jurors who have to have witnesses."[61] Rehnquist sided with Harkin on the crux of his complaint. "The Senate is not simply a jury; it is a court in this case," the chief justice proclaimed. "Therefore, counsel should refrain from referring to the senators as jurors."[62] Harkin's protest reinforced a clear signal to the House prosecutors: the Senate would dictate the terms of the impeachment trial.

The Senate tentatively scheduled votes on competing Democratic and Republican plans, but both Senate party leaders began conferring openly about procedure as soon as the chief justice left the chamber. Senate practice holds that unless senators walk to the side of the chamber to signify they want a private conversation, other senators are welcome to join in.[63] Subsequently, senators started to huddle around Lott and Daschle, until eventually nearly half the Senate encompassed them, as leading negotiators from both parties took their back-room dealing out in the open. For nearly a half hour senators went back and forth, seemingly oblivious to a cluster of reporters eaves-dropping from a nearby balcony.[64] Majority Leader Lott arranged for an unprecedented bipartisan Senate caucus the next day in the Old Senate Chamber, an ornate, ceremonial room in the Capitol that had served as the Senate chamber during its "Golden Age," between 1810 and 1859, when some of the great debates and confrontations over slavery took place. Prior to the bipartisan meeting, Lott had hand picked a group of GOP lieutenants to pass along the mood of the Senate to the House prosecutors. The senators counseled the prosecution team on how best to pursue the issue of witnesses, arguing that new facts, conflicts between witnesses, and the need to clarify individual testimony should be stressed.[65] Perhaps more importantly, the senators reiterated a bipartisan sentiment—that members would jealously protect the dignity of the Senate by retaining sole custody of how the matter would be conducted and concluded.[66]

The Gramm-Kennedy Plan

After about three hours' arguing about the merits of reintroducing witnesses and calling an early vote of dismissal, a bipartisan proposal was finessed to close the impeachment case with dispatch. Ironically, the agreed upon plan came from Republican Phil Gramm of Texas, a strong conservative, and Democrat Kennedy of Massachusetts, a staunch liberal, who made back-to-back statements at the bipartisan caucus. The Gramm-Kennedy arrangement called for a trial lasting two weeks, allowing arguments from both the House managers and Clinton's defense team, and questioning by senators. The trial would get under way in earnest with arguments on any procedural pretrial motions by House prosecutors or White House lawyers. The House would then be provided twenty-four hours in which to present its case against the president, with another twenty-four hours allotted to the White House team to make its case. Neither side would be allowed to present new evidence unrelated to the impeachment record presented in the House. Senators then would have sixteen hours to question the two sides by sending written queries up to Chief Justice Rehnquist. Those deliberations would be followed by debate and a vote on two motions, one to adjourn the trial and the second to call witnesses, each resolved by simple majority votes. If accepted, witnesses would first be questioned in depositions, followed by a second majority vote required to have testimony in front of the full Senate, for each potential witness.

Democrats, who had previously stood adamantly against witnesses, seemed to take solace in the fact that if witnesses were to be called at all, they would initially have to be approved all at once, in a group, which they believed would discourage the House from seeking to call too many. They also anticipated that the senators, who were sitting as jurors under a vow of silence, would be less inclined to call witnesses after listening to the House managers and White House counsel for two weeks. "There's one thing the Senate can't tolerate and that's remaining quiet for very long," Senator Christopher J. Dodd (D-Conn.) said. "And the idea they are going to sit there day after day and listen to House managers and White House counsels, with their inability to respond, is not going to last very long."[67]

Each side made significant concessions in the compromise. In the end, however, it was the Democrats who moved the most, to accept a proposal much like the one the Republicans had originally drafted. Some Senate Democrats expressed private annoyance that Kennedy had been so quick to support Gramm because they thought he gave away a tactical advantage held by the Democrats stemming from the Republicans' fear of looking as partisan as their House counterparts. But despite those Democrats who were wary of the blueprint, many senators from both parties reveled in institutional pride at maintaining a conciliatory tone that had eluded the House. "You know, we didn't ask for this trial," said Senator Leahy. "We didn't ask for the President to conduct himself the way he did, and we didn't ask for the House to make a mishmash of this thing. But all that's happened and now we have to preserve the Senate and give the country a sense of credibility."[68] Sounding much the same, Senator Mitch McConnell (R-Ky.) said, "I think there's a feeling in this situation that the Senate is on trial."[69] Senator Lott, who had been trying for weeks to broker a bipartisan agreement, said in satisfaction, "I think today we have acted in the very best tradition of the Senate, and it is an appropriate approach for this historic, very solemn event."[70] "Stranger things have happened in politics," said Senator John McCain (R-Ariz.) afterwards, "but the Kennedy-Gramm alignment is one of the strangest."[71] Ross K. Baker has observed, "That such a relatively minor point of agreement should have been the occasion for such great celebration underscores the climate of apprehension in the Senate that the Senate would accompany the House in a descent into harsh partisanship."[72]

Ironically, although the impeachment trial of President Clinton was driven primarily by partisanship, it was the possibility of bipartisanship that the White House feared most, especially after the Senate unanimously decided (on January 8, 1999) to hold an impeachment trial. As Gregory Craig, a member of the president's defense team, explained it three months after the trial, matters improved for the White House precisely because of the partisanship that beset the House: "What happened in the House, we thought, was partisan, was unfair, and was illegitimate, and low and behold we now have a united, unanimous Senate voting 100-to-nothing to proceed." Craig added, "This was actually a moment when the president's spirits were very low. He thought the partisan nature and the unfairness of the process had been lost and we were now beginning from scratch."[73]

There were already indications, however, that virtually all the Democratic senators and a handful of moderate Republicans agreed with the president's lawyers, who took the position that Clinton's testimony before a federal grand jury, while clearly evasive, did not rise above the high legal threshold to become perjurious. "One of the things I learned from this trial, contrary to a lay person's notion, is that perjury and lying aren't the same thing," said Senator Susan Collins (R-Maine).[74] But she added that Clinton's "grand jury testimony is replete with lies, half-truths and evasions," noting that "he [Clinton] seems to have navigated the shoals of the perjury laws in a way that may allow him to avoid it."[75] Senators on both sides of the aisle agreed that the prosecution had made a much stronger case that Clinton obstructed justice, a charged based primarily on the allegation that he encouraged Lewinsky to file a false affidavit in the Jones case. But several Democrats said the facts laid out by the prosecutors, while compelling, formed only a circumstantial case. The House managers "were taking only those things that could support their case and holding them up in isolation and saying, 'Look at this,'" said Senator Byron L. Dorgan (D-N.D.). "They just started out with a pretty weak case and didn't do anything to enhance it along the way."[76] "If you look at it in technical terms, the president perjured himself before the grand jury—I have no question about that," said Senator Robert F. Bennett (R-Utah). "But [then] you add the question of materiality: Did it affect anything? In basketball lingo, 'no harm, no foul.'"[77] To the vast majority of Republicans, such objections seemed to be "legal nitpicking."[78] Many focused on what they regarded as the totality of the president's wrongdoing in the Lewinsky affair. And some accused him of misdeeds that went well beyond the case brought by the House managers.

After six days of opening arguments, which amounted to uninterrupted speeches by each side—some, in the words of Senator Arlen Specter (R-Pa.), "laced with grand rhetoric and Shakespearean, biblical, and historical references"—the House Republican managers and the White House lawyers responded to questions from senators and engaged in a feisty debate about whether to remove Clinton from office for perjury and obstruction of justice.[79] But the tone of the senatorial inquiries indicated that views of the case had hardened. The fifty questions read aloud by Chief Justice Rehnquist revealed no possible dissenters on either side of the aisle, again suggesting prosecutors had not won over enough senators to muster the two-thirds vote required for conviction. Indeed, as observed by political journalist Peter Baker, the questions were designed to make debating points rather than elicit new information, with Republicans generally posing "sympathetic queries" to House managers and Democrats mostly tossing "softballs" to Clinton's lawyers. The format, Baker contends, made for an odd "four-way dance" as the two sides waited for questions to be directed their way and as leadership from both sides of the aisle choreographed them to aide their respective camps.[80]

Questions alternated from one party to the next and were often written simply to give a particular side a chance to respond to the other. Rehnquist then read the questions in a flat voice without editorial comment and, while setting a five-minute limit for answers, he was forgiving and rarely cut anyone off, even when the first response dragged on for nine minutes. The central arguments from the two sides echoed the trial's opening presentations. The managers maintained Clinton abused his trust as president by lying under oath before a grand jury and trying to impede the Jones case by encouraging Lewinsky to file a false affidavit denying their affair. The defense lawyers insisted the facts did not fit the prosecution theory of the case and that, even if they did, the crimes were not grave offenses against the state that require the removal of the president. "There is a total lack of proportionality, a total lack of balance in this thing," argued former Arkansas senator and governor Dale Bumpers, who was added late to the Clinton legal team to close the president's defense. "The charge and the punishment are totally out of sync. All of you have heard or read the testimony of the five prosecutors who testified before the House Judiciary Committee—five seasoned prosecutors. Each one of them, veterans, said that under the identical circumstances of this case, they would never charge anybody because they would know they couldn't get a conviction. In this case, the charges brought and the punishments sought are totally out of sync. There is no balance; there is no proportionality."[81]

Deposing Witnesses

On January 27, 1999, a sharply divided Senate refused to throw out the case against President Clinton and agreed to take testimony from Monica S. Lewinsky and two other witnesses. As the Senate convened for two long-awaited showdown votes, the chaplain offered a prayer. "Beyond party loyalties," the Reverend Lloyd J. Ogilvie said, "those on both sides of the aisle long to do what ultimately is best for the nation."[82] With identical 56 to 44 votes, the Senate first defeated a Democratic motion by Senator Byrd to dismiss the charges against Clinton, and then approved a Republican-sponsored motion to depose three witnesses that House impeachment managers insisted were the bare minimum they needed to make their case. They also approved prosecution subpoenas for Lewinsky, presidential confidant Vernon E. Jordan, Jr., and White House aide Sidney Blumenthal. Senator Russell D. Feingold (D-Wis.) was the only lawmaker to cross party lines, joining Republicans to keep the trial going with depositions. Another Democrat who had kept his counsel and been watched nervously by party leaders, Senator Bob Graham of Florida, stayed within the party fold, issuing a brief statement saying that the case against Clinton did not meet "the high standards required by the Constitution for removal" of the president and that "the Senate and the American people have had ample opportunity to review the charges against the president."[83] Senate Majority Leader Lott won over wavering Republican senators by narrowing the number of witnesses and by agreeing to the closed-door terms for depositions. The box that follows shows the Democratic leadership memorandum that was internally circulated before the trial

---

Internal Leadership Memorandum Outlining Senate Deposition Procedures

Location and Time.

Ms. Lewinsky	Monday, February 1 at 9:00 A.M. (Location off Capitol Hill—specific site yet to be determined)[a]
Mr. Jordan	Tuesday, February 2 at 9:00 A.M. S-407
Mr. Blumenthal	Wednesday, February 3 at 9:00 A.M. S-407

Duration. No more than *eight* hours, unless the Majority and Minority Leader agree to extend the time for deposition. Any decision to extend time will be made on a deposition-by-deposition basis. Questioning will be equally divided between the parties, four hours for each side.

Questioning. Examination of witnesses shall be conducted by the Managers or their counsel, and by counsel for the President. Witnesses shall be examined by no more than two persons for each party.

The scope of the questioning shall be "limited to the subject matters reflected in the Senate record."

No exhibits outside of the Senate record shall be employed, except for articles and materials in the press.

The party taking a deposition shall present to the other party, at least eighteen hours in advance of the deposition, copies of all exhibits which the deposing party intends to enter into the deposition.

Objections. Each deposition shall be presided over by two Senators, one appointed by the Majority Leader and one by the Minority Leader. One of the presiding officers will administer the oath.

The Democratic presiding officers are Senators Leahy, Dodd and Edwards. The Republican presiding offers are Senators Specter, Thompson, and DeWine with Senator Kyl serving as an alternate.

Acting jointly, the presiding officers shall have authority to rule, as an initial matter, upon any question arising out of the deposition. Objections to questions shall be noted by the presiding officers, but the examination shall proceed and the witness shall answer such questions. A witness may refuse to answer a question only when necessary to preserve a legally recognized privilege or constitutional right and must identify such privilege cited if refusing to answer a question.

Closed proceedings. Depositions shall be closed except for the two presiding Senators, the witness, counsel for the witness, the Managers, their counsel, the President's counsel, Senate Legal Counsel, persons whose presence is required to make and preserve a record of the proceedings and Senate staff as determined by the Majority Leader and Minority Leader, acting jointly. All persons present, except for the witness and the witness' counsel, shall be required to execute an agreement acknowledging that they are bound by the confidentiality provisions of Senate Rule 29.[b]

Distribution of the deposition records. The presiding officers at the depositions shall file the videotaped and transcribed records of the depositions with the Secretary, who shall maintain them as confidential records of the Senate. These records shall be made available for viewing only in that location by members of the Senate, the Chief Justice, and/or such other persons as jointly designated by the Majority Leader and the Minority Leader.

(SOURCE: Acquired by authors, Washington, D.C., U.S. Senate, January 1999)

[a]Monica Lewinsky was deposed in her hotel room at the Mayflower Hotel, located in downtown Washington, D.C.

[b]Senate Rule 29 relates to executive sessions, in particular, sections 5 and 6, which make any senator, officer, or employee of the Senate liable for divulging any pending confidential business, proceedings of the Senate, or documents related to any matter pending in the Senate, without leave of the Senate.

opened, outlining to senators and their staff the procedures for witness deposition by House prosecutors and White House attorneys.

The back-to-back votes against dismissing the case and for calling witnesses showed that all senators, with one exception, chose their party position as the one best for the nation, leaving the Senate as divided along partisan lines as the House had been when it impeached Clinton. Partisan messages were sharpened on both sides of the aisle. The Democrats argued that the Republicans were scripting open-ended trial agony against the popular will. "This is not 'L.A. Law,'" said Senator Dodd. "This is not 'The Litigators.' This is not 'Judge Judy.' This is not 'Court TV' you're dealing with here."[84] Republicans countered that any slowdown would only come about if the White House made good on its threats to carry out extensive discovery proceedings. "I don't understand the White House threats of scorched earth, drag-this-out-until-next-Memorial-Day kind of strategy," said Senator Bennett, "because the White House has been the one insisting that this ought to come to an end and this is nothing new."[85] Republicans also raised the precedent of former Senator Bob Packwood (R-Ore.), who resigned in a sex scandal, and asked why the White House feared the Senate's hearing for itself from the former intern.

Despite heated rhetoric, the realization that the Senate was nowhere near sixty-seven votes for the president's removal from office left the two parties with the alternatives of working together to find a way to bring the trial to an end or else bracing for endless bloodletting.

Exit Strategies

With the prospects of removing President Clinton from office all but disappearing, senators increasingly puzzled over how they could register their disapproval of Clinton's misbehavior, thereby building upon the House's impeachment, yet vote to acquit him of perjury and obstruction of justice. Consistent with much of the impeachment process, two camps formed to develop a response that roughly followed partisan lines. While sounding similar, with each side trying to wrap its efforts in the mantle of bipartisanship, the competing reprimands served different purposes. Knowing the Senate would acquit Clinton, Republicans wanted a way to voice their displeasure and to make sure the trial did not simply end with an acquittal; they subsequently sought language detailing presidential misconduct before acquitting him of the actual impeachment articles. Democrats, wanting to distance themselves from Clinton but not wanting the GOP to reprimand him in stronger-than-necessary language in the trial, where a motion could pass by a simple majority, preferred a post-trial censure resolution on the Senate floor. Considered "impeachment plus" or "conviction lite," depending on the spin, neither proposed alternative imposed tangible sanctions on the president, and both required only a majority for approval, rather than the two-thirds threshold the Constitution sets for conviction.

Bridging the partisan divide to find a graceful way to end the acrimonious trial proceedings would prove elusive, however. The Republican-driven "finding of fact" would have enabled senators to condemn Clinton for his relationship with Lewinsky and his alleged efforts to cover it up, but also allow him to remain in office. In effect, senators could formally agree on a list of offenses even if they disagreed on whether the conduct warranted removal from office. "We are looking for ways to separate the issue of whether or not the president committed offenses such as obstruction of justice from the issue of whether or not the offenses are sufficient to warrant his removal from office," said Senator Susan Collins (R-Maine), who advocated a finding-of-act resolution against the president.[86] Senators Olympia J. Snowe (R-Maine) and Pete V. Domenici (R-N.M.), who co-chaired the GOP task force charged with drafting the finding-of-fact resolution, avoided legal terms including "guilty," "conviction," "perjury," and "obstruction of justice," opting instead for a declaration that Clinton gave "false and misleading testimony under oath." Senator Domenici argued that such a motion was necessary because failure to convict the president on allegations of perjury and obstruction of justice "will provide history with the wrong interpretation of this case."[87]

The fact-finding resolution appealed to a number of senators, including Democrats Lieberman and Bob Graham of Florida, according to Senator Larry E. Craig (R-Idaho), who believed the president was guilty of certain actions but questioned whether his actions rose to the level of impeachability. Different from a censure, a finding of fact could not be revoked by a subsequent Congress, similar to when Congress repealed the resolution condemning President Jackson that had been passed three years earlier, because the findings would become part of the official trial record.[88] Moreover, as Senator Cochran summarized several Republican senators' thoughts, once President Clinton was indicted "our only option of punishing him was to remove him from office. Censure was a decision for the House to make."[89] Democrats, in the end, closed ranks to reject the proposal, calling it "a strategic retreat for the Republican majority," a "finding of fiction" with no constitutional basis.[90] "This seems like the dumbing down of impeachment," said Senator Schumer, fresh from the House Judiciary Committee.[91] "We see the Senate now degenerating into the snake-pit stage, in which the consuming objective is to win politically," Senator Byrd said.[92]

When the Senate Republican proposal to rebuke President Clinton collapsed, Democrats, led by Senator Diane Feinstein of California, rushed to promote their idea for a freestanding censure, to be considered after the trial. Republicans expressed deep skepticism or outright opposition, accusing Democrats of pushing a weak slap on the wrist that Republicans charged was a political shield designed to deflect criticism away from any Democrat who voted for acquittal. "We want finality, and that's a guilty or not guilty vote, and let the chips fall where they may," proclaimed Senator Charles E. Grassley of Iowa.[93] Aside from the wording, acquiring the needed sixty votes to break a threatened filibuster by Senator Gramm proved an insurmountable hurdle for censure proponents.

Closed Deliberations and Public Statements

In the concluding days of the impeachment trial the Senate cleared its galleries and shut its doors for three days of private deliberation on the fate of President Clinton—in keeping with rules established in 1868 for the Johnson impeachment trial. Although the Senate voted 59 to 41 to open the debate, it fell eight votes short of the two-thirds required to suspend the secrecy rules. Fourteen Republicans joined all forty-five Democrats in supporting public deliberations.[94] Later, openness advocates achieved an agreement to let individual senators insert written transcripts of their own remarks during the closed session into the *Congressional Record*. "However clubby we may think it is, [the Senate] is not a private club," said Senator Harkin, who led the charge to conduct the debate in public. "There's no legitimate reason for why those doors are closed."[95] "I think the deliberations should be in closed session, as all juries in this country are," countered Senator Craig shortly before the vote, adding: "I think they would not be deliberations otherwise, and they should not be called deliberations. They should be called final statements or final speeches or political statements."[96]

With the main drama seemingly settled, members sparred over various ancillary issues. The only view shared by all one hundred senators appeared to be disgust with Clinton's behavior. Virtually all the statements, even from Democrats, condemned the president's conduct in the scandal with language like "disgraceful" and "reprehensible," though the two parties parted company on the proper punishment; Democrats said the president should remain in office, while all but a handful of Republicans affirmed conviction as a just result.[97] Still, beneath the heated rhetoric, the statements and speeches of more than two dozen senators showed a surprising range. Both sides in many cases showed considerable thoughtfulness and took obvious care to make a clear statement, whether to their colleagues, their constituents, or to history. "The views are far afield, from the specifics of the evidence to overarching issues about the future of America," declared Senator Durbin, who said he would vote to acquit. "Each person has his own or her own spin on it."[98]

Overall, ninety-five of one hundred senators made some kind of public statement; as documented by Burdett A. Loomis, these ranged from 130 words by Senator Robert G. Torricelli (D-N.J.) to 31,000 words by Senator Joseph R. Biden (D-Del.).[99] Senators Lieberman and Feinstein, among their party's strongest Clinton critics, had fallen into line with their party colleagues. "No matter how deeply disappointed I am that our president, who has worked so successfully to lift up the lives of so many people, so lowered himself and his office, I conclude that his wrongdoing in this sordid saga does not justify making him the first president to be ousted from office in our history," Lieberman said.[100] Feinstein criticized Clinton's conduct as "deplorable" but argued that the charges remained unproven.[101] The House impeachment was "flawed" and "partisan," she said, criticizing the House's pretrial release of evidence, failure to call witnesses, "vague" drafting of the articles, and what she described as denial of the Democratic minority's rights.[102]

For many senators, the closing speeches were an opportunity to comment on the state of politics in America, to discuss the history of the nation and its Constitution, and even to reflect on their upbringing and intellectual growth. Senator Byrd stated:

This is only the second time that this nation has ever impeached a President. President [Richard] Nixon resigned when it was made clear to him that, if impeached and tried, he would be convicted and removed from office. In that instance, both the country and the Congress were of the same mind that the President's offenses merited his removal. It was not a partisan political impeachment; it was a bipartisan act. But where political partisanship becomes such an overwhelming factor as to put the country and the Congress at odds, as it has with this impeachment, something draws us back. We must be careful of the precedent we set. One political party, alone, should not be enough to bring Goliath's great sword out of the Temple.

Regrettably, this process has become so partisan on both sides of the aisle and particularly in the House and was so tainted from the outset, that the American people have rebelled against it.[103]

In an effort to understand how individual senators approached their constitutional roles as both judges and jurors, Loomis places senators' closing statements into three perspectives within the scholarly literature on the Senate.[104] The first perspective, he suggests, springs from Sarah A. Binder and Steven S. Smith's work[105] on whether Senate filibusters have historically been based on principle or merely employed as a political tactic. Thus, because senators from both parties knew what the outcome would be, they framed their arguments accordingly, only occasionally admitting the political nature of their votes.[106] Among those who voted to convict on both counts, Senator Bennett, for instance, offered one of the most extensive narratives of a principled decision, recounting a strategy of choice that moved him from leaning toward innocent on perjury and undecided on obstruction to eventual guilty votes on each article. In the end, for Senator Bennett, presidential counsel Charles Ruff asked the central question that governed his votes: "Would [the crime] put at risk the liberties of the people?"[107] He convinced himself it would.

Loomis's second framework is derived from Fenno, who has argued that "explaining" is an essential component of legislators' activities.[108] Thus senators' public explanations of their actions during impeachment should tell us a great deal about how they understood their part in the proceedings.[109] Many Republicans, for instance, formulated explanations of their actions in terms of their adherence to the law, and the belief that the House managers' case had effectively demonstrated the president's guilt. Senator Jeff Sessions's (R-Ala.) comments were characteristic of this viewpoint:

> Mr. President, the Constitution of the United States requires the Senate to convict and remove the President of the United States if it is proven that he has committed high crimes while in office. It has been proven beyond a reasonable doubt and to a moral certainty that President William Jefferson Clinton has persisted in a continuous pattern to lie and obstruct justice. The chief law officer of the land, whose oath of office calls on him to preserve, protect and defend the Constitution, crossed the line and failed to protect the law, and, in fact, attacked the law and the rights of a fellow citizen. Under our Constitution, such acts are high crimes and equal justice requires that he forfeit his office. For these reasons, I felt compelled to vote to convict and remove the President from office.[110]

Senator Sessions concluded by saying: "It is crucial to our system of justice that we demand the truth. I fear that an acquittal of this President will weaken the legal system by suggesting that being less than truthful is an option for those who testify under oath in official proceedings. Whereas the handling of the case against President Nixon clearly strengthened the nation's respect for law, justice and truth, by sending a crystal clear message about the requirement for honesty, the Clinton impeachment may unfortunately have the opposite result."[111]

Democrats by contrast explained their opposition to conviction on the grounds that even if the president were technically guilty on one or other of the impeachment articles, the punishment of removal from office was utterly disproportionate to the scale of the crime.[112] This position was summarized by Senator Feingold:

> I cannot justify concluding that the President should be removed from office for committing these federal crimes unless the case is proved by the same standard of proof that any federal prosecutor would be required to meet in a federal criminal case. This standard requires that the President be shown to have committed one of the two crimes alleged "beyond a reasonable doubt," as that standard of proof is understood in our criminal justice system. The "beyond a reasonable doubt" standard is guaranteed to defendants in criminal cases by the due process clause of the Constitution. *Victor* v. *Nebraska*, 511 U.S. 1 (1994). To apply any lesser standard in this trial would be unfair not only to the President, but also to the tens of millions of Americans whose right to have the President finish his term could be overridden by a mere likelihood or possibility that he actually committed such serious crimes.
>
> In other words, the House Managers are free to use the "sword" of the language of the federal criminal law but cannot simultaneously deprive the president of the "shield" that same criminal law provides any defendant by requiring the prosecution to prove its case by the highest standard of proof in our legal system. [113]

"Thus, for me," concurred Senator Max Cleland (D-Ga.), "as one United States Senator, the bar for impeachment and removal from office of a President must be a high one, and I want the record to reflect that my vote to dismiss is based upon a standard of evidence equivalent to that used in criminal proceedings—that is, that guilt must be proven "beyond a reasonable doubt"— and a standard of impeachable offense which, in my view, conforms to the Founders' intentions that such an offense must be one which represents official misconduct threatening grievous harm to our whole system of government."[114]

But while these perspectives proved useful in understanding senators' explanations of their vote, the third perspective, alluded to at the beginning of the chapter, that the Senate has become more partisan in recent decades, has the most explanatory power regarding senators' voting decisions on impeachment. Loomis's study of senatorial rhetoric ultimately demonstrates that senators could find "principled" reasons to vote for or against impeachment, but the correlation between the two predominant sets of reasoning and partisanship—"legalism" for Republicans, "rule of law" for the Democrats—demonstrates how each side in the Senate tried to use the impeachment trial for partisan advantage.[115] The fact that senators nevertheless felt obliged to provide extensive and principled reasoning for their decision is perhaps some indication of the persistence of institutional loyalty in that body relative to the House.

"Senators, How Say You?"

The trial ended as it began, a sober and formal proceeding of little mystery but great power. Dark-suited senators—every single one of them present and attentive—sat stiffly at their desks. Chief Justice Rehnquist read elaborate passages from an antique-sounding script, with the galleries hushed. Upon reading the first article of impeachment, he instructed the senators to stand by their desks when their names were called and deliver their verdict. "Senators," he intoned, "how say you? Is the respondent, William Jefferson Clinton, guilty or not guilty?"[116] When their names were called alphabetically, some senators spoke in a "resolute baritone," others in a "soft whisper," still others seemed to "bow slightly as they cast their votes."[117] Senator Barbara A. Mikulski (D-Md.) emphatically declared, "Not guilty," while Senator Kay Bailey Hutchison (R-Tex.) could not even be heard from the gallery pronouncing Clinton's guilt. Everything went smoothly until Senator Specter defied Rehnquist's instruction and cast his own idiosyncratic vote: "not proved, therefore not guilty."[118] Through scores of names, the clerk had repeated each vote, but he did not seem to know what to do with this one and so forged ahead.[119] The Senate rejected Article 1 by a 55 to 45 vote at 12:22 P.M., as ten Republicans voted with all Senate Democrats in rejecting the charges. The GOP defectors were John H. Chafee (R.I.), Susan Collins (Maine), Slade Gorton (Wash.), James M. Jeffords (Vt.), Richard C. Shelby (Ala.), Arlen Specter (Pa.), Olympia J. Snowe (Maine), Ted Stevens (Alaska), Fred Thompson (Tenn.), and John W. Warner (Va.).

Fifteen minutes later, the second vote on the obstruction article went by quickly, ending in a 50 to 50 tie. Lott had worked hard in the days leading up to the vote to preserve a majority to convict the president on at least one count. He did not quite make it, with five Republican moderates from the Northeast—Chafee, Collins, Jeffords, Snowe, and Specter—joining the unanimous Democrats in rejecting the charge.

Falling short by seventeen votes, the House prosecutors were only able to muster fifty (all Republican) votes of the sixty-seven that they needed for conviction. "We all have our opinion of the president," said Representative Lindsey O. Graham (R-S.C.) with a hint of bitterness. "But under our system, impeachment is hard. It is meant to be hard. And it's over."[120]

After the Democrats failed to get the sixty-seven votes needed to take up a censure of Clinton, exhausted senators headed home for the President's Day recess with a sense of relief that the grueling, five-week trial was over. Lott, who voted for both articles, said he was at peace with the chamber's decision. "While I feel the two articles of impeachment were proven . . . that was not the conclusion of the Senate, so that is done," he said, although he did flatly reject the idea that Clinton's acquittal had merely been a partisan vote—at least for Republicans. "Every Democrat voted against every article," Lott said, noting that only Republicans had been willing to cross the aisle on the votes.[121]

"I hope the score card isn't on which party won or lost," said Senator Graham. "The Constitution won, and a positive spirit has been created to help us move forward."[122] While there was division between the parties—and unhappiness among the House managers—everyone seemed to agree on at least one point: it was time to get a rest. After Rehnquist and the House impeachment managers were given formal escorts from the chamber, a similar courtesy was proposed for the White House lawyers. Lott laughed and pointed to the back way out. "There's the door!" he joked.[123] The jovial mood was soon halted, however, by a bomb threat that forced the evacuation of the Capitol for seventy-five minutes (on an unusually balmy winter afternoon).

The Senate's twin votes acquitting Clinton stood as Congress's last statement on the presidential scandal. But while the notion of an official censure might have died, the statements that senators delivered, either during secret deliberations or to the throng of reporters waiting outside the chamber, left little doubt of their distaste for the president's behavior. In some cases, this was partly designed for political effect, especially the comments of those Democrats facing an impending reelection. "The president has disgraced himself and dishonored his office," said Democratic Senator Jack Reed of Rhode Island, a reliable ally of the president.[124] President Clinton's actions were "boorish, indefensible, even reprehensible," said Senator Richard H. Bryan (D-Nev.). Perhaps the toughest words of all came from Senator Bennett, who voted twice for conviction. "Bill Clinton will go down in history as the most accomplished, polished liar we have ever had serving in the White House," he said. "The name Clinton is entering the political lexicon . . . it's synonymous for an elegant and well-crafted lie."[125]

CONCLUSION

For a variety of reasons, the impeachment case brought by the House never had a realistic chance of crossing the Constitution's formidable two-thirds barrier to conviction. Some Democrats challenged the trial's very legitimacy, on the grounds that the House approved impeachment on near-party-line votes. Senator Feinstein, long considered a swing vote, criticized the managers for infecting the proceedings with the partisan "jaundice" of the House impeachment process.[126] Others maintained the case was flawed because it was based on allegations lodged by a "biased," "reckless" prosecutor, Independent Counsel Kenneth Starr. "Extreme partisanship and prosecutorial zealotry have strained this process in its critical early junctures," charged Senator Leahy, adding, "partisan impeachments are lacking in credibility."[127]

Many Republican senators faced pressure from their party's conservative base to move ahead with the impeachment trial despite the lack of votes necessary for conviction.[128] There was also a growing recognition among Republican senators that the more united their party was on impeachment, the better positioned it would be to tackle a legislative agenda following the trial.[129] Still another reason the Senate moved forward, at times seeming deferential to the House, was that that chamber has become more like the populist House, in that party is now playing a wider role, something largely attributable to the partisan and ideological cohesion of more recently elected senators. Indeed, many senators who pressed most vociferously internally for moving forward with the trial at a deliberate pace were former House members: Senators Don Nickles and James M. Inhofe of Oklahoma, Jon Kyl of Arizona, Rick Santorum of Pennsylvania, and Connie Mack of Florida.

From a historical perspective the Senate has maintained a more supportive role for presidents than has the House of Representatives. Presidential support scores over nearly fifty years of the modern presidency suggest a closer relationship between the Senate and the White House.[130] As illustrated by Table 6.1, of the nine presidents who have served since 1953, all but two enjoyed higher mean support levels in the Senate than in the House. Since Gerald Ford's first full year in office in 1975, presidents have received greater support in Senate votes than in House votes in all but two years. During Clin-

Table 6.1. Presidential Victories on House and Senate Votes, Eisenhower through Clinton (by percentage)

	House	Senate	Difference
Eisenhower (1953–1960)	68.7	73.0	+4.3
(1953–1954)	87.0	85.3	−1.7
(1955–1960)	65.0	70.5	+5.5
Kennedy (1961–1963)	83.7	85.3	+1.8
Johnson (1964–1968)	86.5	79.8	−6.7
Nixon (1969–1974)	72.7	63.0	−9.7
Ford (1974–1976)	51.0	64.2	+13.2
Carter (1977–1980)	73.2	78.9	+5.7
Reagan (1981–1988)	43.6	66.5	+22.9
(1981–1986)	51.2	82.7	+31.5
(1987–1988)	33.0	60.6	+27.6
Bush (1989–1992)	40.6	64.7	+24.1
Clinton (1993–1998)	54.9	69.3	+14.4
(1993–1994)	87.3	85.5	−1.8
(1995–1998)	38.7	61.2	+22.5

SOURCE: Adapted from Roger H. Davidson and Colton C. Campbell, "The Senate and the Executive," in *Esteemed Colleagues: Civility and Deliberation in the Senate*, ed. Burdett A. Loomis (Washington, D.C.: Brookings Institution, 2001).

NOTE: Percentages indicate average numbers of congressional votes supporting the president divided by the total numbers of votes on which the president had taken a position. The final column indicates the differences between Senate and House averages for the years indicated.

ton's two years with a Democratic Congress (1993–1994), he won slightly higher proportions of floor votes in the House than in the Senate. But in those two years Clinton's overall success rates in both chambers were the highest since the Kennedy-Johnson era.

In addition, recent presidents generally have received far gentler treatment at the hands of senators than from representatives, as measured by success in floor votes. As illustrated in Table 6.1, in 1995–1998, the years of the impeachment, Bill Clinton's winning percentages of Senate votes were approaching twice those in the House. Along with predecessors Reagan and Bush, Clinton prevailed in about two-thirds of the Senate's presidential support votes. In the House, these three presidents' success rates were well below 50 percent.[131]

Another phenomenon is that Senate Republicans are more supportive of presidents, regardless of party, than are their House colleagues. Senate Democrats have been less consistent in supporting presidents of their own party.[132] Probably because of the large number of southerners in the party, Senate Democrats gave less support to Presidents Kennedy and Johnson than did House members of their party. Presidents Carter and Clinton received higher support from their own partisans, probably because of the declining numbers of southerners estranged from the Democrats' national agenda.[133] That demographic shift also accounts for declining Democratic support for Republican presidents, though the trend is sharpest in the House.[134]

Senators no doubt wished to shield themselves from the raw partisanship of the House's proceedings, and to protect their personal and institutional reputations for probity and judgment. If survey results are to be trusted, the senators were only mildly successful. Citizens had already concluded that the impeachment process was primarily a political vendetta against a president whose moral failings, they reasoned, were not markedly worse than those of most elected officials. On the night of February 12 CBS News asked respondents whether they thought most senators' votes reflected politics and party loyalty, or whether the senators really believed they were doing the right thing. Nearly three-quarters said most senators followed politics and party interests, whereas only 19 percent said that most senators followed what they thought was right.[135] A large majority of citizens, in other words, had already made up their minds about the impeachment process, and the Senate's actions did little to change their assessment. But as Senator Byrd, the self-proclaimed conscience of the Senate, would later reflect on how the process played out: "The Constitution is a cul-de-sac when it comes to impeachment. There is no escape exit. There is only one way and that is to deal directly with the articles of impeachment."[136]

In the end, according to Loomis, senators' public rationalizations of their behavior during and after the trial were dominated by partisan dimensions.[137] But this partisanship was different in character from that in the House, partly due to the traditionally more individualistic nature of the smaller chamber, and to the greater consideration that senators still give to the traditional norms and reputation of their institution.[138]

7
Conclusion: Lessons Learned

It takes a lot and it should take a lot for Congress to be permitted to overturn an election, and that essentially is what this process was. Whether Nixon would have been convicted in the Senate, had we gone forward in 1974, I don't know. He had engaged in massive misbehavior, using the IRS against his enemies and subverting the FBI. That was sufficient to reach the standard. But if one party can use this tool, which was put in the Constitution as a tool to save the Republic from disaster, for a partisan purpose, then other parties can do the same, and that is worrisome to me.
—Representative Zoe Lofgren (D-Calif.)

The fact that it is very hard, requiring a two-thirds vote of the Senate, and that only two presidents have been impeached is a good thing, because you are removing an elected official. The deterrent effect is profound, and Mr. Clinton will always have an asterisk after his name as Andrew Johnson does, throughout history. Just enduring an impeachment is a punishment of sorts. The dramatic nature of the remedy—expulsion from office—means that it will only be upheld in the most serious and egregious cases.
—Representative Henry J. Hyde (R-Ill.)

The congressional impeachment proceedings against President Bill Clinton were highly politicized, with nearly all Democrats supporting the president and almost all Republicans opposing him. Throughout the impeachment process in the House and often, if in a more subdued manner, in the Senate, party stood out as the core distinguishing characteristic between Clinton's accusers and his defenders.[1] It is thus difficult to conclude that impeachment was anything but a partisan affair.

Clinton's defenders argued that lying about sex was a private matter, not an abuse of governmental authority, and that impeachment was the culminating event in a long partisan witch-hunt. Representative Zoe Lofgren recalled: "In 1974, when the [Judiciary] committee vote to impeach Nixon was finished, Chairman Rodino went to his office, called his wife, broke into tears, and said it was a sad day for the country. On the 19th of December 1998, as soon as the vote was over on the House floor there was a little cheer on the Republican side. There's the difference."[2]

Clinton's detractors, however, adamantly maintained that he had violated the law, and that by purposely misleading the American public he undermined the integrity of the office of the presidency.[3] When recalling what standard of evidence merited congressional impeachment, Republican Representative Howard Coble said: "I didn't mind the affair bit; lots of folks here [Capitol Hill] have them. I didn't even mind the fact that he [Clinton] had an affair with an intern; that, too, can happen here. But Clinton violated the sanctity of the oath of office he swore to uphold."[4]

Drawing heavily on Independent Counsel Kenneth Starr's extensive record of the investigation and his recommendations, the House majority relied on a highly partisan and polarized Judiciary Committee to sort out the charges. Both Republicans and Democrats on the Judiciary Committee reflected the partisan extremes of their respective parties, leaving little chance for members on either side of the aisle to reach some middle-ground solution, such as censure, that would have satisfied the overwhelming majority of the American public. Led by conservative (and historically fair-minded) Representative Henry J. Hyde (R-Ill.), the majority called no witnesses and expeditiously marched toward impeachment in the weeks after the 1998 midterm election. At the start of the impeachment proceedings, Chairman Hyde evoked the spirit of his predecessor, Peter Rodino (D-N.J.), and observed that the process would have to be bipartisan to avoid failure. Yet as the investigative hearings progressed, little work the committee did reflected this call for bipartisanship.

Each party in the House has grown more homogeneous, and the Judiciary Committee's composition exaggerated such a trend. The committee included no Republican moderates.[5] Rather, its roster was dominated by cultural conservatives from the South and the West, who vented their anger on a symbol of the counterculture—someone whose opposition to the Vietnam War and his "want of military service, marijuana smoking and numerous infidelities" made him an easy target of traditionalists.[6] Judiciary Committee Democrats were correspondingly left of center, disproportionately liberal, representing especially safe districts, deliberately appointed by the party leadership for the primary task of blocking Republican-sponsored measures dealing with highly charged issues from ever getting out of the committee.

Such polarizing partisanship and the absence of deliberation spilled onto the House floor. Republican Majority Whip Tom Delay made sure that debate was confined to the impeachment articles voted out of committee and that members were denied a vote on a censure motion, which would have commanded an overwhelming bipartisan consensus among House members. As a consequence, the four articles of impeachment became the only opportunity for Republican members to show their disapproval of Clinton's conduct to the party faithful back in their districts, and two of them were adopted on virtually party-line votes. The near certainty that the Senate would not convict meant, moreover, that Republican members could vote for impeachment without suffering any electoral backlash from centrist voters for the removal of a popular president.

The partisanship of the House debate and the subsequent votes probably doomed any real chance of convicting President Clinton in the Senate. At no point during the Senate trial did it ever appear likely that there would be anything like the twelve Democratic votes required to combine with the fifty-five Republicans and convict Clinton on either count. Such a foreordained outcome contributed to a less rancorous process in the Senate, but the final tally did break down, for the most part, along party lines.[7] In fact, as Burdett A. Loomis observes, the Senate Democrats, who voted unanimously against impeachment on both articles, acted more as a bloc than their Republican counterparts in the Senate or either of the parties in the House.[8]

The congressional Republicans were thus able to galvanize their electoral base against Clinton without inflicting any significant long-term electoral damage to the party. Indeed, in the 2000 presidential election, the 1998 impeachment undoubtedly undermined the Clinton administration's record and forced Clinton's vice president, Democratic candidate Al Gore, into a much closer contest than the prosperous economic situation would have predicted. His relationship to Clinton bedeviled Gore throughout the 2000 campaign, muddling his general election strategy and distracting from his message at several crucial points.[9] In addition to his eventual triumph in the Florida post-election fracas, Republican George W. Bush's narrow electoral college win hinged on his winning several culturally conservative states that had voted twice for Clinton in 1992 and 1996: Missouri, Kentucky, West Virginia, Arkansas, Louisiana, and Gore's home state of Tennessee. The pattern reoccurred in the 2002 congressional elections, when the Republicans narrowly regained control of the Senate through victories in critical "Bible belt" Senate races in Missouri, Georgia, North Carolina, South Carolina, Tennessee, and Texas. Thus despite the widespread commentary at the time, whatever long-term electoral consequences there were from the Clinton impeachment may have redounded to the Republicans' benefit, as they effectively utilized the memory of the former president and his indiscretions to rally their own electoral base.

Did the impeachment proceedings reflect well or poorly on the contemporary American governmental process? Some suggest that an impeachment proceeding is a reminder that the process works by design to give the legislative branch a check on the other branches when officials in those other branches exceed or misuse their power.[10] There are many checks and balances in the American constitutional system of separate institutions sharing governmental powers, and impeachment is one of these. Moreover, the arduous nature of impeachment is intended to minimize the possibility that so serious a course will be pursued without fair and due deliberation by the elected officials themselves. By making impeachment a "bungling business," in Thomas Jefferson's words, the Constitution discourages regular legislative intrusions into the business of the judicial and executive branches.[11] But, without careful handling, impeachment can turn into a "vote of no confidence," on policy grounds—a cheap way to change the government without invoking new elections and bending the presidency to congressional will.[12] While in theory we may want impeachment "locked away in a gun safe somewhere in the House," in practice, "it really is just a loaded pistol lying out there on the coffee table."[13]

Congressional partisanship on Capitol Hill in the 1990s was more than a construct of voting patterns. Throughout the congressional impeachment of President Clinton, party loyalty also included an element of hostility that extended both across the aisle within Congress, especially the House, and across the branches of government, with many Republican members expressing extensive hostility toward the president, and Democrats replying with bitter counterattacks against his accusers.[14] A valuable lesson future congresses might therefore heed is that impeachment is a weapon of last resort to be used only when there is a broad consensus that a president has seriously abused the powers of his office, and is more than likely to be removed from office by a Senate trial.[15] In short, while impeachment is ultimately a political process, it will succeed only if directed at what an overwhelming preponderance of public opinion regards as illegitimate presidential acts, rather than as a weapon in the partisan conflict of the moment.[16]

Besides serving as an instance of the relative importance of party pressures in understanding contemporary congressional behavior, the congressional impeachment of President Bill Clinton can also be understood as an example of institutional assertiveness. Congressional assertiveness has historically followed episodes of presidential activism. Abraham Lincoln's centralized control in the Civil War brought a succession of weak chief executives and strong congresses; the strong presidencies of Theodore Roosevelt and Woodrow Wilson brought the shift to congressional dominance in the 1920s; and President Franklin D. Roosevelt's expansion of executive power and four election victories led to the 22nd Amendment to the Constitution limiting presidents to two terms. Since the New Deal, presidential power has often been seen as nearly limitless, in part because of the rise of the modern, post–World War II administrative state with its emphasis on national security bureaucracies that propelled the executive branch to the forefront of the American governmental system. Following the reaction against the "imperial presidency" after Vietnam and Watergate, and with the collapse of the Soviet Union and the end of the cold war, a more complex and confrontational relationship has evolved between Congress and the presidency.

When parties are strong in Congress, party leaders are also strong, and this cohesiveness in turn means that Congress is better able to assert itself vis-à-vis the executive branch, as was demonstrated during the Clinton impeachment in 1998. Newt Gingrich and his 1994 Republican House majority held a "Whiggish" view of Congress as a dominant first branch of government and the prime mover in national politics, able to set and implement policy.[17] A strong party leadership, embodied by the House Speakership in both its formal and informal powers, conducted the ambitious reform effort by the new Republican majority in 1995. This revitalized Speakership was the culmination of events begun in the 1970s, when Democratic party reformers attacked the power of committee barons not only with caucus restrictions but also with enhanced powers for elected leaders.[18]

The impeachment and near conviction of Andrew Johnson arguably eviscerated the power of the presidency as an institution for the following quarter century. It has also been argued that the near impeachment of Richard Nixon damaged the presidency and American standing in the world during the 1970s.[19] In the case of the long-term impact of the Clinton impeachment and acquittal, it appears unlikely that the impact will be so drastic, simply because a strong presidency has become so integral to the modern American governing structure abroad and at home. The adverse public reaction to the Clinton impeachment may also make even the most partisan Congress more reluctant to use this particular constitutional device to try to restrain an assertive president of the opposing party in the near future.

Finally, the Clinton impeachment also raises issues of congressional partisanship and its implications. Newt Gingrich did more than inspire institutional loyalty among Republican House members; he also provided a glimpse of party responsibility. More than fifty years have passed since the American Political Science Association published "Toward a More Responsible Two-Party System," a report that urged the major American parties to offer voters clear ideological choices in the hope of promoting greater governmental accountability.[20] When political scientists refer to an *ideological party,* they mean a party with clear and consistent principles on questions ranging from the purpose of government to the pitfalls and possibilities of human nature.[21] Throughout their histories, however, the American parties have tended to be pragmatic rather than ideological, focusing on concrete problems and building broad coalitions of electoral support rather than on protecting the purity of their principles.[22]

In a move spearheaded by Gingrich and a core of Republican lawmakers and aspirants, the great majority of Republicans running for House seats in 1994 signed a widely publicized "national" agenda they called the "Contract with America." In it, they pledged that if voters would give Republicans a House majority (the first time in forty years), they would reform the way Congress did its business as well as approve an ambitious legislative agenda (with ten points), embodying conservative principles, within the first hundred days of the next Congress.[23] The statement concluded, in words that would gladden the hearts of responsible party government advocates: "If we break this contract, throw us out. We mean it."[24]

The benefit of such *responsible party government,* according to its proponents, is that it can offer clear, distinguishable solutions to social and economic problems. American governing institutions may have been well suited to the limited expectations of government characteristic of the early years of American history, but they are ineffective in the modern context, when more vigorous government action appears to be required across the entire gamut of policy.[25] Undisciplined parties containing diverse interests, moreover, appear to exacerbate the situation.

The problem, however, with more disciplined, homogeneous, and ideological major parties, as evidenced by the congressional impeachment of President Bill Clinton, is a more intense, bitter, divisive, dogmatic politics, as well as a Congress unrepresentative of a general public that still does not share the intense partisan or ideological preoccupations of the party elites. Congressional deliberation and the ability to forge legislative and public consensus on pressing issues becomes harder to achieve, and instead partisan considerations guide debate and dictate legislative outcomes or non-outcomes. Moreover, in a system of "separated institutions sharing powers" intense partisanship is likely to give rise only to frustration, exasperation, and impasse on the part of both national political actors and the wider public.[26] This, in turn, ratchets up partisan animosity even further, culminating in apparently bizarre events such as the impeachment of the president of the United States by the legislative body constitutionally closest to the citizenry in defiance of the clearly expressed views of that citizenry.

Perhaps the bitterness engendered by the Clinton impeachment has prompted something of a "timeout" on the part of the most important participants in this partisan conflict. As evidenced by the 2000 elections, the major American parties are simply too finely balanced electorally, as we advance into the new millennium, for "responsible party government" to be a viable governing strategy—if it ever was in the American context. Even when such a strategy has been seriously attempted, the electorate—while admittedly somewhat more partisan than was the case thirty years ago—invariably still tends to apply a corrective by dividing the legislative and executive branches between the parties. Moreover, the terrorist attacks on the American homeland on September 11, 2001, may concentrate the minds of partisan elites on matters of national and international security, issues that transcend the cultural cleavages that fomented and sustained the partisan politics of the 1990s.

Nevertheless, the rise of partisanship in Congress has deep roots in a wider change in the American political environment. This environment of low overall political participation, selective mobilization of partisan constituencies, and the domination of the national parties by polarized single-issue and ideological activists, with the national news media as the main locus of partisan debate, appears unlikely to change dramatically anytime soon. No matter how much tragic events or sudden crises may temporarily bring political elites together, the imperatives of party competition in modern American politics are likely to soon pull them apart once more. While the Clinton impeachment demonstrated the unsuitability of that particular constitutional procedure as an instrument of partisan competition, partisan antagonists are likely to find other, though perhaps less drastic, weapons to deploy in their unflagging struggle for supremacy within the American national government.

Appendixes

METHODOLOGY

For the analysis of the factors leading to the congressional impeachment and subsequent trial of President Bill Clinton we relied principally on interviews with Republican and Democratic members, especially those who sat on the Judiciary Committee in the fall of 1998. Throughout the work, we also include non-interview data—descriptive, analytical summary of the steps in the legislative and political history of impeachment as well as background material on committee members and their constituencies. But the interviews provide the leading edge of the description. How reliable and valid are data collected in this fashion? In the end, each reader will have to make some judgments. The data do suggest that congressional decision making is a more nuanced and complex process than mere calculation of career goals and electoral interests.

This methodological approach may prove to be more illuminating than formal rational-choice models because of the varied nature of the issues surrounding the motives to impeach President Clinton. As other congressional scholars who use what Richard F. Fenno, Jr., calls the "soaking and poking" approach suggest, in exploratory research the focus is on discovering relationships or motives and on generating ideas about them rather than using rational-choice or formal models which may assume answers to the very questions under investigation.[1] Interviews are most useful for this, especially when the conversation is frank and spontaneous. As Fenno says, "You watch, you accompany, and you talk with people you are studying. Much of what you see, therefore, is dictated by what they say and do. If something is important to members of Congress, it becomes important to you."[2]

A range of public records was also examined. These included transcripts of committee and subcommittee hearings as well as the *Congressional Record,* particularly the debates behind each case study commission, which were studied to assess the positions taken by the key legislators in the formation of each case study commission. Other information was derived from the *Congressional Directory,* the *Congressional Yellow Book,* the *U.S. Code: Congressional and Administrative News,* the Library of Congress computer search systems (SCORPIO and THOMAS), the Library of Congress Information Service (LOCIS), and the media (NEXIS-LEXIS). Major *Congressional Quarterly* publications were consulted, such as *Congressional Quarterly Almanac,* an annual compendium of biographical and organizational data, summaries of action taken in each session of Congress, roll-call votes, and analyses of congressional voting; *Congress and the Nation,* a summary of all major legislation and a biographical index to members of Congress and key roll-call votes; and *Congressional Quarterly Weekly Report,* a weekly summary of important congressional news, roll calls, and analyses of congressional voting.

CONGRESSIONAL TIME LINE: IMPEACHMENT AND TRIAL

1998

September 9	Independent Counsel Kenneth W. Starr delivers his report and eighteen boxes of supporting documents to the House of Representatives. The report lists eleven possible grounds for impeachment as well as accuses the president of obstruction of justice and abusing his authority as president.
September 11	The House of Representative votes to receive the Starr report. The House Judiciary Committee takes possession of the eighteen boxes of materials and promptly releases the first 445 pages to the public.
September 18	House Judiciary Committee agrees to release President Clinton's videotaped grand jury testimony and more than three thousand pages of supporting material from the Starr Report, including sexually explicit testimony from Monica Lewinsky.
September 21	House Judiciary Committee releases Clinton's videotaped grand jury testimony to the public. Along with the videotape, the Judiciary Committee also releases the appendix to the Starr's report, which includes 3,183 pages of testimony and other evidence.
September 24	House Judiciary Committee announces the committee will consider a resolution to begin an impeachment inquiry against President Clinton in an open session.
October 8	House of Representatives votes to hold an impeachment inquiry.
November 3	Democrats pick up five House seats in the midterm election.
November 5	House Judiciary Committee Chair Henry J. Hyde (R-Ill.) submits eighty-one questions to the president regarding his affair with Monica Lewinsky.
November 6	House Speaker Newt Gingrich (R-Ga.) announces resignation.
November 27	President Clinton responds to eighty-one questions from Chairman Hyde, writing that his testimony in the Lewinsky affair was "not false and misleading."
December 11	Judiciary Committee approves impeachment articles I, II, and III, which accuse the president of perjury in the Jones deposition and in his grand jury testimony and obstruction of justice in the Jones case.
December 12	Judiciary Committee approves a fourth and final article, including charges of perjury regarding Clinton's responses to its questions. The committee rejects a substitute resolution backed by Democrats that would instead censure Clinton for "reprehensible conduct."
December 17	House delays debate on articles of impeachment after the United States launches military strikes against Iraq.
December 19	Speaker-elect Robert L. Livingston (R-La.) resigns from the House; House votes to impeach Clinton on two articles and appoints thirteen Republicans on the House Judiciary Committee to be floor managers.

1999

January 7	Impeachment trial begins in Senate.
January 8	Bipartisan plan adopted unanimously.
January 11	Response by the House Judiciary trial managers to the summons for an impeachment trial in the Senate.
January 24	Monica Lewinsky questioned privately by House managers.
January 25	Text of ten questions submitted by Senate Republicans to the president; Senate rejects a motion 57 to 43 by Senator Robert Byrd (D-W.Va.) to open Senate deliberations on a motion to dismiss articles of impeachment against President Clinton.
January 26	House managers motion to call Monica Lewinsky, Vernon Jordan, and Sidney Blumenthal.
January 27	Senate votes to depose witnesses.
January 28	Senate passes GOP plan for witnesses.
February 1–3	Witness depositions.
February 6	Clips from the videotaped testimonies of Ms. Lewinsky, Mr. Jordan, and Mr. Blumenthal, as well as videotaped testimony from Clinton, are played publicly at Senate trial.
February 4	Six roll call votes: admitting depositions into evidence; calling Monica Lewinsky as live witnesses; using only the transcripts; presenting videotaped depositions on the Senate floor during closing arguments; begin closing arguments; requiring House managers to notify Senate of parts of videotaped deposition being used in closing arguments.
February 8	House managers and White House lawyers present closing arguments.
February 9	Senate declines to change rules to allow open deliberations on impeachment articles and begins private deliberations.
February 10–11	Senate continues private deliberations.
February 12	Senate votes to acquit Clinton of impeachment charges; Senator Diane Feinstein (D-Calif.) moves to suspend the rules for a censure resolution; movement is blocked procedurally by Senator Phil Gramm (R-Tex.).

PRESIDENT CLINTON'S RESPONSE TO QUESTIONS BY CHAIRMAN HENRY J. HYDE (R-ILL.)

1. Do you admit or deny that you are the chief law-enforcement officer of the United States of America?

Response: The President is frequently referred to as the chief law-enforcement officer, although nothing in the Constitution specifically designates the President as such. Article II, Section 1 of the United States Constitution states that "the executive power shall be vested in a President of the United States of America," and the law-enforcement function is a component of the executive power.

2. Do you admit or deny that upon taking your oath of office that you swore you would faithfully execute the office of President of the United States, and would to the best of your ability, preserve, protect and defend the Constitution of the United States?

Response: At my Inaugurations in 1993 and 1997, I took the following oath: "I do solemnly swear that I will faithfully execute the Office of President of the United States, and will to the best of my ability, preserve, protect and defend the Constitution of the United States."

3. Do you admit or deny that, pursuant to Article II, Section 2 of the Constitution, you have a duty to "take care that the laws be faithfully executed"?

Response: Article II, Section 3 (not Section 2), of the Constitution states that the President "shall take care that the Laws be faithfully executed," and that is a Presidential obligation.

4. Do you admit or deny that you are a member of the bar and officer of the court of a state of the United States, subject to the rules of professional responsibility and ethics applicable to the bar of that state?

Response: I have an active license to practice law (inactive for continuing legal education purposes) issued by the Supreme Court of Arkansas. The license, No. 73017, was issued in 1973.

5. Do you admit or deny that you took an oath in which you swore or affirmed to tell the truth, the whole truth, and nothing but the truth, in a deposition conducted as part of a judicial proceeding in the case of *Jones v. Clinton* on January 17, 1998?

Response: I took an oath to tell the truth on January 17, 1998, before my deposition in the *Jones v. Clinton* case. While I do not recall the precise wording of that oath, as I previously stated in my grand jury testimony on August 17, 1998, in taking the oath "I believed then that I had to answer the questions truthfully."

6. Do you admit or deny that you took an oath in which you swore or affirmed to tell the truth, the whole truth, and nothing but the truth, before a grand jury impaneled as part of a judicial proceeding by the United States District Court for the District of Columbia Circuit on August 17, 1998?

Response: As the August 17, 1998, videotape reflects, I was asked, "Do you solemnly swear that the testimony you are about to give in this matter will be the truth, the whole truth, and nothing but the truth, so help you God?" and I answered, "I do."

7. Do you admit or deny that on or about October 7, 1997, you received a letter composed by Monica Lewinsky in which she expressed dissatisfaction with her search for a job in New York?

Response: At some point I learned of Ms. Lewinsky's decision to seek suitable employment in New York. I do not recall receiving a letter in which she expressed dissatisfaction about her New York job search. I understand Ms. Lewinsky has stated that she sent a note indicating her decision to seek employment in New York, but I do not believe she has said the note expressed dissatisfaction about her search for a job there.

8. Do you admit or deny that you telephoned Monica Lewinsky early in the morning on October 10, 1997, and offered to assist her in finding a job in New York?

Response: I understand that Ms. Lewinsky testified that I called her on the 9th of October, 1997. I do not recall that particular telephone call.

9. Do you admit or deny that on or about October 11, 1997, you met with Monica Lewinsky in or about the Oval Office dining room?

10. Do you admit or deny that on or about October 11, 1997, Monica Lewinsky furnished to you, in or about the Oval Office dining room, a list of jobs in New York in which she was interested?

11. Do you admit or deny that on or about October 11, 1997, you suggested to Monica Lewinsky that Vernon Jordan may be able to assist her in her job search?

12. Do you admit or deny that on or about October 11, 1997, after meeting with Monica Lewinsky and discussing her search for a job in New York, you telephoned Vernon Jordan?

Response to Requests Nos. 9, 10, 11, and 12: At some point, Ms. Lewinsky either discussed with me or gave me a list of the kinds of jobs she was interested in, although I do not know whether it was on Saturday, October 11, 1997. Records included in the O.I.C. Referral indicate that Ms. Lewinsky visited the White House on October 11, 1997, and I may have seen her on that day.

I do not believe I suggested to Ms. Lewinsky that Mr. Jordan might be able to assist her in her job search, and I understand that Ms. Lewinsky has stated that she asked me if Mr. Jordan could assist her in finding a job in New York.

I speak to Mr. Jordan often, and I understand that records included in the O.I.C. Referral indicate that he telephoned me shortly after Ms. Lewinsky left the White House complex. I understand that Mr. Jordan testified that he and I did not discuss Ms. Lewinsky during that call.

13. Do you admit or deny that you discussed with Monica Lewinsky prior to December 17, 1997, a plan in which she would pretend to bring you papers with a work-related purpose, when in fact such papers had no work-related purpose, in order to conceal your relationship?

14. Do you admit or deny that you discussed with Monica Lewinsky prior to December 17, 1997, that Betty Currie should be the one to clear Ms. Lewinsky in to see you so that Ms. Lewinsky could say that she was visiting with Ms. Currie instead of with you?

15. Do you admit or deny that you discussed with Monica Lewinsky prior to December 17, 1997, that if either of you were questioned about the existence of your relationship you would deny its existence?

19. Do you admit or deny that on or about December 17, 1997, you suggested to Monica Lewinsky that she could say to anyone inquiring about her relationship with you that her visits to the Oval Office were for the purpose of visiting with Betty Currie or to deliver papers to you?

Response to Requests Nos. 13, 14, 15, and 19: I was asked essentially these same questions by O.I.C. lawyers. I testified that Ms. Lewinsky and I "may have talked about what to do in a nonlegal context at some point in the past, but I have no specific memory of that conversation." That continues to be my recollection today— that is, any such conversation was not in connection with her status as a witness in the *Jones v. Clinton* case.

16. Do you admit or deny that on or about December 6, 1997, you learned that Monica Lewinsky's name was on a witness list in the case of *Jones v. Clinton?*

Response: As I stated in my August 17 grand jury testimony, I believe that I found out that Ms. Lewinsky's name was on a witness list in the *Jones v. Clinton* case late in the afternoon on the 6th of December, 1997.

17. Do you admit or deny that on or about December 17, 1997, you told Monica Lewinsky that her name was on the witness list in the case of *Jones v. Clinton?*

18. Do you admit or deny that on or about December 17, 1997, you suggested to Monica Lewinsky that the submission of an affidavit in the case of *Jones v. Clinton* might suffice to prevent her from having to testify personally in that case?

Response to Requests Nos. 17 and 18: As I previously testified, I recall telephoning Ms. Lewinsky to tell her Ms. Currie's brother had died, and that call was in the middle of December. I do not recall other particulars of such a call, including whether we discussed the fact that her name was on the *Jones v. Clinton* witness list. As I stated in my August 17 grand jury testimony in response to essentially the same questions, it is quite possible that that happened. . . . I don't have any memory of it, but I certainly wouldn't dispute that I might have said that she was on the witness list.

I recall that Ms. Lewinsky asked me at some time in December whether she might be able to get out of testifying in the *Jones v. Clinton* case because she knew nothing about Ms. Jones or the case. I told her I believed other witnesses had executed affidavits, and there was a chance they would not have to testify. As I stated in my August 17 grand jury testimony, "I felt strongly that . . . Ms. Lewinsky could execute an affidavit that would be factually truthful, that might get her out of having to testify." I never asked or encouraged Ms. Lewinsky to lie in her affidavit, as Ms. Lewinsky herself has confirmed.

19. For the response to Request No. 19, see the response to Request No. 13 et al.

20. Do you admit or deny that you gave false and misleading testimony under oath when you stated during your deposition in the case of *Jones v. Clinton* on January 17, 1998, that you did not know if Monica Lewinsky had been subpoenaed to testify in that case?

Response: It is evident from my testimony on pages 69 to 70 of the deposition that I did know on January 17, 1998, that Ms. Lewinsky had been subpoenaed in the *Jones v. Clinton* case. Ms. Jones's lawyer's question, "Did you talk to Mr. Lindsey about what action, if any, should be taken as a result of her being served with a subpoena?" and my response, "No," reflected my understanding that Ms. Lewinsky had been subpoenaed. That testimony was not false and misleading.

21. Do you admit or deny that you gave false and misleading testimony under oath when you stated before the grand jury on August 17, 1998, that you did know prior to January 17, 1998, that Monica Lewinsky had been subpoenaed to testify in the case of *Jones v. Clinton?*

Response: As my testimony on January 17 reflected, and as I testified on August 17, 1998, I knew prior to January 17, 1998, that Ms. Lewinsky had been subpoenaed to testify in *Jones v. Clinton.* That testimony was not false and misleading.

22. Do you admit or deny that on or about December 28, 1997, you had a discussion with Monica Lewinsky at the White House regarding her moving to New York?

Response: When I met with Ms. Lewinsky on December 28, 1997, I knew she was planning to move to New York, and we discussed her move.

23. Do you admit or deny that on or about December 28, 1997, you had a discussion with Monica Lewinsky at the White House in which you suggested to her that she move to New York soon because by moving to New York, the lawyers representing Paula Jones in the case of *Jones v. Clinton* may not contact her?

Response: Ms. Lewinsky had decided to move to New York well before the end of December 1997. By December 28, Ms. Lewinsky had been subpoenaed. I did not suggest that she could avoid testifying in the *Jones v. Clinton* case by moving to New York.

24. Do you admit or deny that on or about December 28, 1997, you had a discussion with Monica Lewinsky at the White House regarding gifts you had given to Ms. Lewinsky that were subpoenaed in the case of *Jones v. Clinton?*

25. Do you admit or deny that on or about December 28, 1997, you expressed concern to Monica Lewinsky about a hatpin you had given to her as a gift which had been subpoenaed in the case of *Jones v. Clinton?*

Response to Requests Nos. 24 and 25: As I told the grand jury, "Ms. Lewinsky said something to me like, what if they ask me about the gifts you've given me," but I do not know whether that conversation occurred on December 28, 1997, or earlier.

Whenever this conversation occurred, I testified, I told her "that if they asked her for gifts, she'd have to give them whatever she had. . . ." I simply was not concerned about the fact that I had given her gifts. Indeed, I gave her additional gifts on December 28, 1997. I also told the grand jury that I do not recall Ms. Lewinsky telling me that the subpoena specifically called for a hat pin that I had given her.

26. Do you admit or deny that on or about December 28, 1997, you discussed with Betty Currie gifts previously given by you to Monica Lewinsky?

27. Do you admit or deny that on or about December 28, 1998, you requested, instructed, suggested to or otherwise discussed with Betty Currie that she take possession of gifts previously given to Monica Lewinsky by you?

Response to Requests Nos. 26 and 27: I do not recall any conversation with Ms. Currie on or about December 28, 1997, about gifts I had previously given to Ms. Lewinsky. I never told Ms. Currie to take possession of gifts I had given Ms. Lewinsky; I understand Ms. Currie has stated that Ms. Lewinsky called Ms. Currie to ask her to hold a box.

28. Do you admit or deny that you had a telephone conversation on January 6, 1998, with Vernon Jordan during which you discussed Monica Lewinsky's affidavit, yet to be filed, in the case of *Jones v. Clinton?*

Response: White House records included in the O.I.C. Referral reflect that I spoke to Mr. Jordan on January 6, 1998. I do not recall whether we discussed Ms. Lewinsky's affidavit during a telephone call on that date.

29. Do you admit or deny that you had knowledge of the fact that Monica Lewinsky executed for filing an affidavit in the case of *Jones v. Clinton* on January 7, 1998?

30. Do you admit or deny that on or about January 7, 1998, you had a discussion with Vernon Jordan in which he mentioned that Monica Lewinsky executed for filing an affidavit in the case of *Jones v. Clinton?*

Response to Requests Nos. 29 and 30: As I testified to the grand jury, "I believe that Mr. Jordan did notify us when she signed her affidavit." While I do not recall the timing, as I told the grand jury, I have no reason to doubt Mr. Jordan's statement that he notified me about the affidavit around January 7, 1998.

31. Do you admit or deny that on or about January 7, 1998, you had a discussion with Vernon Jordan in which he mentioned that he was assisting Monica Lewinsky in finding a job in New York?

Response: I told the grand jury that I was aware that Mr. Jordan was assisting Ms. Lewinsky in her job search in connection with her move to New York. I have no recollection as to whether Mr. Jordan discussed it with me on or about January 7, 1998.

32. Do you admit or deny that you viewed a copy of the affidavit executed by Monica Lewinsky on January 7, 1998, in the case of *Jones v. Clinton,* prior to your deposition in that case?

33. Do you admit or deny that you had knowledge that your counsel viewed a copy of the affidavit executed by Monica Lewinsky on January 7, 1998, in the case of *Jones v. Clinton,* prior to your deposition in that case?

Response to Requests Nos. 32 and 33: I do not believe I saw this affidavit before my deposition, although I cannot be absolutely sure. The record indicates that my counsel had seen the affidavit at some time prior to the deposition.

34. Do you admit or deny that you had knowledge that any facts or assertions contained in the affidavit executed by Monica Lewinsky on January 7, 1998, in the case of *Jones v. Clinton* were not true?

40. Do you admit or deny that during your deposition in the case of *Jones v. Clinton* on January 17, 1998, you affirmed that the facts or assertions stated in the affidavit executed by Monica Lewinsky on January 7, 1998, were true?

Response to Requests Nos. 34 and 40: I was asked at my deposition in January about two paragraphs of Ms. Lewinsky's affidavit. With respect to Paragraph 6, I explained the extent to which I was able to attest to its accuracy.

With respect to Paragraph 8, I stated in my deposition that it was true. In my August 17 grand jury testimony, I sought to explain the basis for that deposition answer: "I believe at the time that she filled out this affidavit, if she believed that the definition of sexual relationship was two people having intercourse, then this is accurate."

35. Do you admit or deny that you viewed a copy of the affidavit executed by Monica Lewinsky on January 7, 1998, in the case of *Jones v. Clinton,* at your deposition in that case on January 17, 1998?

36. Do you admit or deny that you had knowledge that your counsel viewed a copy of the affidavit executed by Monica Lewinsky on January 7, 1998, in the case of *Jones v. Clinton,* at your deposition in that case on January 17, 1998?

Response to Requests Nos. 35 and 36: I know that Mr. Bennett saw Ms. Lewinsky's affidavit during the deposition because he read portions of it aloud at the deposition. I do not recall whether I saw a copy of Ms. Lewinsky's affidavit during the deposition.

37. Do you admit or deny that on or about January 9, 1998, you received a message from Vernon Jordan indicating that Monica Lewinsky had received a job offer in New York?

Response: At some time, I learned that Ms. Lewinsky had received a job offer in New York. However, I do not recall whether I first learned it in a message from Mr. Jordan or whether I learned it on that date.

38. Do you admit or deny that between January 9, 1998, and January 15, 1998, you had a conversation with Erskine Bowles in the Oval Office in which you stated that Monica Lewinsky received a job offer and had listed John Hilley as a reference?

39. Do you admit or deny that you asked Erskine Bowles if he would ask John Hilley to give Ms. Lewinsky a positive job recommendation?

Response to Requests Nos. 38 and 39: As I testified to the grand jury, I recall at some point talking to Mr. Bowles "about whether Monica Lewinsky could get a recommendation that was not negative from the Legislative Affairs Office," or that "was at least neutral," although I am not certain of the date of the conversation. To suggest that I told Mr. Bowles that Ms. Lewinsky had received a job offer and had listed John Hilley as a reference is, as I testified, a "little bit" inconsistent with my memory. It is possible, as I also indicated, that she had identified Mr. Hilley as her supervisor on her résumé and in that respect had already listed him as a reference.

40. For the response to Request No. 40, see response to Request No. 34 et al.

41. As to each, do you admit or deny that you gave the following gifts to Monica Lewinsky at any time in the past?

    a. A lithograph
    b. A hatpin
    c. A large Black Dog canvas bag
    d. A large Rockettes blanket
    e. A pin of the New York skyline
    f. A box of "cherry chocolates"
    g. A pair of novelty sunglasses
    h. A stuffed animal from the Black Dog
    i. A marble bear's head
    j. A London pin
    k. A shamrock pin
    l. An Annie Lennox compact disk
    m. Davidoff cigars

Response: In my deposition in the Jones case, I testified that I "certainly . . . could have" given Ms. Lewinsky a hat pin and that I gave her "something" from the Black Dog. In my grand jury testimony, I indicated that in late December 1997, I gave Ms. Lewinsky a Canadian marble bear's head carving, a Rockettes blanket, some kind of pin, and a bag (perhaps from the Black Dog) to hold these objects. I also stated that I might have given her such gifts as a box of candy and sunglasses, although I did not recall doing so, and I specifically testified that I had given Ms. Lewinsky gifts on other occasions. I do not remember giving her the other gifts listed in Question 41, although I might have. As I have previously testified,

I receive a very large number of gifts from many different people, sometimes several at a time. I also give a very large number of gifts. I gave Ms. Lewinsky gifts, some of which I remember and some of which I do not.

42. Do you admit or deny that when asked on January 17, 1998, in your deposition in the case of *Jones v. Clinton* if you had ever given gifts to Monica Lewinsky, you stated that you did not recall, even though you actually had knowledge of giving her gifts in addition to gifts from the Black Dog?

Response: In my grand jury testimony, I was asked about this same statement. I explained that my full response was "I don't recall. Do you know what they were?" By that answer, I did not mean to suggest that I did not recall giving gifts; rather, I meant that I did not recall what the gifts were, and I asked for reminders.

43. Do you admit or deny that you gave false and misleading testimony under oath in your deposition in the case of *Jones v. Clinton* when you responded "once or twice" to the question "has Monica Lewinsky ever given you any gifts"?

Response: My testimony was not false and misleading. As I have testified previously, I give and receive numerous gifts. Before my January 17, 1998, deposition, I had not focused on the precise number of gifts Ms. Lewinsky had given me. My deposition testimony made clear that Ms. Lewinsky had given me gifts; at the deposition, I recalled "a book or two" and a tie. At the time, those were the gifts I recalled. In response to O.I.C. inquiries, after I had had a chance to search my memory and refresh my recollection, I was able to be more responsive. However, as my counsel have informed the O.I.C., in light of the very large number of gifts I receive, there might still be gifts from Ms. Lewinsky that I have not identified.

44. Do you admit or deny that on January 17, 1998, at or about 5:38 P.M., after the conclusion of your deposition in the case of *Jones v. Clinton*, you telephoned Vernon Jordan at his home?

Response: I speak to Mr. Jordan frequently, so I cannot remember specific times and dates. According to White House records included in the O.I.C. Referral, I telephoned Mr. Jordan's residence on January 17, 1998, at or about 5:38 P.M.

45. Do you admit or deny that on January 17, 1998, at or about 7:02 P.M., after the conclusion of your deposition in the case of *Jones v. Clinton*, you telephoned Betty Currie at her home?

46. Do you admit or deny that on January 17, 1998, at or about 7:02 P.M., after the conclusion of your deposition in the case of *Jones v. Clinton*, you telephoned Vernon Jordan at his office?

47. Do you admit or deny that on January 17, 1998, at or about 7:13 P.M., after the conclusion of your deposition in the case of *Jones v. Clinton*, you telephoned Betty Currie at her home and asked her to meet with you the next day, Sunday, January 18, 1998?

Response to Requests Nos. 45, 46, and 47: According to White House records included in the O.I.C. Referral, I placed a telephone call to Ms. Currie at her residence at 7:02 P.M. and spoke to her at or about 7:13 P.M. I recall that when I spoke to her that evening, I asked if she could meet with me the following day. According to White House records included in the O.I.C. Referral, I telephoned Mr. Jordan's office on January 17, 1998, at or about 7:02 P.M.

48. Do you admit or deny that on January 18, 1998, at or about 6:11 A.M., you learned of the existence of tapes of conversations between Monica Lewinsky and Linda Tripp recorded by Linda Tripp?

Response: I did not know on January 18, 1998, that tapes existed of conversations between Ms. Lewinsky and Ms. Tripp recorded by Ms. Tripp. At some point on Sunday, January 18, 1998, I knew about the Drudge Report. I understand that, while the report talked about tapes of phone conversations, it did not identify Ms. Lewinsky by name and did not mention Ms. Tripp at all. The report did not state who the parties to the conversations were or who taped the conversations.

49. Do you admit or deny that on January 18, 1998, at or about 12:50 P.M., you telephoned Vernon Jordan at his home?

Response: According to White House records included in the O.I.C. Referral, I telephoned Mr. Jordan's residence on January 18, 1998, at or about 12:50 P.M.

50. Do you admit or deny that on January 18, 1998, at or about 1:11 P.M., you telephoned Betty Currie at her home?

Response: According to White House records included in the O.I.C. Referral, I telephoned Ms. Currie's residence on January 18, 1998, at or about 1:11 P.M.

51. Do you admit or deny that on January 18, 1998, at or about 2:55 P.M., you received a telephone call from Vernon Jordan?

Response: According to White House records included in the O.I.C. Referral, Mr. Jordan telephoned me from his residence on January 18, 1998, at or about 2:55 P.M.

52. Do you admit or deny that on January 18, 1998, at or about 5 P.M., you had a meeting with Betty Currie at which you made statements similar to any of the following regarding your relationship with Monica Lewinsky?

    a. "You were always there when she was there, right? We were never really alone."
    b. "You could see and hear everything."
    c. "Monica came on to me, and I never touched her, right?"
    d. "She wanted to have sex with me, and I couldn't do that."

Response: When I met with Ms. Currie, I believe that I asked her certain questions, in an effort to get as much information as quickly as I could, and made certain statements, although I do not remember exactly what I said.

Some time later, I learned that the Office of Independent Counsel was involved and that Ms. Currie was going to have to testify before the grand jury.

After learning this, I stated in my grand jury testimony, I told Ms. Currie, "Just relax, go in there and tell the truth."

53. Do you admit or deny that you had a conversation with Betty Currie within several days of January 18, 1998, in which you made statements similar to any of the following regarding your relationship with Monica Lewinsky?

    a. "You were always there when she was there, right? We were never really alone."
    b. "You could see and hear everything."

c. "Monica came on to me, and I never touched her, right?"

d. "She wanted to have sex with me and I couldn't do that."

Response: I previously told the grand jury that "I don't know that I" had another conversation with Ms. Currie within several days of January 18, 1998, in which I made statements similar to those quoted above. "I remember having this conversation one time." I further explained, "I do not remember how many times I talked to Betty Currie or when. I don't. I can't possibly remember that. I do remember, when I first heard about this story breaking, trying to ascertain what the facts were, trying to ascertain what Betty's perception was. I remember that I was highly agitated, understandably. I think."

I understand that Ms. Currie has said a second conversation occurred the next day that I was in the White House (when she was), which would have been Tuesday, January 20, before I knew about the grand jury investigation.

54. Do you admit or deny that on January 18, 1998, at or about 11:02 P.M., you telephoned Betty Currie at her home?

Response: According to White House records included in the O.I.C. Referral, I called Ms. Currie's residence on January 18, 1998, at or about 11:02 P.M.

55. Do you admit or deny that on Monday, January 19, 1998, at or about 8:50 A.M., you telephoned Betty Currie at her home?

Response: According to White House records included in the O.I.C. Referral, I called Ms. Currie's residence on January 19, 1998, at or about 8:50 A.M.

56. Do you admit or deny that on Monday, January 19, 1998, at or about 8:56 A.M., you telephoned Vernon Jordan at his home?

Response: According to White House records included in the O.I.C. Referral, I called Mr. Jordan's residence on January 19, 1998, at or about 8:56 A.M.

57. Do you admit or deny that on Monday, January 19, 1998, at or about 10:58 A.M., you telephoned Vernon Jordan at his office?

Response: According to White House records included in the O.I.C. Referral, I called Mr. Jordan's office on January 19, 1998, at or about 10:58 A.M.

58. Do you admit or deny that on Monday, January 19, 1998, at or about 1:45 P.M., you telephoned Betty Currie at her home?

Response: According to White House records included in the O.I.C. referral, I called Ms. Currie's residence on January 19, 1998, at or about 1:45 P.M.

59. Do you admit or deny that on Monday, January 19, 1998, at or about 2:44 P.M., you met with individuals including Vernon Jordan, Erskine Bowles, Bruce Lindsey, Cheryl Mills, Charles Ruff, and Rahm Emanuel?

60. Do you admit or deny that on Monday, January 19, 1998, at or about 2:44 P.M., at any meeting with Vernon Jordan, Erskine Bowles, Bruce Lindsey, Cheryl Mills, Charles Ruff, Rahm Emanuel, and others, you discussed the existence of tapes of conversations between Monica Lewinsky and Linda Tripp recorded by Linda Tripp, or any other matter related to Monica Lewinsky?

Response to Requests Nos. 59 and 60: I do not believe such a meeting occurred. White

House records included in the O.I.C. referral indicate that Mr. Jordan entered the White House complex that day at 2:44 P.M. According to Mr. Jordan's testimony, he and I met alone in the Oval Office for about 15 minutes.

I understand that Mr. Jordan testified that we discussed Ms. Lewinsky at that meeting and also the Drudge Report, in addition to other matters. Please also see my Response: 48.

61. Do you admit or deny that on Monday, January 19, 1998, at or about 5:56 P.M., you telephoned Vernon Jordan at his office?

Response: According to White House records included in the O.I.C. Referral, I called Mr. Jordan's office on January 19, 1998, at or about 5:56 P.M.

62. Do you admit or deny that on January 21, 1998, the day the Monica Lewinsky story appeared for the first time in *The Washington Post,* you had a conversation with Sidney Blumenthal, in which you stated that you rebuffed alleged advances from Monica Lewinsky and in which you made a statement similar to the following? "Monica Lewinsky came at me, and made a sexual demand on me."

63. Do you admit or deny that on January 21, 1998, the day the Monica Lewinsky story appeared for the first time in *The Washington Post,* you had a conversation with Sidney Blumenthal, in which you made a statement similar to the following in response to a question about your conduct with Monica Lewinsky? "I haven't done anything wrong."

64. Do you admit or deny that on January 21, 1998, the day the Monica Lewinsky story appeared for the first time in *The Washington Post,* you had a conversation with Erskine Bowles, Sylvia Matthews and John Podesta, in which you made a statement similar to the following? "I want you to know I did not have sexual relationships with this woman Monica Lewinsky. I did not ask anybody to lie. And when the facts come out, you'll understand."

65. Do you admit or deny that on or about January 23, 1998, you had a conversation with John Podesta, in which you stated that you had never had an affair with Monica Lewinsky?

66. Do you admit or deny that on or about January 23, 1998, you had a conversation with John Podesta, in which you stated that you were not alone with Monica Lewinsky in the Oval Office and that Betty Currie was either in your presence or outside your office with the door open while you were visiting with Monica Lewinsky?

67. Do you admit or deny that on or about January 26, 1998, you had a conversation with Harold Ickes, in which you made statements to the effect that you did not have an affair with Monica Lewinsky?

68. Do you admit or deny that on or about January 26, 1998, you had a conversation with Harold Ickes, in which you made statements to the effect that you had not asked anyone to change their story, suborn perjury or obstruct justice if called to testify or otherwise respond to a request for information from the Office of Independent Counsel or in any other legal proceeding?

Responses to Requests Nos. 62–68: As I have previously acknowledged, I did not want my family, friends, or colleagues to know the full nature of my relationship with Ms. Lewinsky. In the days following the January 21, 1998, *Washington Post* article, I misled people about this relationship. I have repeatedly apologized for doing so.

69. Do you admit or deny that on or about January 21, 1998, you and Richard (Dick) Morris discussed the possibility of commissioning a poll to determine public opinion following the *Washington Post* story regarding the Monica Lewinsky matter?

70. Do you admit or deny that you had a later conversation with Richard (Dick) Morris in which he stated that the polling results regarding the Monica Lewinsky matter suggested that the American people would forgive you for adultery but not for perjury or obstruction of justice?

71. Do you admit or deny that you responded to Richard (Dick) Morris's explanation of these polling results by making a statement similar to the following: "Well, we just have to win, then"?

Response to Requests Nos. 69, 70, and 71: At some point after the O.I.C. investigation became public, Dick Morris volunteered to conduct a poll on the charges reported in the press. He later called back. What I recall is that he said the public was most concerned about obstruction of justice or subornation of perjury. I do not recall saying, "Well, we just have to win then."

72. Do you admit or deny the past or present existence of or the past or present direct or indirect employment of individuals, other than counsel representing you, whose duties include making contact with or gathering information about witnesses or potential witnesses in any judicial proceeding related to any matter in which you are or could be involved?

Response: I cannot respond to this inquiry because of the vagueness of its terms ("indirect," "potential," "could be involved"). To the extent it may be interpreted to apply to individuals assisting counsel, please see my responses to Request Nos. 73–75. To the extent the inquiry addresses specific individuals, as in Request Nos. 73–75, I have responded and stand ready to respond to any other specific inquiries.

73. Do you admit or deny having knowledge that Terry Lenzner was contacted or employed to make contact with or gather information about witnesses or potential witnesses in any judicial proceeding related to any matter in which you are or could be involved?

Response: My counsel stated publicly on February 24, 1998, that Mr. Terry Lenzner and his firm have been retained since April 1994 by two private law firms that represent me. It is commonplace for legal counsel to retain such firms to perform legal and appropriate tasks to assist in the defense of clients. See also response to No. 72.

74. Do you admit or deny having knowledge that Jack Palladino was contacted or employed to make contact with or gather information about witnesses or potential witnesses in any judicial proceeding related to any matter in which you are or could be involved?

Response: My understanding is that during the 1992 Presidential campaign, Mr. Jack Palladino was retained to assist legal counsel for me and the campaign on a variety of matters arising during the campaign. See response to No. 72.

75. Do you admit or deny having knowledge that Betsy Wright was contacted or employed to make contact with or gather information about witnesses or potential witnesses in any judicial proceeding related to any matter in which you are or could be involved?

Response: Ms. Betsey Wright was my longtime chief of staff when I was Governor of Arkansas, and she remains a good friend and trusted adviser. Because of her great knowledge of Arkansas, from time to time my legal counsel and I have consulted with her on a wide range of matters. See also response to No. 72.

76. Do you admit or deny that you made false and misleading public statements in response to questions asked on or about January 21, 1998, in an interview with "Roll Call," when you stated "Well, let me say, the relationship was not improper, and I think that's important enough to say. But because the investigation is going on and because I don't know what is out—what's going to be asked of me, I think I need to cooperate, answer the questions, but I think it's important for me to make it clear what is not. And then, at the appropriate time, I'll try to answer what is. But let me answer—it is not an improper relationship and I know what the word means"?

Response: The tape of this interview reflects that in fact I said: "Well, let me say the relationship's not improper and I think that's important enough to say. . . ." With that revision, the quoted words accurately reflect my remarks. As I stated in response to Request Nos. 62 to 68, in the days following the January 21, 1998, disclosures, I misled people about this relationship, for which I have apologized.

77. Do you admit or deny that you made false and misleading public statements in response to questions asked on or about January 21, 1998, in the Oval Office during a photo opportunity, when you stated: "Now, there are a lot of other questions that are, I think, very legitimate. You have a right to ask them; you and the American people have a right to get answers. We are working very hard to comply and get all the requests for information up here, and we will give you as many answers as we can, as soon as we can, at the appropriate time, consistent with our obligation to also cooperate with the investigations. And that's not a dodge, that's really what I've—I've talked with our people. I want to do that. I'd like for you to have more rather than less, sooner rather than later. So we'll work through it as quickly as we can and get all those questions out there to you"?

Response: I made this statement (as corrected), according to a transcript of a January 22, 1998, photo opportunity in the Oval Office. This statement was not false and misleading. It accurately represented my thinking.

78. Do you admit or deny that you discussed with Harry Thomasson, prior to making public statements in response to questions asked by the press in January 1998, relating to your relationship with Monica Lewinsky, what such statements should be or how they should be communicated?

Response: Mr. Thomasson was a guest at the White House in January 1998, and I recall his encouraging me to state my denial forcefully.

79. Do you admit or deny that you made a false and misleading public statement in response to a question asked on or about January 26, 1998, when you stated "But I want to say one thing to the American people. I want you to listen to me. I'm going to say this again. I did not have sexual relations with that woman, Ms. Lewinsky"?

Response: I made this statement on January 26, 1998, although not in response to any question. In referring to "sexual relations," I was referring to sexual intercourse. As I stated in response to Request Nos. 62 to 68, in the days following the January 21, 1998, disclosures, answers like this misled people about this relationship, for which I have apologized.

80. Do you admit or deny that you made a false and misleading public statement in response to a question asked on or about January 26, 1998, when you stated "I never told anybody to lie, not a single time. Never"?

Response: This statement was truthful: I did not tell Ms. Lewinsky to lie, and I did not tell anybody to lie about my relationship with Ms. Lewinsky. I understand that Ms. Lewinsky also has stated that I never asked or encouraged her to lie.

81. Do you admit or deny that you directed or instructed Bruce Lindsey, Sidney Blumenthal, Nancy Hernreich and Lanny Breuer to invoke executive privilege before a grand jury impaneled as part of a judicial proceeding by the United States District Court for the District of Columbia Circuit in 1998?

Response: On the recommendation of Charles Ruff, counsel to the President, I authorized Mr. Ruff to assert the Presidential communications privilege (which is one aspect of executive privilege) with respect to questions that might be asked of witnesses called to testify before the grand jury to the extent that those questions sought disclosure of matters protected by that privilege. Thereafter, I understand that the Presidential communications privilege was asserted as to certain questions asked of Sidney Blumenthal and Nancy Hernreich. Further, I understand that, as to Mr. Blumenthal and Ms. Hernreich, all claims of official privilege were subsequently withdrawn and they testified fully on several occasions before the grand jury.

Mr. Lindsey and Mr. Breuer testified at length before the grand jury about a wide range of matters, but declined, on the advice of the White House counsel, to answer certain questions that sought disclosure of discussions that they had with me and my senior advisers concerning, among other things, their legal advice as to the assertion of executive privilege. White House counsel advised Mr. Lindsey and Mr. Breuer that these communications were protected by the attorney-client privilege, as well as executive privilege. Mr. Lindsey also asserted my personal attorney-client privilege as to certain questions relating to his role as an intermediary between me and my personal counsel in the *Jones v. Clinton* case, a privilege that was upheld by the Federal appeals court in the District of Columbia.

(SOURCE: *New York Times,* "Testing of a President; Clinton's Responses to Questions from the House Judiciary Committee," November 28, 1998: A12.)

ARTICLE I

In his conduct while President of the United States, William Jefferson Clinton, in violation of his constitutional oath faithfully to execute the office of President of the United States and, to the best of his ability, preserve, protect, and defend the Constitution of the United States, and in violation of his constitutional duty to take care that the laws be faithfully executed, has willfully corrupted and manipulated the judicial process of the United States for his personal gain and exoneration, impeding the administration of justice, in that:

On August 17, 1998, William Jefferson Clinton swore to tell the truth, the whole truth, and nothing but the truth before a Federal grand jury of the United States. Contrary to that oath, William Jefferson Clinton willfully provided perjurious, false and misleading testimony to the grand jury concerning one or more of the following: (1) the nature and details of his relationship with a subordinate Government employee; (2) prior perjurious, false and misleading testimony he gave in a Federal civil rights action brought against him; (3) prior false and misleading statements he allowed his attorney to make to a Federal judge in that civil rights action; and (4) his corrupt efforts to influence the testimony of witnesses and to impede the discovery of evidence in that civil rights action.

In doing this, William Jefferson Clinton has undermined the integrity of his office, has brought disrepute on the Presidency, has betrayed his trust as President, and has acted in a manner subversive of the rule of law and justice, to the manifest injury of the people of the United States.

Wherefore, William Jefferson Clinton, by such conduct, warrants impeachment and trial, and removal from office and disqualification to hold and enjoy any office of honor, trust or profit under the United States.

ARTICLE II

In his conduct while President of the United States, William Jefferson Clinton, in violation of his constitutional oath faithfully to execute the office of President of the United States and, to the best of his ability, preserve, protect, and defend the Constitution of the United States, and in violation of his constitutional duty to take care that the laws be faithfully executed, has willfully corrupted and manipulated the judicial process of the United States for his personal gain and exoneration, impeding the administration of justice, in that:

(1) On December 23, 1997, William Jefferson Clinton, in sworn answers to written questions asked as part of a Federal civil rights action brought against him, willfully provided perjurious, false and misleading testimony in response to questions deemed relevant by a Federal judge concerning conduct and proposed conduct with subordinate employees.

(2) On January 17, 1998, William Jefferson Clinton swore under oath to tell the truth, the whole truth, and nothing but the truth in a deposition given as part of a Federal civil rights action brought against him. Contrary to that oath, William Jefferson Clinton willfully provided perjurious, false and misleading testimony in response to questions deemed relevant by a Federal judge concerning the nature and details of his relationship with a subordinate Government employee, his knowledge of that employee's involvement and participation in the civil rights action brought against him, and his corrupt efforts to influence the testimony of that employee.

In all of this, William Jefferson Clinton has undermined the integrity of his office, has brought disrepute on the Presidency, has betrayed his trust as President, and has acted in a manner subversive of the rule of law and justice, to the manifest injury of the people of the United States.

Wherefore, William Jefferson Clinton, by such conduct, warrants impeachment and trial, and removal from office and disqualification to hold and enjoy any office of honor, trust or profit under the United States.

ARTICLE III [ARTICLE II IN THE SENATE]

In his conduct while President of the United States, William Jefferson Clinton, in violation of his constitutional oath faithfully to execute the office of President of the United States and, to the best of his ability, preserve, protect, and defend the Constitution of the United States, and in violation of his constitutional duty to take care that the laws be faithfully executed, has prevented, obstructed, and impeded the administration of justice, and has to that end engaged personally, and through his subordinates and agents, in a course of conduct or scheme designed to delay, impede, cover up, and conceal the existence of evidence and testimony related to a Federal civil rights action brought against him in a duly instituted judicial proceeding.

The means used to implement this course of conduct or scheme included one or more of the following acts:

(1) On or about December 17, 1997, William Jefferson Clinton corruptly encouraged a witness in a Federal civil rights action brought against him to execute a sworn affidavit in that proceeding that he knew to be perjurious, false and misleading.

(2) On or about December 17, 1997, William Jefferson Clinton corruptly encouraged a witness in a Federal civil rights action brought against him to give perjurious, false and misleading testimony if and when called to testify personally in that proceeding.

(3) On or about December 28, 1997, William Jefferson Clinton corruptly engaged in, encouraged, or supported a scheme to conceal evidence that had been subpoenaed in a Federal civil rights action brought against him.

(4) Beginning on or about December 7, 1997, and continuing through and including January 14, 1998, William Jefferson Clinton intensified and succeeded in an effort to secure job assistance to a witness in a Federal civil rights action brought against him in order to corruptly prevent the truthful testimony of that witness in that proceeding at a time when the truthful testimony of that witness would have been harmful to him.

(5) On January 17, 1998, at his deposition in a Federal civil rights action brought against him, William Jefferson Clinton corruptly allowed his attorney to make false and misleading statements to a Federal judge characterizing an affidavit, in order to prevent questioning deemed relevant by the judge. Such false and misleading statements were subsequently acknowledged by his attorney in a communication to that judge.

(6) On or about January 18 and January 20–21, 1998, William Jefferson Clinton related a false and misleading account of events relevant to a Federal civil rights action brought against him to a potential witness in that proceeding, in order to corruptly influence the testimony of that witness.

(7) On or about January 21, 23 and 26, 1998, William Jefferson Clinton made false and misleading statements to potential witnesses in a Federal grand jury proceeding in order to corruptly influence the testimony of those witnesses. The false and misleading statements made by William Jefferson Clinton were repeated by the witnesses to the grand jury, causing the grand jury to receive false and misleading information.

In all of this, William Jefferson Clinton has undermined the integrity of his office, has brought disrepute on the Presidency, has betrayed his trust as President, and has acted in a manner subversive of the rule of law and justice, to the manifest injury of the people of the United States.

Wherefore, William Jefferson Clinton, by such conduct, warrants impeachment and trial, and removal from office and disqualification to hold and enjoy any office of honor, trust or profit under the United States.

ARTICLE IV

Using the powers and influence of the office of President of the United States, William Jefferson Clinton, in violation of his constitutional oath faithfully to execute the office of President of the United States and, to the best of his ability, preserve, protect, and defend the

Constitution of the United States, and in disregard of his constitutional duty to take care that the laws be faithfully executed, has engaged in conduct that resulted in misuse and abuse of his high office, impaired the due and proper administration of justice and the conduct of lawful inquiries, and contravened the authority of the legislative branch and the truth-seeking purpose of a coordinate investigative proceeding in that, as President, William Jefferson Clinton refused and failed to respond to certain written requests for admission and willfully made perjurious, false and misleading sworn statements in response to certain written requests for admission propounded to him as part of the impeachment inquiry authorized by the House of Representatives of the Congress of the United States.

William Jefferson Clinton, in refusing and failing to respond, and in making perjurious, false and misleading statements, assumed to himself functions and judgments necessary to the exercise of the sole power of impeachment vested by the Constitution in the House of Representatives and exhibited contempt for the inquiry.

In doing this, William Jefferson Clinton has undermined the integrity of his office, has brought disrepute on the Presidency, has betrayed his trust as President, and has acted in a manner subversive of the rule of law and justice, to the manifest injury of the people of the United States.

Wherefore, William Jefferson Clinton, by such conduct, warrants impeachment and trial, and removal from office and disqualification to hold and enjoy any office of honor, trust or profit under the United States.

SENATE VOTE ON ARTICLE I: PERJURY. (YEA—GUILTY; NAY—NOT GUILTY)

Yea – 45	Nay – 55	Present – 0	NV – 0
45 R; 0 D	10 R; 45 D	0 R; 0 D	0 R; 0 D

Abraham, Spencer (R-Mich.)	Chafee, John H. (R-R.I.)
Allard, Wayne (R-Colo.)	Collins, Susan (R-Maine)
Ashcroft, John (R-Mo.)	Gorton, Slade (R-Wash.)
Bennett, Robert F. (R-Utah)	Jeffords, James M. (R-Vt.)
Bond, Christopher S. (R-Mo.)	Shelby, Richard C. (R-Ala.)
Brownback, Sam (R-Kan.)	Snowe, Olympia J. (R-Maine)
Bunning, Jim (R-Ky.)	Specter, Arlen (R-Pa.)
Burns, Conrad R. (R-Mont.)	Stevens, Ted (R-Alaska)
Campbell, Ben Nighthorse	Thompson, Fred (R-Tenn.)
(R-Colo.)	Warner, John W. (R-Va.)
Cochran, Thad (R-Miss.)	Akaka, Daniel K. (D-Hawaii)
Coverdell, Paul (R-Ga.)	Baucus, Max (D-Mont.)
Craig, Larry E. (R-Idaho)	Bayh, Evan (D-Ind.)
Crapo, Michael (R-Idaho)	Biden, Joseph R., Jr. (D-Del.)
DeWine, Mike (R-Ohio)	Bingaman, Jeff (D-N.M.)
Domenici, Pete V. (R-N.M.)	Boxer, Barbara (D-Calif.)
Enzi, Mike (R-Wyo.)	Breaux, John B. (D-La.)
Fitzgerald, Peter (R-Ill.)	Bryan, Richard H. (D-Nev.)
Frist, William H. (R-Tenn.)	Byrd, Robert C. (D-W.Va.)

SENATE VOTE ON ARTICLE I, *continued*

Yea – 45	Nay – 55	Present – 0	NV – 0
45 R; 0 D	10 R; 45 D	0 R; 0 D	0 R; 0 D

Yea – 45	Nay – 55
Gramm, Phil (R-Tex.)	Cleland, Max (D-Ga.)
Grams, Rod (R-Minn.)	Conrad, Kent (D-N.D.)
Grassley, Charles (R-Iowa)	Daschle, Thomas A. (D-S.D.)
Gregg, Judd (R-N.H.)	Dodd, Christopher J. (D-Conn.)
Hagel, Chuck (R-Neb.)	Dorgan, Byron L. (D-N.D.)
Hatch, Orrin G. (R-Utah)	Durbin, Richard (D-Ill.)
Helms, Jesse (R-N.C.)	Edwards, John (D-N.C.)
Hutchison, Kay Bailey	Feingold, Russell D. (D-Wis.)
(R-Tex.)	Feinstein, Dianne (D-Calif.)
Hutchinson, Tim (R-Ark.)	Graham, Bob (D-Fla.)
Inhofe, James M. (R-Okla.)	Harkin, Tom (D-Iowa)
Kyl, Jon (R-Ariz.)	Hollings, Ernest F. (D-S.C.)
Lott, Trent (R-Miss.)	Inouye, Daniel K. (D-Hawaii)
Lugar, Richard G. (R-Ind.)	Johnson, Tim (D-S.D.)
Mack, Connie (R-Fla.)	Kennedy, Edward M. (D-Mass.)
McCain, John (R-Ariz.)	Kerrey, J. Robert (D-Neb.)
McConnell, Mitch (R-Ken.)	Kerry, John F. (D-Mass.)
Murkowski, Frank H.	Kohl, Herb (D-Wis.)
(R-Alaska)	Landrieu, Mary (D-La.)
Nickles, Don (R-Okla.)	Lautenberg, Frank R. (D-N.J.)
Roberts, Pat (R-Kan.)	Leahy, Patrick J. (D-Vt.)
Roth, William V., Jr. (R-Del.)	Levin, Carl (D-Mich.)
Santorum, Rick (R-Pa.)	Lieberman, Joseph I. (D-Conn.)
Sessions, Jeff (R-Ala.)	Lincoln, Blanche Lambert
Smith, Bob (R-N.H.)	(D-Ark.)
Smith, Gordon (R-Ore.)	Mikulski, Barbara A. (D-Md.)
Thomas, Craig (R-Wyo.)	Moynihan, Daniel Patrick
Thurmond, Strom (R-S.C.)	(D-N.Y.)
Voinovich, George (R-Ohio)	Murray, Patty (D-Wash.)
	Reed, Jack (D-R.I.)
	Reid, Harry (D-Nev.)
	Robb, Charles S. (D-Va.)
	Rockefeller, John D., IV
	(D-W.Va.)
	Sarbanes, Paul S. (D-Md.)
	Schumer, Charles (D-N.Y.)
	Torricelli, Robert (D-N.J.)
	Wellstone, Paul D. (D-Minn.)
	Wyden, Ron (D-Ore.)

SENATE VOTE ON ARTICLE II: OBSTRUCTION OF JUSTICE.
(YEA—GUILTY; NAY—NOT GUILTY)

Yea – 50	*Nay – 50*	*Present – 0*	*NV – 0*
50 R; 0 D	*5 R; 45 D*	*0 R; 0 D*	*0 R; 0 D*

Abraham, Spencer (R-Mich.)
Allard, Wayne (R-Colo.)
Ashcroft, John (R-Mo.)
Bennett, Robert F. (R-Utah)
Bond, Christopher S.
    (R-Mo.)
Brownback, Sam (R-Kan.)
Bunning, Jim (R-Ky.)
Burns, Conrad R. (R-Mont.)
Campbell, Ben Nighthorse
    (R-Colo.)
Cochran, Thad (R-Miss.)
Coverdell, Paul (R-Ga.)
Craig, Larry E. (R-Idaho)
Crapo, Michael (R-Idaho)
DeWine, Mike (R-Ohio)
Domenici, Pete V. (R-N.M.)
Enzi, Mike (R-Wyo.)
Fitzgerald, Peter (R-Ill.)
Frist, William H. (R-Tenn.)
Gorton, Slade (R-Wash.)
Gramm, Phil (R-Tex.)
Grams, Rod (R-Minn.)
Grassley, Charles (R-Iowa)
Gregg, Judd (R-N.H.)
Hagel, Chuck (R-Neb.)
Hatch, Orrin G. (R-Utah)
Helms, Jesse (R-N.C.)
Hutchison, Kay Bailey
    (R-Tex.)
Hutchinson, Tim (R-Ark.)
Inhofe, James M. (R-Okla.)
Kyl, Jon (R-Ariz.)
Lott, Trent (R-Miss.)
Lugar, Richard G. (R-Ind.)
Mack, Connie (R-Fla.)
McCain, John (R-Ariz.)
McConnell, Mitch (R-Ky.)
Murkowski, Frank H.
    (R-Alaska)

Chafee, John H. (R-R.I.)
Collins, Susan (R-Maine)
Jeffords, James M. (R-Vt.)
Snowe, Olympia J. (R-Maine)
Specter, Arlen (R-Pa.)
Akaka, Daniel K. (D-Hawaii)
Baucus, Max (D-Mont.)
Bayh, Evan (D-Ind.)
Biden, Joseph R., Jr. (D-Del.)
Bingaman, Jeff (D-N.M.)
Boxer, Barbara (D-Calif.)
Breaux, John B. (D-La.)
Bryan, Richard H. (D-Nev.)
Byrd, Robert C. (D-W.Va.)
Cleland, Max (D-Ga.)
Conrad, Kent (D-N.D.)
Daschle, Thomas A. (D-S.D.)
Dodd, Christopher J. (D-Conn.)
Dorgan, Byron L. (D-N.D.)
Durbin, Richard (D-Ill.)
Edwards, John (D-N.C.)
Feingold, Russell D. (D-Wis.)
Feinstein, Dianne (D-Calif.)
Graham, Bob (D-Fla.)
Harkin, Tom (D-Iowa)
Hollings, Ernest F. (D-S.C.)
Inouye, Daniel K. (D-Hawaii)
Johnson, Tim (D-S.D.)
Kennedy, Edward M. (D-Mass.)
Kerrey, J. Robert (D-Neb.)
Kerry, John F. (D-Mass.)
Kohl, Herb (D-Wis.)
Landrieu, Mary (D-La.)
Lautenberg, Frank R. (D-N.J.)
Leahy, Patrick J. (D-Vt.)
Levin, Carl (D-Mich.)
Lieberman, Joseph I. (D-Conn.)
Lincoln, Blanche Lambert
    (D-Ark.)
Mikulski, Barbara A. (D-Md.)

SENATE VOTE ON ARTICLE II, *continued*

Yea – 50	*Nay – 50*	*Present – 0*	*NV – 0*
50 R; 0 D	*5 R; 45 D*	*0 R; 0 D*	*0 R; 0 D*

Nickles, Don (R-Okla.)	Moynihan, Daniel Patrick
Roberts, Pat (R-Kan.)	(D-N.Y.)
Roth, William V., Jr. (R-Del.)	Murray, Patty (D-Wash.)
Santorum, Rick (R-Pa.)	Reed, Jack (D-R.I.)
Sessions, Jeff (R-Ala.)	Reid, Harry (D-Nev.)
Shelby, Richard C. (R-Ala.)	Robb, Charles S. (D-Va.)
Smith, Bob (R-N.H.)	Rockefeller, John D., IV
Smith, Gordon (R-Ore.)	(D-W.Va.)
Stevens, Ted (R-Alaska)	Sarbanes, Paul S. (D-Md.)
Thomas, Craig (R-Wyo.)	Schumer, Charles (D-N.Y.)
Thompson, Fred (R-Tenn.)	Torricelli, Robert (D-N.J.)
Thurmond, Strom (R-S.C.)	Wellstone, Paul D. (D-Minn.)
Voinovich, George (R-Ohio)	Wyden, Ron (D-Ore.)
Warner, John W. (R-Va.)	

QUANTIFYING THE IMPEACHMENT PROCEEDINGS

Days since the Monica Lewinsky story broke and Senate acquittal	387
Witnesses who testified before the Starr grand jury	67
Pages in Starr report to the House of Representatives	453
Questions House Judiciary Committee submitted to President Clinton	81
Days full House spent on impeachment	2
House Democrats who voted for article of impeachment alleging perjury	5
House Republicans who opposed perjury article	5
House Democrats who voted for obstruction of justice article	5
House Republicans who opposed obstruction of justice article	12
House Republican Judiciary members who were prosecutors in the Senate trial	13
Days Senate spent on impeachment trial	21
Approximate hours Senate spent in final deliberations	20
Senate votes that were needed to convict the president	67

(SOURCE: Adapted from "Quantifying the Impeachment Proceedings," *Washington Post*, February 13, 1999, A32.)

Notes

1. A RANCOROUS PARTISAN ATMOSPHERE

1. See, for example, Peter Baker, *The Breach: Inside the Impeachment and Trial of William Jefferson Clinton* (New York: Scribner's, 2000); Jeffrey Toobin, *A Vast Conspiracy: The Real Story of the Sex Scandal That Nearly Brought Down a President* (New York: Random House, 2000); and Richard A. Posner, *An Affair of State: The Investigation, Impeachment, and Trial of President Clinton* (Cambridge, Mass.: Harvard University Press, 1999).

2. Steven E. Schier, *By Invitation Only: The Rise of Exclusive Politics in the United States* (Pittsburgh, Pa.: University of Pittsburgh Press, 2000).

3. Irwin L. Morris, *Votes, Money, and the Clinton Impeachment* (Boulder, Colo.: Westview Press, 2002).

4. Chris Lawrence, "Impeaching the President: Representatives' Behavior on a Highly Salient Issue," paper presented at the Annual Meeting of the American Political Science Association, Washington, D.C., August 31–September 3, 2000.

5. Morris P. Fiorina, "Legislator Uncertainty, Legislative Control, and the Delegation of Legislative Authority," in *Regulatory Policy and the Social Sciences*, ed. Roger G. Noll (Berkeley: University of California Press, 1986, 175–199); and David R. Mayhew, *Congress: The Electoral Connection* (New Haven, Conn.: Yale University Press, 1974).

6. R. Douglas Arnold, *The Logic of Congressional Action* (New Haven, Conn.: Yale University Press, 1990).

7. David J. Lanoue and Craig F. Emmert, "Voting in the Glare of the Spotlight: Representatives' Votes on the Impeachment of President Clinton," *Polity* 32 (1999): 253–269.

8. Richard Hall, *Participation in Congress* (New Haven, Conn.: Yale University Press, 1996), 66.

9. Thomas P. O'Neill, *Man of the House* (New York: St. Martin's, 1987).

10. Florida International University, Miami, Florida, March 2000.

11. The concept of *ideology* or a *belief system* as a theoretical construct is meant to *link beliefs,* whether beliefs about facts or values, and *attitudes,* defined as predispositions to act in certain ways toward certain sets of objects or events, with *behavior.* It is a pattern of intercorrelated positions across a set of issues. See Jerrold E. Schneider, *Ideological Coalitions in Congress* (Westport, Conn.: Greenwood Press, 1979); and Phillip E. Converse, "The Nature of Belief Systems in Mass Politics," in *Ideology and Discontent,* ed. David E. Apter (New York: Free Press, 1964).

12. Quoted in Janet Hook, "Divisiveness Rules as Debate Opens," *Los Angeles Times,* December 19, 1998, A1.

13. Ibid. Representative Meek was not a member of the Judiciary Committee, but her comments do reflect the sentiments of a majority of committee Democrats.

14. Ralph K. Huitt, "The Congressional Committee: A Case Study," *American Political Science Review* 48 (1954): 340.

15. Roger H. Davidson, "Building the Republican Regime: Leadership and Committees," in *New Majority or Old Minority? The Impact of Republicans on Congress,* ed. Nicol C. Rae and Colton C. Campbell (Lanham, Md.: Rowman & Littlefield, 1999), 69–90; and Robin Kolodny, "Moderate Success: Majority Status and the Changing Nature of Factionalism in the House Republican Party," in *New Majority or Old Minority?,* ed. Rae and Campbell, 153–172.

16. Donald R. Wolfensberger, *Congress and the People: Deliberative Democracy on Trial* (Washington, D.C.: Woodrow Wilson Center Press; Baltimore, Md.: Johns Hopkins University Press, 2000).

17. Roger H. Davidson, "Congressional Parties, Leaders, and Committees: 1900, 2000, and Beyond," in *American Political Parties: Decline or Resurgence?,* ed. Jeffrey E. Cohen, Richard Fleisher, and Paul Kantor (Washington, D.C.: CQ Press, 2001), 187–208.

18. Ibid., 203.

19. Peter Carlson, "130 Years Ago, Parallels Up to a Boiling Point," *Washington Post,* December 13, 1998, A1.

20. Ibid.

21. Leon D. Epstein, *Political Parties in Western Democracies* (New York: Praeger, 1967); and Maurice Duverger, *Political Parties: Their Organization and Activity in the Modern State,* 3d ed. (London: Methuen, 1964).

22. See, for example, Louis Hartz, *The Liberal Tradition in America: An Interpretation of American Political Thought since the Revolution* (New York: Harcourt, Brace, 1955); and Richard Hofstadter, *The American Political Tradition and the Men Who Made It* (New York: Knopf, 1948).

23. See, for example, Moisei I. Ostrogorski, *Democracy and the Party System in the United States* (New York: Arno Press, 1974); Joel H. Silbey, *The American Political Nation, 1838–1893* (Palo Alto, Calif.: Stanford University Press, 1991); and Joel H. Silbey, *The Shrine of Party: Congressional Voting Behavior, 1841–1852* (Pittsburgh, Pa.: University of Pittsburgh Press, 1967).

24. Richard A. Hofstadter, *The Age of Reform: From Bryan to FDR* (New York: Knopf, 1955).

25. Walter Dean Burnham, "The Changing Shape of the American Political Universe," *American Political Science Review* 59 (1965): 7–28; and Walter Dean Burnham, *The Current Crisis in American Politics* (New York: Oxford University Press, 1982).

26. James L. Sundquist, *The Decline and Resurgence of Congress* (Washington, D.C.: Brookings Institution, 1981).

27. Mayhew, *Congress: The Electoral Connection;* Gary C. Jacobson, *The Politics of Congressional Elections,* 5th ed. (New York: Longman, 2001); and Paul S. Herrnson, *Congressional Elections: Campaigning at Home and in Washington,* 2d ed. (Washington, D.C.: CQ Press, 1998).

28. James T. Patterson, *Congressional Conservatism and the New Deal: The Growth of the Conservative Coalition in Congress* (Lexington: University of Kentucky Press, 1967).

29. Duverger, *Political Parties.*

30. Ibid.

31. Epstein, *Political Parties in Western Democracies.*

32. Burnham, *The Current Crisis in American Politics.*

33. American Political Science Association, Committee on Political Parties, "Toward a More Responsible Two-Party System," *American Political Science Review* 44 (Supplement, 1950).

34. Walter Dean Burnham, *Critical Elections and the Mainsprings of American Politics* (New York: Norton, 1970), and *The Current Crisis in American Politics;* Everett Carll Ladd, Jr., with Charles C. Hadley, *Transformations of the American Party System: Political Coalitions from the New Deal to the 1970s,* 2d ed. (New York: Norton, 1978).

35. Burnham, *The Current Crisis in American Politics.*

36. James Q. Wilson, *The Amateur Democrat: Club Politics in Three Cities* (Chicago, Ill.: University of Chicago Press, 1962); and Aaron B. Wildavsky, *The Revolt against the Masses and Other Essays in Politics and Public Policy* (New York: Basic Books, 1971).

37. Sundquist, *The Decline and Resurgence of Congress.*

38. David R. Mayhew, "Congressional Elections: The Case of the Vanishing Marginals," *Polity* 6 (1974): 295–315.

39. Mayhew, *Congress: The Electoral Connection.*

40. Richard F. Fenno, Jr., *Home Style: House Members in Their Districts* (Boston, Mass.: Little, Brown, 1978).

41. Samuel C. Patterson, "The Semi-Sovereign Congress," in *The New American Political System,* ed. Anthony King (Washington, D.C.: American Enterprise Institute, 1979), 125–177.

42. David W. Rohde, *Parties and Leaders in the Postreform House* (Chicago, Ill.: University of Chicago Press, 1991).

43. Wilson, *The Amateur Democrat;* Wildavsky, *The Revolt against the Masses;* and Jeane J. Kirkpatrick, *The New Presidential Elite: Men and Women in National Politics* (New York: Sage Foundation, 1976).

44. Schier, *By Invitation Only;* Gary C. Jacobson, "Party Polarization in National Politics: The Electoral Connection," in *Polarized Politics: Congress and the President in a Partisan Era,* ed. Jon R. Bond and Richard Fleisher (Washington, D.C.: CQ Press, 2000), 9–30; and John H. Aldrich and David W. Rohde, "The Logic of Conditional Party Government: Revisiting the Electoral Connection," in *Congress Reconsidered,* 7th ed., ed. Lawrence C. Dodd and Bruce I. Oppenheimer (Washington, D.C.: CQ Press, 2001), 269–292.

45. Jacobson, *The Politics of Congressional Elections,* and Herrnson, *Congressional Elections.*

46. Herrnson, *Congressional Elections,* and Victoria A. Farrar-Myers and Diana Dwyre, "Parties and Campaign Finance," in *American Political Parties: Decline or Resurgence?,* ed. Jeffrey E. Cohen, Richard Fleisher, and Paul Kantor (Washington, D.C.: CQ Press, 2001), 138–161.

47. Kevin A. Hill and John E. Hughes, *Cyberpolitics: Citizen Activism in the Age of the Internet* (Lanham, Md.: Rowman & Littlefield, 1998).

48. Kevin A. Hill, "Does the Creation of Majority Black Districts Aid Republicans? An Analysis of the 1992 Congressional Elections in Eight Southern States," *Journal of Politics* 57 (1995): 384–401; and Kevin A. Hill and Nicol C. Rae, "What Happened to the Democrats in the South? U.S. House Elections, 1992–1996," *Party Politics* 6 (2000), 5–22.

49. Barry C. Burden, "The Polarizing Effect of Congressional Primaries," in *Congressional Primaries and the Politics of Representation*, ed. Peter F. Galderisi, Marni Ezra, and Michael Lyons (Lanham, Md.: Rowman & Littlefield, 2001), 95–115.

50. From 1910 to 1970, for example, the House Rules Committee operated independently, often tabling legislation at the whims of its chairman or a cross-party conservative majority. Since the Speaker was given the authority to name its Democratic members in 1975, the Rules Committee has reverted to being an arm of the party leadership, drafting rules for floor debate per the leadership's requirements.

51. Barbara Sinclair, *Legislators, Leaders, and Lawmaking: The U.S. House of Representatives in the Postreform Era* (Baltimore, Md.: Johns Hopkins University Press, 1995).

52. Ibid., and John H. Aldrich and David W. Rohde, "The Consequences of Party Organization in the House: The Role of the Majority and Minority Parties in Conditional Party Government," in *Polarized Politics: Congress and the President in a Partisan Era*, ed. Jon R. Bond and Richard Fleisher (Washington, D.C.: CQ Press, 2000), 31–72.

53. William F. Connelly, Jr., and John J. Pitney, Jr., *Congress' Permanent Minority? Republicans in the U.S. House* (Lanham, Md.: Rowman & Littlefield, 1994).

54. John M. Barry, *The Ambition and the Power* (New York: Viking, 1989).

55. Nicol C. Rae and Colton C. Campbell, "Party Politics and Ideology in the Contemporary Senate," in *The Contentious Senate: Partisanship, Ideology, and the Myth of Cool Judgment*, ed. Colton C. Campbell and Nicol C. Rae (Lanham, Md.: Rowman & Littlefield, 2001), 1–18.

56. C. Lawrence Evans and Walter J. Oleszek, *Congress under Fire: Reform Politics and the Republican Majority* (New York: Houghton-Mifflin, 1997).

57. Nicol C. Rae, *Conservative Reformers: The Republican Freshmen and the Lessons of the 104th Congress* (Armonk, N.Y.: M. E. Sharpe, 1998).

58. Aldrich and Rohde, in *Polarized Politics*, ed. Bond and Fleisher; and Richard F. Fenno, Jr., *Learning to Govern: An Institutional View of the 104th Congress* (Washington, D.C.: Brookings Institution, 1997).

59. Roger H. Davidson, "The 2000 Elections: A New Gilded Age?" in *Congressional Parity: Where Do We Go from Here? Extensions of Remarks*, ed. Burdett A. Loomis (Lawrence: University Press of Kansas, 2001).

60. John J. Pitney, Jr., "War on the Floor," in *Congressional Parity*, ed. Loomis.

61. Norman J. Ornstein, Thomas E. Mann, and Michael J. Malbin, *Vital Statistics on Congress, 1999–2000* (Washington, D.C.: American Enterprise Institute, 2000), 194.

62. Eric Uslaner, *The Decline of Comity in Congress* (Ann Arbor: University of Michigan Press, 1993).

63. Hook, "Divisiveness Rules As Debate Opens."

64. Roger H. Davidson and Walter J. Oleszek, *Congress and Its Members*, 7th ed. (Washington, D.C.: CQ Press, 2000); and Gary W. Cox and Mathew D. McCubbins, *Legislative Leviathan: Party Government in the House* (Berkeley: University of California Press, 1993).

65. Davidson and Oleszek, *Congress and Its Members*, 267.

66. Shortly before losing control of the Senate, Republican leaders of the 107th Congress (2001–2003) dismissed the chamber's parliamentarian because of their frustration over his rulings on tax and budget matters. See Colton C. Campbell and Paul S. Herrnson, "Lessons from the Battlefield," in *War Stories from Capitol Hill*, ed. Colton C. Campbell and Paul S. Herrnson (Upper Saddle River, N.J.: Prentice Hall, 2004).

67. Pitney, "War on the Floor."

68. Robin Kolodny, *Pursuing Majorities: Congressional Campaign Committees in American Politics* (Norman: University of Oklahoma Press, 1998); and Norman J. Ornstein and Thomas E. Mann, eds., *The Permanent Campaign and Its Future* (Washington, D.C.: AEI Press, 2000).

69. William S. Cohen, "Farewell Address," in *Lessons and Legacies: Farewell Addresses from the Senate,* ed. Norman J. Ornstein (New York: Addison-Wesley, 1997), 46.

70. James Davison Hunter, *Culture Wars: The Struggle to Define America* (New York: Basic Books, 1991).

71. Geoffrey Layman, *The Great Divide: Religious and Cultural Conflict in American Party Politics* (New York: Columbia University Press, 2001); and Alan Wolfe, *One Nation, After All: What Middle-Class Americans Really Think About: God, Country, Family, Racism, Welfare, Immigration, Homosexuality, Work, the Right, the Left, and Each Other* (New York: Viking, 1998).

72. Charles O. Jones, *Clinton and Congress: 1993–1996: Risk, Restoration, and Reelection* (Norman: University of Oklahoma Press, 1999); and Barbara Sinclair, "Trying to Govern Positively in a Negative Era," in *The Clinton Presidency: First Appraisals,* ed. Colin Campbell and Bert A. Rockman (New York: Chatham House, 1996), 88–123.

73. James G. Gimpel, *Legislating the Revolution: The Contract with America in Its First Hundred Days* (Boston, Mass.: Allyn & Bacon, 1996).

74. Fenno, *Learning to Govern,* and Rae, *Conservative Reformers.*

75. Elizabeth Drew, *Showdown: The Struggle between the Gingrich Congress and the Clinton White House* (New York: Simon & Schuster, 1996); David Maraniss and Michael Weisskopf, *Tell Newt to Shut Up!* (New York: Touchstone, 1996); and Jones, *Clinton and Congress.*

76. James Stewart, *Blood Sport: The President and His Adversaries* (New York: Simon & Schuster, 1996).

77. All three participants denied that they had discussed dumping Fiske at the lunch. According to Senator Helms they talked of "Western wear, old friends, and prostate problems." Congressional Democrats remained unconvinced. Ibid., 424. See also Posner, *An Affair of State,* 65–66; and Toobin, *A Vast Conspiracy,* 72–73.

78. Susan Schmidt and Michael Weisskopf, *Truth at Any Cost: Ken Starr and the Unmaking of Bill Clinton* (New York: HarperCollins, 2000).

79. Stewart, *Blood Sport.*

80. Barbara Sinclair, "The President as Legislative Leader," in *The Clinton Legacy,* ed. Colin Campbell and Bert A. Rockman (New York: Chatham House, 2000), 70–95.

81. James L. Guth, "Clinton, Impeachment, and the Culture Wars," in *The Postmodern Presidency: Bill Clinton's Legacy in U.S. Politics,* ed. Steven E. Schier (Pittsburgh, Pa.: University of Pittsburgh Press, 2000), 203–222.

2. CONGRESSIONAL GUILLOTINE

1. Article I, sections 2 and 3; Article II, section 4.

2. Dan Carney, "Hyde Staying above Clinton Fray but Tries to Raise Panel Profile," *Congressional Quarterly Weekly Report,* March 7, 1998, 563–568.

3. Alexander Hamilton, James Madison, and John Jay, *The Federalist* (New York: Bantom Books, 1982), 331.

4. John R. Labovitz, *Presidential Impeachment* (New Haven, Conn.: Yale University Press, 1978).

5. Hamilton, Madison, and Jay, *The Federalist,* 346.

6. Ibid.

7. United States Senate Historical Office, www.senate.gov.

8. Ibid.

9. Ibid.

10. Ibid.

11. Mary L. Volcansek, *Judicial Impeachment: None Called for Justice* (Urbana, Ill.: University of Illinois Press, 1993).

12. U.S. Congress, House of Representatives, Committee on Administration, *History of the United States House of Representatives, 1789–1994,* 103d Cong., 2d sess. (Washington, D.C.: Government Printing Office, 1994); Peter C. Hoffer and N. E. H. Hull, *Impeachment in America, 1635–1805* (New Haven, Conn.: Yale University Press, 1984); and Charles L. Black, Jr., *Impeachment: A Handbook* (New Haven, Conn.: Yale University Press, 1974).

13. Committee on Administration, *History of the United States House of Representatives, 1789–1994,* 340.

14. Michael J. Remington, "Impeachment," in *The Encyclopedia of the United States Congress,* vol. 2., ed. Donald C. Bacon, Roger H. Davidson, and Morton Keller (New York: Simon & Schuster, 1995).

15. Quoted in Max Farrand, Records of the Federal Convention (New Haven, Conn.: Yale University Press, 1966), 550.

16. Hamilton, Madison, and Jay, *The Federalist,* No. 65.

17. Quoted in David Y. Thomas, "The Law of Impeachment in the United States," *American Political Science Review* 2 (1908): 383.

18. Steven W. Stathis and David C. Huckabee, *Congressional Resolutions on Presidential Impeachment: A Historical Overview,* CRS Report, No. 98-763 GOV (Washington, D.C.: Congressional Research Service, 1998).

19. Ibid.

20. David C. Huckabee, Paul S. Rundquist, and Thomas H. Neale, *Impeachment: Frequently Asked Questions,* CRS Report, No. 98-919 GOV (Washington, D.C.: Congressional Research Service, 1998).

21. See U.S. House Rules, sections 601–602.

22. Roger H. Davidson and Walter J. Oleszek, *Congress and Its Members,* 8th ed. (Washington, D.C.: CQ Press, 2002), 339–340.

23. Labovitz, *Presidential Impeachment,* 180. President Richard Nixon discharged Special Prosecutor Archibald Cox and accepted the resignations of Attorney General Elliot L. Richardson and Deputy Attorney General William D. Ruckelshaus to avoid any formal investigation into the Watergate scandal by the Justice Department. The president also abolished the office of the special prosecutor and turned over to the Justice Department the entire responsibility for further investigation and prosecution of suspects and defendants in Watergate and related cases.

24. Ibid.

25. See U.S. House Rules, sections 601–602.

26. Huckabee, Rundquist, and Neale, *Impeachment: Frequently Asked Questions.*

27. Ibid.

28. David C. King, *Turf Wars: How Congressional Committees Claim Jurisdiction* (Chicago, Ill.: University of Chicago Press, 1997).

29. See U.S. House Rules, Rule XXII, cl. 4, annot. section 854; and Labovitz, *Presidential Impeachment.*

30. Labovitz, *Presidential Impeachment,* 184.

31. Ibid.

32. Ibid.

33. Ibid.

34. Lewis Deschler, *Deschler's Precedents of the United States House of Representatives,* 94th Cong., 2d sess., H. Doc. 661 (Washington, D.C.: Government Printing Office, 1977). See chapter 14, section 7.1.

35. Congressional Quarterly, Inc., *Guide to Congress,* 4th ed. (Washington, D.C.: Congressional Quarterly, Inc., 1991), 29.

36. Ibid.

37. Ibid.

38. Asher C. Hinds, ed., *Hind's Precedents of the House of Representatives,* 5 vols. (Washington, D.C.: Government Printing Office, 1907).

39. Clarence Cannon, *Cannon's Precedents of the United States House of Representatives* (Washington, D.C.: Government Printing Office, 1936). See chapter 6, section 501.

40. Kevin Merida, "The Senate Vigil of a House Democrat," *Washington Post,* January 22, 1999, C1.

41. Ibid.

42. Quoted in ibid.

43. Richard A. Baker, *The Senate of the United States: A Bicentennial History* (Malabar, Fla.: Robert E. Krieger Publishing, 1988).

44. Ibid.

45. Hamilton, Madison, and Jay, *The Federalist,* No. 65.

46. R. A. Baker, *The Senate of the United States: A Bicentennial History.*

47. Ibid.

48. Richard A. Baker, "Senate Adopts First Impeachment Rules," in *Series of Historical Minutes,* United States Senate Historical Office (Washington, D.C.: http://www.senate.gov/learning/min).

49. Ibid.

50. Ibid.

51. Roger H. Davidson and Colton C. Campbell, "The Senate and the Executive," in *Esteemed Colleagues: Civility and Deliberation in the U.S. Senate,* ed. Burdett A. Loomis (Washington, D.C.: Brookings Institution, 2000), 194–219.

52. Ibid.

53. *Nixon v. United States,* 506 U.S. 224, 1993.

54. *Nixon v. United States,* 506 U.S. 224, 1993, 236.

55. *Nixon v. United States,* 506 U.S. 224, 1993 citing, 938 F.2d 239 [D.C. Cir. 1991], 246.

56. Thomas B. Ripey, *Standard of Proof in Senate Impeachment Proceedings,* CRS Report, No. 98-990 A (Washington, D.C.: Congressional Research Service, 1998).

57. Ibid.

58. Elizabeth A. Bazan, *Impeachment: An Overview of Constitutional Provisions, Procedure, and Practice,* CRS Report, No. 98-186 A (Washington, D.C.: Congressional Research Service, 1998).

59. Ibid.

60. In a contemporary example, former federal judge Alcee Hastings was impeached on grounds of bribery, and subsequently tried, convicted, and removed from office by the Senate. Not having been specifically barred from holding future public or federal office, Judge Hastings has served as a member of the U.S. House from Florida since 1993.

61. Bazan, *Impeachment: An Overview of Constitutional Provisions, Procedure, and Practice;* Richard S. Beth, *Censure of Executive and Judicial Branch Officials: Past Congressional Proceedings,* CRS Report, No. 98-983 GOV (Washington, D.C.: Congressional Research Service, 1998); Charles Doyle, *Impeachment Grounds: Part 4A: Articles of Past Impeachments,* CRS Report, No. 98-896 (Washington, D.C.: Congressional Research Service, 1998); and Charles Doyle, *Impeachment Grounds: Part 4B: Articles of Past Impeachments,* CRS Report, No. 98-896 (Washington, D.C.: Congressional Research Service, 1998).

62. Ibid.

63. Richard A. Baker, "To Arrest an Impeached Senator," in *Series of Historical Minutes,* United States Senate Historical Office (Washington, D.C.: http://www.senate.gov/learning/min).

64. Bazan, *Impeachment: An Overview of Constitutional Provisions, Procedure, and Practice.*

65. Ibid.

66. William H. Masterson, *William Blount* (Westport, Conn.: Greenwood Press, 1969 [1954]).

67. Committee on Administration, *History of the United States House of Representatives, 1789–1994,* 342.

68. Eleanore Bushnell, *Crimes, Follies, and Misfortunes: The Federal Impeachment Trials* (Urbana: University of Illinois Press, 1992).

69. Congressional Quarterly, Inc., *Guide to Congress.*

70. Ibid.

71. Anne M. Butler and Wendy Wolff, *United States Senate: Election, Expulsion, and Censure Cases, 1793–1990* (Washington, D.C.: Government Printing Office, 1995).

72. Emily Van Tassel and Paul Finkelman, *Impeachable Offenses: A Documentary History from 1787 to the Present* (Washington, D.C.: Congressional Quarterly, Inc., 1999), 91.

73. Elaine L. Swift, *The Making of an American Senate: Reconstitutive Change in Congress, 1787–1841* (Ann Arbor, Mich.: University of Michigan Press, 1996).

74. Van Tassel and Finkelman, *Impeachable Offenses: A Documentary History,* 91.

75. Ibid.

76. Hoffer and Hull, *Impeachment in America, 1635–1805,* 208.

77. Ibid.

78. Richard E. Ellis, "Impeachment," in *The Oxford Companion to the Supreme Court of the United States,* ed. Kermit L. Hall (New York: Oxford University Press, 1992).

79. Ibid.

80. Ibid.

81. Ibid.

82. Committee on Administration, *History of the United States House of Representatives, 1789–1994,* 346.

83. Michael Les Benedict, "A New Look at the Impeachment of Andrew Johnson," *Political Science Quarterly* 88 (1973): 349–367.

84. James L. Sundquist, *The Decline and Resurgence of Congress* (Washington, D.C.: Brookings Institution, 1981).

85. Michael Les Benedict, *The Impeachment Trial of Andrew Johnson* (New York: W.W. Norton, 1973).

86. James T. Currie, *The United States House of Representatives* (Malabar, Fla.: Robert E. Krieger Publishing Company, 1988).

87. *Congressional Digest,* "Impeachment of the President" (Washington, D.C.: Congressional Quarterly, Inc., 1999).

88. Donald A. Ritchie, *Press Gallery: Congress and the Washington Correspondents* (Cambridge, Mass.: Harvard University Press, 1991).

89. United States Senate Historical Office, www.senate.gov.

90. Ibid.

91. Ibid.

92. Ibid.

93. Ibid.

94. Ibid.

95. Bushnell, *Crimes, Follies, and Misfortunes: The Federal Impeachment Trials.*

96. United States Senate Historical Office, www.senate.gov.

97. Ibid.

98. Ibid.

99. Ibid.

100. Bushnell, *Crimes, Follies, and Misfortunes: The Federal Impeachment Trials.*

101. Quoted in Van Tassel and Finkelman, *Impeachable Offenses,* 168.

102. Ibid.

103. Ibid.

104. The latter measure includes Senate consideration of impeachments before senators were sworn in as well as actual days when the cases were tried.

105. Other impeachment resolutions, inquiries, or investigations which, for various reasons, did not result in articles of impeachment being voted by the House included those related to the conduct of the following judges: Lebbeus R. Wilfley, Judge of United States Court for China (1908); Cornelius H. Hanford, U.S. Circuit Judge for the Western District of Washington (1912); Emory Speer, U.S. District Judge for the Southern District of Georgia (1913); Daniel Thew Wright, Associate Justice of the Supreme Court of the District of Columbia (1914); Alston G. Dayton, U.S. District Judge for the Northern District of West Virginia (1915); Kenesaw Mountain Landis, U.S. District Judge for the Northern District of Illinois (1921); William E. Baker, U.S. District Judge for the Northern District of West Virginia (1925); Frank Cooper, U.S. District Judge for the Northern District of New York (1927); Francis A. Winslow, U.S. District Judge for the Southern District of New York (1929); Harry B. Anderson, U.S. District Judge for the Western District of Tennessee (1930); Grover M. Moscowitz, U.S. District Judge for the Eastern District of New York (1930); Harry B. Anderson, U.S. District Judge for the Western District of Tennessee (1931); James Lowell, U.S. District Judge for the District of Massachusetts (1933–1934); Joseph Molyneaux, U.S. District Judge for the District of Minnesota (1934); Samuel Alschuler, U.S. Circuit Judge for the Seventh Circuit (1935); Albert Johnson, U.S. District Judge for the Middle District

of Pennsylvania; Albert Watson, U.S. District Judge for the Middle District of Pennsylvania (1944); Alfred Murrah, Chief Judge of the Court of Appeals for the Tenth Circuit; Stephen Chandler, U.S. District Judge for the Western District of Oklahoma; Luther Bohanon, U.S. District Judge for the Eastern, Northern, and Western Districts of Oklahoma (1936) (resolution referred to the House Committee on Rules, but not acted upon); and William O. Douglas, Associate Justice of the U.S. Supreme Court (1970).

Among the inquiries into conduct of executive branch officers that did not lead to Senate trials were those regarding H. Snowden Marshall, U.S. District Attorney for the Southern District of New York (1916–1917); Attorney General Harry M. Daugherty (1922–1924); Clarence C. Chase, Collector of Customs at the Port of El Paso, Texas (1924); Andrew W. Mellon, as Secretary of the Treasury (1932) (discontinued before completion of the investigation upon his nomination and confirmation as Ambassador to Court of St. James); President Herbert Hoover (1933) (motion to impeach laid on the table); Frances Perkins, Secretary of Labor; James L. Houghteling, Commissioner of the Immigration and Naturalization Service of the Department of Labor; Gerard K. Reilly, Solicitor of the Department of Labor (1939); President Harry S Truman (1952) (Truman left office before articles of impeachment were voted upon by the House); President Richard M. Nixon (1973–1974) (House adopted a resolution accepting the report of the Judiciary Committee recommending impeachment and including articles of impeachment submitted to House, but no further action was taken); and Andrew Young, U.S. Ambassador to the United Nations (1978) (measure considered in the House; motion to table was passed by House).

106. Bazan, *Impeachment: An Overview of Constitutional Provisions, Procedure, and Practice.*

107. Beth, *Censure of Executive and Judicial Branch Officials: Past Congressional Proceedings.*

108. Stephen Gettinger, "An Alternative to Impeachment," *Congressional Quarterly Weekly Report,* March 7, 1998, 566. See also Jack Maskell, *Censure of the President by the Congress,* CRS Report, No. 98-843 A (Washington, D.C.: Congressional Research Service, 1998). According to Maskell, the authority of Congress to censure is rooted in the constitutional provision permitting it to "punish its members for disorderly behavior." Many House censures have been applied for discourteous comments on the floor, assaults on other members, or "insults to the House by introducing offensive resolutions." Others have dealt with some form of corrupt act, such as taking kickbacks from staff and sexual misconduct. The House has a range of disciplinary actions it may take, from removal of one's committee or subcommittee chairmanships or seats for the remainder of that Congress. In many cases the House stops its censure proceedings when members apologize for those actions that prompted censure against them. Senators have been censured for disloyalty during the Civil War, fracas on the floor, rude or offensive remarks to colleagues, and financial infractions.

109. Beth, *Censure of Executive and Judicial Branch Officials: Past Congressional Proceedings.*

110. Maskell, *Censure of the President by the Congress,* 3.

111. Ibid.

112. Ibid.

113. Ibid.

114. Labovitz, *Presidential Impeachment,* ix.

115. Davidson and Oleszek, *Congress and Its Members,* 21–22.

116. Ibid.

117. Michael J. Gerhardt, *The Federal Impeachment Process: A Constitutional and Historical Analysis,* 2d ed. (Chicago, Ill.: University of Chicago Press, 2000).

118. Ibid.

119. Davidson and Oleszek, *Congress and Its Members,* 21–22.

120. Ibid.

121. Ibid.

122. United States Senate Historical Office, www.senate.gov.

123. Quoted in Warren S. Grimes, "Hundred-Ton Gun Control: Preserving Impeachment As the Exclusive Removal Mechanism for Federal Judges," *UCLA Law Review* 38 (1991): 1209.

124. Ibid.

125. Van Tassel and Finkelman, *Impeachable Offenses: A Documentary History;* and Norman J. Ornstein, "Civility, Deliberation, and Impeachment," in *Esteemed Colleagues: Civility and Deliberation in the U.S. Senate,* ed. Burdett A. Loomis (Washington, D.C.: Brookings Institution, 2000), 223–240.

126. See Ross K. Baker, "Examining Senate Individualism versus Senate Folkways in the Aftermath of the Clinton Impeachment," in *U.S. Senate Exceptionalism,* ed. Bruce I. Oppenheimer (Columbus: Ohio State University Press, 2002), 305–321.

127. See Roger H. Davidson, "Congressional Parties, Leaders, and Committees: 1900, 2000, and Beyond," in *American Political Parties: Decline or Resurgence?,* ed. Jeffrey E. Cohen, Richard Fleisher, and Paul Kantor (Washington, D.C.: CQ Press, 2001), 187–208; Peter Baker, *The Breach: Inside the Impeachment and Trial of William Jefferson Clinton* (New York: Scribner's, 2000); and Posner, *An Affair of the State: The Investigation, Impeachment, and Trial of President Clinton.*

3. IGNORING ELECTORAL OUTCOMES: REPUBLICAN MEMBERS OF THE HOUSE JUDICIARY COMMITTEE

1. Barbara Sinclair, *Legislators, Leaders, and Lawmaking: The U.S. House of Representatives in the Postreform Era* (Baltimore, Md.: Johns Hopkins University Press, 1995); David R. Mayhew, *Congress: The Electoral Connection* (New Haven, Conn.: Yale University Press, 1974); and Richard F. Fenno, Jr., *Congressmen in Committees* (Boston, Mass.: Little, Brown, 1973).

2. Gary C. Jacobson, "Impeachment Politics in the 1998 Congressional Elections," *Political Science Quarterly* 114 (1999): 31–51.

3. Michael R. Kagay, "Presidential Address: Public Opinion during Presidential Scandal and Impeachment," *Public Opinion Quarterly* 63 (1999): 449–463.

4. In his pioneering 1978 study of House members' relationship with their districts, Richard Fenno, Jr., argues that House members have to respond to four concentric constituencies ("geographic," "reelection," "primary," and "personal") of differing size and intensity. "The strategies developed for getting and keeping electoral support involve the manipulation of these scopes and intensities" (p. 27). See Richard F. Fenno, Jr., *Home Style: House Members in Their Districts* (New York: HarperCollins, 1978), 1–30.

5. Christopher J. Deering and Steven S. Smith, *Committees in Congress,* 2d ed. (Washington, D.C.: CQ Press, 1990); and Fenno, *Congressmen in Committees.*

6. Interview with Representative Charles T. Canady, December 21, 1999.

7. Interview with Representative Howard Coble, March 7, 2000.

8. Michael Barone and Grant Ujifusa, *The Almanac of American Politics 2000* (Washington, D.C.: National Journal, 1999). ADA scores rate members on a zero (most conservative) to 100 (most liberal) scale based on a series of key votes during a congressional session.

9. Norman J. Ornstein, Thomas E. Mann, and Michael J. Malbin, *Vital Statistics on Congress: 1997–1998* (Washington, D.C.: American Enterprise Institute, 1998). The "Conservative Coalition" score rates members according to how often they vote with a majority of Republicans and a majority of southern Democrats on votes where the coalition appears.

10. Interview with Representative Henry J. Hyde, March 8, 2000.

11. Interview with Representative Howard Coble, March 7, 2000.

12. Interview with Representative Lindsey O. Graham, March 8, 2000.

13. Jeffrey Toobin, *A Vast Conspiracy: The Real Story of the Sex Scandal That Nearly Brought Down a President* (New York: Simon & Schuster, 2000), 279–282.

14. Interview with Representative Howard Coble, March 7, 2000.

15. Interview with Representative Charles T. Canady, December 21, 1999.

16. Interview with Representative Christopher B. Cannon, March 9, 2000.

17. Interview with Representative Asa Hutchinson, March 9, 2000.

18. Interview with Representative Lindsey O. Graham, March 8, 2000.

19. Interview with Representative Henry J. Hyde, March 8, 2000.

20. Interview with Representative Charles T. Canady, 21 December 1999.

21. Jacobson, "Impeachment Politics in the 1998 Congressional Elections."

22. David E. Price, *The Congressional Experience,* 2d ed. (Boulder, Colo.: Westview Press, 2000), 181–185.

23. The Judiciary Committee recommended that President Richard M. Nixon be impeached for obstruction of justice, abuse of power, and contempt of Congress in relation to his role in spearheading and then covering up a burglary at Democratic National Headquarters in the Watergate hotel-apartment complex in Washington, D.C.

24. Interview with Representative Henry J. Hyde, March 8, 2000.

25. Interview with Representative Charles T. Canady, December 21, 1999.

26. Interview with Representative Asa Hutchinson, March 9, 2000.

27. Interview with Representative Charles T. Canady, December 21, 1999.

28. Interview with Representative Lindsey O. Graham, March 8, 2000.

29. Interview with Representative Charles T. Canady, December 21, 1999.

30. Interview with Representative Howard Coble, March 7, 2000.

31. Newt Gingrich never lost his boyhood fascination with paleontology, and when the House GOP swept to power in 1995, he decorated one of his offices with the skull of a tyrannosaurus rex, on loan from the Smithsonian Institute.

32. Interview with Representative Henry J. Hyde, March 8, 2000.

33. Interview with Representative Lindsey O. Graham, March 8, 2000.

34. Interview with Representative Asa Hutchinson, March 9, 2000.

35. Interview with Representative Henry J. Hyde, March 8, 2000.

36. Interview with Representative Christopher B. Cannon, March 9, 2000.

37. Interview with Representative Henry J. Hyde, March 8, 2000.

38. Interview with Representative Howard Coble, March 7, 2000.

39. Interview with Representative Christopher B. Cannon, March 9, 2000.

40. Interview with Representative Charles T. Canady, December 21, 1999.

41. Interview with Representative Lindsey O. Graham, March 8, 2000.

42. Hanna F. Pitkin, *The Concept of Representation* (Berkeley, Calif.: University of California Press, 1978).

43. Interview with Representative Henry J. Hyde, March 8, 2000.

44. Quoted in Stephen M. Nichols, "Schiff Defeats Rogan in California's 27th District Race," in *The Roads to Congress, 2000,* ed. Sunil Ahuja and Robert Dewhirst (Stamford, Conn.: Wadsworth, 2002), 107.

45. Ibid.

46. Interview with Representative Lindsey O. Graham, March 8, 2000.

4. STANDING BY THEIR MAN: DEMOCRATIC MEMBERS OF THE HOUSE JUDICIARY COMMITTEE

1. Interview with Representative Martin Frost, June 20, 2002.

2. Barbara Sinclair, "Trying to Govern Positively in a Negative Era," in *The Clinton Presidency: First Appraisals,* ed. Colin Campbell and Bert A. Rockman (Chatham, N.J.: Chatham House Publishers, Inc., 1996), 88–123.

3. James W. Ceaser and Andrew E. Busch, *Losing to Win: The 1996 Elections and American Politics* (Lanham, Md.: Rowman & Littlefield, 1997); and Nicol C. Rae, "Clinton and the Democrats: The President As Party Leader," in *The Postmodern Presidency: Bill Clinton's Legacy in U.S. Politics,* ed. Steven E. Schier (Pittsburgh, Pa.: University of Pittsburgh Press, 2000), 183–200.

4. Paul J. Quirk and Joseph Hinchcliffe, "Domestic Policy: The Trials of a Centrist Democrat," in *The Clinton Presidency: First Appraisals,* ed. Colin Campbell and Bert A. Rockman (Chatham, N.J.: Chatham House, 1996), 262–289.

5. Theda Skocpol, *Boomerang: Healthcare Reform and the Turn against Government* (New York: W. W. Norton, 1997).

6. Sinclair, "Trying to Govern Positively in a Negative Era."

7. Ceaser and Busch, *Losing to Win: The 1996 Elections and American Politics.*

8. Rae, "Clinton and the Democrats."

9. James G. Gimpel, *Legislating the Revolution: The Contract with America in Its First Hundred Days* (Boston, Mass.: Allyn & Bacon, 1996).

10. Nicol C. Rae, *Conservative Reformers: The Republican Freshmen and the Lessons of the 104th Congress* (Armonk, N.Y.: M. E. Sharpe, 1998).

11. Barbara Sinclair, *Unorthodox Lawmaking: New Legislative Processes in the U.S. Congress,* 2d ed. (Washington, D.C.: CQ Press, 2000), 184–219.

12. Jackie Kosczuk, "Democrats' Resurgence Fueled by Pragmatism," *Congressional Quarterly Weekly Report,* May 4, 1996, 1205–1210.

13. Rae, "Clinton and the Democrats."

14. Elizabeth Drew, *Whatever It Takes: The Real Struggle for Political Power in America* (New York: Viking, 1997).

15. Interview with Representative Barney Frank, May 1, 2001.

16. Barbara Sinclair, "The President As Legislative Leader," in *The Clinton Legacy,* ed. Colin Campbell and Bert A. Rockman (Chatham, N.J.: Chatham House, 1999), 70–95.

17. Interview with Representative Jerrold Nadler, May 3, 2001.

18. Interview with Representative Barney Frank, May 1, 2001.

19. On Sentelle, Helms, and the replacement of Fiske, see Chapter 1, at note 77.

20. Interview with Representative Jerrold Nadler, May 3, 2001.

21. Ibid.

22. Interview with Representative Barney Frank, May 1, 2001.

23. Peter Baker, *The Breach: Inside the Impeachment and Trial of William Jefferson Clinton* (New York: Simon & Schuster, 2000), 59–62.

24. Howard Fields, *High Crimes and Misdemeanors: The Dramatic Story of the Rodino Committee* (New York: W. W. Norton, 1978).

25. Interview with Representative Barney Frank, May 1, 2001.

26. Interview with Representative Jerrold Nadler, May 3, 2001.

27. Interview with Representative Barney Frank, May 1, 2001.

28. Roger H. Davidson, "Congressional Parties, Leaders, and Committees: 1900, 2000, and Beyond," in *American Political Parties: Decline or Resurgence?* ed. Jeffrey E. Cohen, Richard Fleisher, and Paul Kantor (Washington, D.C.: CQ Press, 2001), 203.

29. Interview with Representative Barney Frank, May 1, 2001.

30. Interview with Representative Zoe Lofgren, May 2, 2001.

31. P. Baker, *The Breach: Inside the Impeachment and Trial of William Jefferson Clinton,* 84–87.

32. Interview with Representative Jerrold Nadler, May 3, 2001.

33. P. Baker, *The Breach: Inside the Impeachment and Trial of William Jefferson Clinton,* 114–117.

34. Interview with Representative Zoe Lofgren, May 2, 2001.

35. Ibid. Representative Lofgren worked for Representative William Donlon (Don) Edwards (D-Calif.), whose seat she now holds.

36. Interview with Representative Barney Frank, May 1, 2001.

37. P. Baker, *The Breach: Inside the Impeachment and Trial of William Jefferson Clinton,* 111–139.

38. Interview with Representative Zoe Lofgren, May 2, 2001.

39. Ibid.

40. Ibid.

41. Interview with Representative Barney Frank, May 1, 2001.

42. Interview with Representative Jerrold Nadler, May 3, 2001.

43. Interview with Representative Barney Frank, May 1, 2001.

44. Steven E. Schier, *By Invitation Only: The Rise of Exclusive Politics in the United States* (Pittsburgh, Pa.: University of Pittsburgh Press, 2000).

45. Ibid.; and Barbara Sinclair, *Legislators, Leaders, and Lawmaking: The U.S. House of Representatives in the Postreform Era* (Baltimore, Md.: Johns Hopkins University Press, 1995).

46. Benjamin Ginsburg and Martin Shefter, *Politics by Other Means: The Declining Importance of Elections in America* (New York: Basic Books, 1991).

47. Interview with Representative Zoe Lofgren, May 2, 2001.

5. HOUSE FLOOR DEBATE

1. Alexander Hamilton, James Madison, and John Jay, *The Federalist Papers* (New York: New American Library, 1961), 327.

2. For these terms, see Richard F. Fenno, Jr., *Home Style: House Members in Their Districts* (Boston, Mass.: Little, Brown, 1979), 1–30. For Fenno a House member's "reelection" constituency is "composed of those people in the district who he thinks vote for him" (see page 8), while his "primary" constituency is a further subset within the reelection constituency of the member's strongest supporters: "the ones each Congressman believes would provide his last line of electoral defense in a primary contest" (see page 18).

3. On the failed 1997 coup against Gingrich see Jackie Koszcuk, "Coup Attempt Throws GOP off Legislative Track," *Congressional Quarterly Weekly Report,* July 19, 1997, 1671–1674; and Ronald M. Peters, Jr., "Institutional Context and Leadership Style: The Case of Newt Gingrich," in *New Majority or Old Minority? The Impact of Republicans on Congress,* ed. Nicol C. Rae and Colton C. Campbell (Lanham, Md.: Rowman & Littlefield, 1999), 43–65.

4. Interview with Representative David E. Price, June 19, 2002.

5. See Gary C. Jacobson, *The Politics of Congressional Elections,* 5th ed. (New York: Longman, 2001), 189–194; and Karen Foerstal, "Elections Expected to Produce Modest Gains for Republicans," *Congressional Quarterly Weekly Report,* October 24, 1998, 2866–2867.

6. Carroll J. Doherty, "Riding the Omnibus off into the Sunset," *Congressional Quarterly Weekly Report,* October 17, 1998, 2794–2796.

7. Alan Greenblatt, "Negative Campaigning: Denounced, Denied—and Indispensable," *Congressional Quarterly Weekly Report,* October 31, 1998, 2950–2951.

8. Interview with Representative Martin Frost, June 20, 2002.

9. Quoted in Jeffrey L. Katz, "Shakeup in the House," *Congressional Quarterly Weekly Report,* November 7, 1998, 2989–2991.

10. Ibid.

11. Andrew Taylor, "Is Livingston the Manager the House Needs?" *Congressional Quarterly Weekly Report,* November 14, 1998, 3050–3054.

12. Jeffrey L. Katz and Carroll J. Doherty, "New GOP Leaders' Watchword Is Realism, Not Revolution," *Congressional Quarterly Weekly Report,* November 21, 1998, 3161–3166.

13. Gebe Martinez, with Jackie Koszcuk, "Tom Delay: The Hammer That Drives the House GOP," *Congressional Quarterly Weekly Report,* June 5, 1999, 1322–1328.

14. Dan Carney, "Impeachment: Seeking Closure," *Congressional Quarterly Weekly Report,* November 7, 1998, 2986–2988.

15. Ibid.

16. Peter Baker, *The Breach: Inside the Impeachment and Trial of William Jefferson Clinton* (New York: Simon & Schuster, 2000), 179–180.

17. Dan Carney and Andrew Taylor, "105th's Final Vote May Be against Impeachment," *Congressional Quarterly Weekly Report,* November 21, 1998, 3154–3160.

18. Ibid., 3158.

19. Ibid., 3160.

20. Ibid., 3154.

21. P. Baker, *The Breach,* 164–187.

22. Ibid., 178.

23. David R. Mayhew, *Congress: The Electoral Connection* (New Haven, Conn.: Yale University Press, 1974).

24. Richard F. Fenno, Jr., *Home Style: House Members in Their Districts* (Boston, Mass.: Little, Brown, 1978), 1–30.

25. Barry C. Burden, "The Polarizing Effect of Congressional Primaries," in *Congressional Primaries and the Politics of Representation*, ed. Peter F. Galderisi, Marni Ezra, and Michael Lyons (Lanham, Md.: Rowman & Littlefield, 2001), 95–115.

26. Gary C. Jacobson, *The Politics of Congressional Elections*, 5th ed. (New York: Longman, 2001); and Paul S. Herrnson, *Congressional Elections: Campaigning at Home and in Washington*, 2d ed. (Washington, D.C.: Congressional Quarterly Press, 1998).

27. Steven E. Schier, *By Invitation Only: The Rise of Exclusive Politics in the United States* (Pittsburgh, Pa.: University of Pittsburgh Press, 2000).

28. Barbara Sinclair, *Legislators, Leaders, and Lawmaking: The U.S. House of Representatives in the Postreform Era* (Baltimore, Md.: Johns Hopkins University Press, 1995).

29. Martinez and Koszcuk, "Tom Delay: The Hammer That Drives the House GOP."

30. Michael Barone and Richard E. Cohen, with Charles E. Cook, Jr., *The Almanac of American Politics, 2002* (Washington, D.C.: National Journal, 2001), 1498.

31. Martinez and Koszcuk, "Tom Delay: The Hammer That Drives the House GOP."

32. Interview with Representative Peter King, June 18, 2002.

33. Quoted in P. Baker, *The Breach*, 180.

34. Ibid., 179–181.

35. Ibid., 181.

36. Ibid., 179.

37. Nicol C. Rae, *Conservative Reformers: The Republican Freshmen and the Lessons of the 104th Congress* (Armonk, N.Y.: M. E. Sharpe, 1998), 125–127.

38. Interview with Representative Mark Souder, June 18, 2002.

39. Ibid.

40. Interview with Representative Peter King, June 18, 2002.

41. Ibid.

42. P. Baker, *The Breach*, 217.

43. Interview with Representative David E. Price, June 19, 2002. See also David E. Price, *The Congressional Experience*, 2d ed. (Boulder, Colo.: Westview Press, 2000), 183–185.

44. Carroll J. Doherty and Jeffrey L. Katz, "House Opens Historic Drama of Morality, Law, and Politics," *Congressional Quarterly Weekly Report*, December 12, 1998, 3282–3286.

45. Interview with Representative Mark Souder, June 18, 2002.

46. Ibid.

47. Joseph M. Bessette, *The Mild Voice of Reason: Deliberative Democracy and American National Government* (Chicago, Ill.: University of Chicago Press, 1994).

48. Robert T. Oliver, *History of Public Speaking in America* (Boston, Mass.: Allyn and Bacon, 1965).

49. Stephen E. Lucas, "Debate and Oratory," in *The Encyclopedia of the United States Congress*, vol. 1, ed. Donald C. Bacon, Roger H. Davidson, and Morton Keller (New York: Simon & Schuster, 1995).

50. Barbara Sinclair, *Unorthodox Lawmaking: New Legislative Processes in the U.S. Congress*, 1st ed. (Washington, D.C.: CQ Press, 1997), 228.

51. George E. Connor and Bruce I. Oppenheimer, "Deliberation: An Untimed Value in a Time Game," in *Congress Reconsidered*, 5th ed., ed. Lawrence C. Dodd and Bruce I. Oppenheimer (Washington, D.C.: CQ Press, 1993), 317.

52. Roger H. Davidson and Colton C. Campbell, "Deliberation in Congress: Past Tradi-

tions and Future Directions," paper presented at the Annual Meeting of the American Political Science Association, Washington, D.C., August 28–August 31, 1997.

53. Walter Kravitz, *American Congressional Dictionary* (Washington, D.C.: Congressional Quarterly, Inc., 1993). One-minute speeches (commonly called "one minutes") provide one of the few opportunities for nonlegislative debate in the House. Recognition for one-minute speeches is the prerogative of the Speaker. A period for one minutes usually takes place at the beginning of the legislative day following the daily prayer, the Pledge of Allegiance, and approval of the previous day's *Journal* (the official record of the proceedings of the House of Representatives). During this time, representatives ask unanimous consent to address the chamber for one minute on a topic of their choice. In addition, one minutes are often permitted after legislative business ends but before special order speeches begin. Special order speeches, provided by unanimous consent, permit members to address the House on any subject when it is not considering business. The House limits each special order speech to one hour and permits them after the program of the day has been completed.

54. Steven S. Smith, *Call to Order: Floor Politics in the House and Senate* (Washington, D.C.: Brookings Institution, 1989), 238–239.

55. Davidson and Campbell, "Deliberation in Congress: Past Traditions and Future Directions."

56. Giraud Chester, "Contemporary Senate Debate: A Case Study," *Quarterly Journal of Speech* 31 (1945): 410.

57. Donald C. Bacon, "Violence in Congress," in *The Encyclopedia of the United States Congress,* vol. 3, ed. Donald C. Bacon, Roger H. Davidson, and Morton Keller (New York: Simon & Schuster, 1995).

58. Lucas, "Debate and Oratory."

59. Neil MacNeil, *Forge of Democracy: The House of Representatives* (New York: David McKay, 1963), 309.

60. Davidson and Campbell, "Deliberation in Congress: Past Traditions and Future Directions."

61. William Granstaff, *Losing Our Democratic Spirit: Congressional Deliberation and the Dictatorship of Propaganda* (Westport, Conn.: Praeger Publishers, 1999).

62. Davidson and Campbell, "Deliberation in Congress: Past Traditions and Future Directions."

63. Ibid.

64. Stanley Bach, *Some Devices for Post-Cloture Delay in the Senate,* CRS Report, No. 88-1298 GOV (Washington, D.C.: Congressional Research Service, 1988); and Keith Krehbiel, "Unanimous Consent Agreements: Going along in the Senate," *Journal of Politics* 48 (1986): 541–564.

65. MacNeil, *Forge of Democracy,* 328.

66. Kathleen Hall Jamieson, "Civility in the House of Representatives: The 105th Congress," report prepared by the Annenberg Public Policy Center, University of Pennsylvania, March 1999.

67. Davidson and Campbell, "Deliberation in Congress: Past Traditions and Future Directions."

68. Ibid.

69. Ibid.

70. P. Baker, *The Breach,* 232–236.

71. Peter Baker and Juliet Eilperin, "Divided House Debates Impeachment; Republicans are Poised Today to Force Senate Trial of Clinton," *Washington Post,* December 19, 1998, A01.

72. Quoted in Edward Walsh, "The Bitterness of Being in the Minority; House Democrats Watch Helplessly As Republican Juggernaut Rolls On," *Washington Post,* December 19, 1998, A27.

73. Quoted in ibid.

74. Quoted in Jamie Dettmer, "The Impeachment," *Insight on the News,* January 11, 1999, 7.

75. Interview with Representative Martin Frost, June 20, 2002.

76. *Congressional Record,* 105th Cong., 2d sess., December 18, 1998, H11786.

77. Ibid.

78. Dettmer, "The Impeachment."

79. Quoted in Congressional Quarterly, Inc., *Almanac,* vol. 54 (Washington, D.C.: Congressional Quarterly, Inc., 1998), 12.

80. Baker and Eilperin, "Divided House Debates Impeachment; Republicans Are Poised Today to Force Senate Trial of Clinton."

81. *Congressional Record,* 105th Cong., 2d sess., December 18, 1998, H11882.

82. Dettmer, "The Impeachment."

83. Walsh, "The Bitterness of Being in the Minority; House Democrats Watch Helplessly As Republican Juggernaut Rolls On."

84. Quoted in ibid.

85. On the events surrounding Livingston's resignation and his replacement as Speaker elect by Chief Deputy Whip Dennis Hastert (R-Ill.) see P. Baker, *The Breach,* 238–258.

86. These moderate Republican lawmakers included: Representatives Connie Morella (Md.), Christopher Shays (Conn.), Mark Souder (Ind.), Amo Houghton (N.Y.), and Peter King (N.Y.). The twelve Republicans who broke ranks to oppose Article III were: Representatives Shays, Morella, Houghton, King, Mike Castle (Del.), Jay Kim (Calif.), Nancy Johnson (Conn.), Jim Leach (Iowa), Sherwood Boehlert (N.Y.), John McHugh (N.Y.), Phil English (Pa.), and Ralph Regula (Ohio).

87. These Democratic lawmakers included Gene Taylor (Miss.), Paul McHale (Pa.), Ralph M. Hall (Tex.), Charlie W. Stenholm (Tex.), and Virgil H. Goode, Jr. (Va.).

6. HERDING CATS TO TRIAL

1. Burdett A. Loomis, "Explaining Impeachment: The Exceptional Institution Confronts the Unique Experience," in *U.S. Senate Exceptionalism,* ed. Bruce I. Oppenheimer (Columbus: Ohio State University Press, 2002), 322–338.

2. "Scenes from the Senate Trial," *The Hill,* January 20, 1999, 1.

3. Senator George L. Murphy (D-Calif.) began the custom in 1968. The former Hollywood actor had a sweet tooth and always kept candies in his desk drawer. Given the senatorial traffic that regularly passed his new location, Murphy invited other senators to help themselves. The desk became fondly known as "the candy desk" and each senator who has subsequently occupied it has carried on the tradition, stocking the desk with assorted sweets. The current occupant, Senator Rick Santorum (R-Pa.), routinely fills the desk with Hershey chocolate candies. See Senate Historical Office, http://www.senate.gov/learning.

4. Peter Baker, *The Breach: Inside the Impeachment and Trial of William Jefferson Clinton* (New York: Simon & Schuster, 2000).

5. Spencer S. Hsu, "The Jurors; Senate's Partisan Lines Don't Foreclose Partnerships," *Washington Post,* January 31, 1999, A20.

6. Norman J. Ornstein, "Civility, Deliberation, and Impeachment," in *Esteemed Colleagues: Civility and Deliberation in the U.S. Senate,* ed. Burdett A. Loomis (Washington, D.C.: Brookings Institution, 2000), 223–240; and David S. Broder and Dan Balz, "A Year of Scandal with No Winners; Public Trust in Institutions Has Suffered, but Long-term Damage Remains in Doubt," *Washington Post,* February 13, 1999, A1.

7. Ross K. Baker, "Examining Individualism versus Senate Folkways in the Aftermath of the Clinton Impeachment," in *U.S. Senate Exceptionalism,* ed. Bruce I. Oppenheimer (Columbus: Ohio State University Press, 2002), 305–321; and Ornstein, "Civility, Deliberation, and Impeachment."

8. Colton C. Campbell and Nicol C. Rae, eds., *The Contentious Senate: Partisanship, Ideology, and the Myth of Cool Judgment* (Lanham, Md.: Rowman & Littlefield, 2001).

9. Interview with Senator Thad Cochran, June 20, 2002.

10. Eric M. Uslaner, *The Decline of Comity in Congress* (Ann Arbor: University of Michigan Press, 1993).

11. Eric M. Uslaner, *The Movers and the Shirkers: Representatives and Ideologues in the Senate* (Ann Arbor: University of Michigan Press, 1999); and Nicol C. Rae, *Conservative Reformers: The Republican Freshmen and the Lessons of the 104th Congress* (Armonk, N.Y.: M. E. Sharpe, 1998).

12. Burdett Loomis, "Senate Leaders, Minority Voices: From Dirksen to Daschle," in *The Contentious Senate: Partisanship, Ideology, and the Myth of Cool Judgment,* ed. Colton C. Campbell and Nicol C. Rae (Lanham, Md.: Rowman & Littlefield, 2001), 91–106; Barbara Sinclair, "The Senate Leadership Dilemma: Passing Bills and Pursuing Partisan Advantage in a Nonmajoritarian Chamber," in ibid., 65–89; and Christopher J. Deering, "Principle or Party? Foreign National Security Policymaking in the Senate," in ibid., 43–61.

13. Norman J. Ornstein, Robert L. Peabody, and David W. Rohde, "The U.S. Senate: Toward the 21st Century," in *Congress Reconsidered,* 6th ed., ed. Lawrence C. Dodd and Bruce I. Oppenheimer (Washington, D.C.: CQ Press, 1997), 1–28; and Steven S. Smith, "Forces of Change in Senate Party Leadership and Organization," in *Congress Reconsidered,* 5th ed., ed. Lawrence C. Dodd and Bruce I. Oppenheimer (Washington, D.C.: CQ Press, 1993), 259–290.

14. Nicol C. Rae, *Southern Democrats* (New York: Oxford University Press, 1994).

15. Barbara Sinclair, *Unorthodox Lawmaking: New Legislative Processes in the U.S. Congress* (Washington, D.C.: CQ Press, 1997).

16. Sarah A. Binder, "The Disappearing Political Center," *Brookings Review* 15 (1996): 36–39.

17. Quoted in Michael Grunwald and Helen Dewar, "Strains Drive Hill toward Gridlock: Parties Stress Difference, No Deals," *Washington Post,* August 1, 1999, A1.

18. Norman J. Ornstein, Thomas E. Mann, and Michael J. Malbin, *Vital Statistics on Congress: 1999–2000* (Washington, D.C.: American Enterprise Institute, 2000), 201.

19. Barbara Sinclair, *The Transformation of the U.S. Senate* (Baltimore, Md.: Johns Hopkins University Press, 1989).

20. Roger H. Davidson, "Senate Leaders: Janitors for an Untidy Chamber?" in *Congress Reconsidered,* 3d ed., ed. Lawrence C. Dodd and Bruce I. Oppenheimer (Washington, D.C.: CQ Press, 1985), 225–252; Norman J. Ornstein, Robert L. Peabody, and David W. Rohde, "The Senate through the 1980s: Cycles of Change," in *Congress Reconsidered,* 3d ed., ed. Lawrence C. Dodd and Bruce I. Oppenheimer (Washington, D.C.: CQ Press, 1985), 13–33; and Michael Foley, *The New Senate: Liberal Influence in a Conservative Institution, 1959–1972* (New Haven, Conn.: Yale University Press, 1980).

21. Nicol C. Rae and Colton C. Campbell, "Party Politics and Ideology in the Contemporary Senate," in *The Contentious Senate: Partisanship, Ideology, and the Myth of Cool Judgment,* ed. Colton C. Campbell and Nicol C. Rae (Lanham, Md.: Rowman & Littlefield, 2001), 1–18.

22. Quoted in Frank Ahrens, "The Unyielding Robert Byrd," *Washington Post,* February 11, 1999, C1.

23. Peter Baker, Juliet Eilperin, Guy Gugliotta, John F. Harris, Dan Morgan, Eric Pianin, and David Von Drehle, "The Train That Wouldn't Stop; Key Players Thwarted Attempts to Derail Process," *Washington Post,* February 14, 1999, A1.

24. Interview with Senator Thad Cochran, June 20, 2002.

25. Senator Lott did not speak publicly about a possible plan for impeachment proceedings in the Senate until December 29, 1998.

26. Ornstein, "Civility, Deliberation, and Impeachment."

27. Quoted in P. Baker et al., "The Train That Wouldn't Stop; Key Players Thwarted Attempts to Derail Process," 9.

28. Ibid.

29. Sinclair, *The Transformation of the U.S. Senate;* Randall B. Ripley, "Power in the Post–World War II Senate," in *Studies of Congress,* ed. Glenn R. Parker (Washington, D.C.: CQ Press, 1985), 297–320; Charles E. Bullock, III, and David W. Brady, "Party, Constituency, and Roll-call Voting in the U.S. Senate," *Legislative Studies Quarterly* 8 (1983): 29–43; and Robert L. Peabody, "Senate Party Leadership from the 1950s to the 1980s," in *Understanding Congressional Leadership,* ed. Frank H. Mackaman (Washington, D.C.: CQ Press, 1981), 51–115.

30. *Congressional Record,* 105th Cong., 2d sess., July 16, 1998, S8374.

31. P. Baker et al., "The Train That Wouldn't Stop; Key Players Thwarted Attempts to Derail Process."

32. Interview with Senator Thad Cochran, June 20, 2002. See also Natasha Hritzuk, "The Impeachment of President Bill Clinton: Background," in *Presidential Power: Forging the Presidency for the Twenty-first Century,* ed. Robert Y. Shapiro, Martha Joynt Kumar, and Lawrence R. Jacobs (New York: Columbia University Press, 2000), 462–472; and Ruth Marcus, "With Precedents As a Guide: Senators' Decisions, As Well As Rules, Will Affect Process," *Washington Post,* January 14, 1999, A17.

33. Donald R. Matthews, *U.S. Senators and Their World* (Chapel Hill, N.C.: University of North Carolina Press, 1960); and R. K. Baker, "Examining Individualism versus Senate Folkways in the Aftermath of the Clinton Impeachment." See also Sinclair, *The Transformation of the U.S. Senate.*

34. Fenno, *Home Style: U.S. House Members in Their Districts,* 167. See also R. K. Baker, "Examining Individualism versus Senate Folkways in the Aftermath of the Clinton Impeachment," 311. According to Baker, based on interviews with nine senators, eight of

whom had previously served in the House of Representatives, senators appeared to believe that they had a larger stake in the reputation of their institution than did House members. "For the Senate to fall into acrimonious partisan disarray as the House had done would have damaged members of a body who thought well of themselves and who seemed to have a stake in the reputation of the Senate that was larger than that of the average House member" (311). Baker suggests several reasons for this cleavage. One is the greater dispersion of power in the Senate. Whereas in the more hierarchical House, the distance, in power terms, is much greater between the leaders and senior members on the one hand and the recently elected members of the other, the difficulty of individual senators is in distancing themselves from the actions of the smaller collectivity with its more even distribution of power. A second reason is the relatively high public profile of senators, as compared to the relative anonymity of most House members. And a third reason, ascribed by Senator Wayne Allard (R-Colo.), is the longer term and greater intimacy of the Senate. See pp. 318–320.

35. Ornstein, "Civility, Deliberation, and Impeachment," 232.

36. J. McIver Weatherford, *Tribes on the Hill: The U.S. Congress, Rituals and Realities,* rev. ed. (South Hadley, Mass.: Bergin & Garvey, 1985).

37. Ahrens, "The Unyielding Robert Byrd," C1.

38. Quoted in ibid.

39. Authors' observation during meetings for Senate Democratic legislative directors, U.S. Capitol, Washington, D.C., January 1999.

40. R. K. Baker, "Examining Individualism versus Senate Folkways in the Aftermath of the Clinton Impeachment," 312.

41. Michael Barone and Richard E. Cohen, with Charles E. Cook, Jr., *The Almanac of American Politics, 2002* (Washington, D.C.: National Journal, 2001), 325.

42. *Congressional Record,* 105th Cong., 2d sess., September 3, 1998, S9923.

43. Ibid.

44. Quoted in Alison Mitchell, "Congress Returns to a Shadow Cast by Impeachment," *New York Times,* January 4, 1999, A1.

45. Ibid.

46. Authors' observation during a meeting for Senate Democratic Legislative Directors, U.S. Capitol, Washington, D.C., January 1999.

47. A. B. Stoddard, "Lott Relied on Key Senators As Link to House," *The Hill,* February 17, 1999, 1.

48. Quoted in "Scenes from Senate Trial," *The Hill,* January 20, 1999, 1.

49. See Senate Historical Office, http://www.senate.gov/learning.

50. Ibid.

51. Elected as a Whig to the Senate to fill the vacancy in the term commencing March 4, 1851, Wade was reelected as a Republican in 1856 and again in 1863 and served from March 15, 1851, to March 3, 1869. He was an unsuccessful Republican candidate for the vice presidential nomination in 1868.

52. See Senate Historical Office, http://www.senate.gov/learning.

53. Ibid.

54. Ibid.

55. See Floyd M. Riddick and Robert B. Dove, *Procedure and Guidelines for Impeachment Trials in the United States Senate,* rev. ed., U.S. Congress, Senate, 99th Cong., 2d sess., S. Doc. 99-33, August 15 (Washington, D.C.: GPO, 1986), 77–78; and David Y. Thomas,

"The Law of Impeachment in the United States," *American Political Science Review* 2 (May 1908): 378–395.

56. Terry M. Neal, "Senate Is Full of Conflicts; Lawmakers Vow Impartiality Despite Personal Connections," *Washington Post,* January 15, 1999, A18.

57. Quoted in Joan Biskupic, "Enter the Chief Justice; Rehnquist to Transform Senate into Jury," *Washington Post,* January 7, 1999, A12.

58. Joan Biskupic, "In the Court He Doesn't Rule, Chief Justice Now Finds His Role," *Washington Post,* January 23, 1999, A13.

59. Quoted in Joan Biskupic, "Rehnquist Departs Trying Experience," *Washington Post,* February 13, 1999, A33.

60. Joan Biskupic, "For High Court's Stern Taskmaster, a New Role in Senate Trial," *Washington Post,* December 22, 1998, A12.

61. Quoted in Tom Baxter and Rebecca Carr, "Barr Presentation Interrupted by Trial's First Objection," Cox News Service, accessed on Lexis-Nexis, 1999.

62. Ibid.

63. Arlen Specter, with Charles Robbins, *Passion for Truth: From Finding JFK's Single Bullet to Questioning Anita Hill to Impeaching Clinton* (New York: William Morrow, 2000), 460–461.

64. Paul West, "In the Senate, a Solemn Ritual: Chamber Now Enters Unchartered Waters," *Baltimore Sun,* January 8, 1999, 1A.

65. Stoddard, "Lott Relied on Key Senators As Link to House." Under pressure from Senate Republicans, the House prosecutors pared their wish list of witnesses from fifteen to five to three. In the end, they left off the one witness whom many Republicans considered a secret weapon—Betty Currie, the president's secretary—disappointing some senators who believed she could resolve factual discrepancies. The prosecutors shuffled their final two choices as they gauged the mood of the Senate and analyzed which witnesses could swing wavering senators. According to Representative George W. Gekas (R-Pa.), this was a question of making judicious decisions as to which witnesses would give the managers the best chance to convert senators into a vote for conviction. The House managers believed that Currie's testimony about President Clinton's recollections of his relationship with Lewinsky seemed immovable. Clinton's lawyers repeatedly insisted that Currie testified that she did not feel pressured when the president uttered a series of statements about Lewinsky in which he claimed to Currie that they were never alone. House prosecutors interpreted that as witness tampering. Another reason prosecutors felt they did not need Currie was their confidence that Lewinsky's testimony was sufficient to support their accusations that President Clinton had directed Currie to pick up gifts that were under subpoena by the lawyers for Paula Jones. See Eric Schmitt, "Obstruction Charge Drove Managers' Witness Choices," *New York Times,* January 28, 1999, A1.

66. Ibid.

67. *Congressional Record,* 106th Cong., 1st sess., February 23, 1998, S1790.

68. Quoted in Alison Mitchell, "The Trial of a President: The Overview; Senate, in Unanimity, Sets Rules for Trial," *New York Times,* January 9, 1999, A1.

69. Ibid.

70. Quoted in Helen Dewar and Peter Baker, "Senate Votes Rules for President's Trial; Proceedings to Begin Next Week; Decision on Witnesses Deferred," *Washington Post,* January 9, 1999, A1.

71. Ibid.

72. R. K. Baker, "Examining Individualism versus Senate Folkways in the Aftermath of the Clinton Impeachment," 317–318.

73. Quoted in Al Kamen, "United He Falls," *Washington Post,* April 28, 1999, A23.

74. Quoted in Guy Gugliotta and Eric Pianin, "Perjury Charge Is Faltering; Some Republicans Remain Skeptical of House's Case," *Washington Post,* February 7, 1999, A1.

75. Quoted in Eric Schmitt, "The President's Trial: The Overview; Democrats Urge Censure Measure but G.O.P. Balks," *New York Times,* February 8, 1999, A1.

76. Quoted in Gugliotta and Pianin, "Perjury Charge Is Faltering; Some Republicans Remain Skeptical of House's Case," A1.

77. Ibid.

78. Ibid.

79. Specter, with Robbins, *Passion for Truth,* 474.

80. Peter Baker, "Lobbing Softballs and Sympathetic Queries; In Trial's New Phase, Senators Ask Questions through Chief Justice," *Washington Post,* January 23, 1999, A13.

81. Quoted in ibid.

82. *Congressional Record,* 106th Cong., 1st sess., January 21, 1999, S846.

83. Quoted in Alison Mitchell, "The President's Trial: The Assessment," *New York Times,* January 28, 1999, A24.

84. Quoted in Francis X. Clines, "Partisan Parade in the Capitol Corridors," *New York Times,* January 28, 1999, A23.

85. Quoted in Mitchell, "The President's Trial: The Assessment," A24.

86. Quoted in Jeffrey L. Katz, "Exit Strategies Divide Senate," *Congressional Quarterly Weekly Report,* January 30, 1999, 249.

87. Quoted in John Bresnahan, "Republicans Debate Opinions on Fact Bills, Democrats Call Any Version Unconstitutional," *Roll Call,* February 4, 1999, 1.

88. The Senate's resolution concerning President Jackson did not expressly contain the word "censure" or any other specific word of condemnation. Some critics of Congress's authority to adopt such resolutions of censure have subsequently categorized the 1834 resolution as one other than a "censure" of the executive. See Jack Maskell, *Censure of the President by the Congress,* CRS Report No. 98-843 A (Washington, D.C.: Congressional Research Service, 1998), citing *Congressional Globe,* 36th Cong., 1st sess., June 13, 1860, 2938–2939.

89. Interview with Senator Thad Cochran, June 20, 2002.

90. Ibid.

91. Quoted in Katz, "Exit Strategies Divide Senate," 249.

92. Quoted in Eric Pianin and Guy Gugliotta, "Senate's Fiercest Partisan Battle Possible over 'Findings of Fact,'" *Washington Post,* February 4, 1999, A7.

93. Quoted in Schmitt, "The President's Trial," A23.

94. The fourteen Republicans who voted against secret deliberations included: Spencer Abraham (Mich.), Susan Collins (Maine), Mike DeWine (Ohio), Slade Gorton (Wash.), Chuck Hagel (Nebr.), Kay Bailey Hutchison (Tex.), James M. Jeffords (Vt.), Jon Kyl (Ariz.), Richard G. Lugar (Ind.), John McCain (Ariz.), Gordon H. Smith (Ore.), Olympia J. Snowe (Maine), Arlen Specter (Pa.), and Ted Stevens (Alaska).

95. Quoted in Helen Dewar and Peter Baker, "Clinton Fate Is Debated in Private; Proceedings to Begin Next Week; Decision on Witnesses Deferred," *Washington Post,* January 9, 1999, A1.

96. Ibid.

97. Guy Gugliotta and Eric Pianin, "Acquittal Nears Majority on Both Articles," *Washington Post,* February 12, 1999, A1.

98. Quoted in ibid.

99. Loomis, "Explaining Impeachment," 325.

100. Quoted in Gugliotta and Pianin, "Acquittal Nears Majority on Both Articles," A1.

101. Ibid.

102. Ibid.

103. Quoted in "Sen. Byrd: 'Impeachment Is a Sword of Damocles'; Quotes from Senators and Other Key Players in the Senate," *Roll Call,* February 15, 1999, 1.

104. Loomis, "Explaining Impeachment," 324.

105. Sarah A. Binder and Steven S. Smith, *Politics or Principle: Filibustering in the United States Senate* (Washington, D.C.: Brookings Institution, 1997).

106. Loomis, "Explaining Impeachment."

107. Quoted in ibid., 334.

108. Richard F. Fenno, Jr., *Home Style: U.S. House Members in Their Districts* (Boston, Mass.: Little, Brown, 1978).

109. Loomis, "Explaining Impeachment."

110. *Congressional Record,* 106th Cong., 1st sess., February 23, 1999, p. S1791.

111. Ibid.

112. Loomis, "Explaining Impeachment."

113. *Congressional Record,* 106th Cong., 1st sess., February 22, 1999, S1718.

114. *Congressional Record,* 106th Cong., 1st sess., January 28, 1999, S1105.

115. Loomis, "Explaining Impeachment," 334–337.

116. Quoted in David Von Drehle, "Hushed Galleries, Somber Senators, Powerful Moment," *Washington Post,* February 13, 1999, A1.

117. Ibid.

118. Ibid. Senator Specter was attempting to give a verdict—"not proven"—available only under Scots law. His reasons for doing so are explained in Specter, *Passion for Truth,* 513–530.

119. Carroll J. Doherty, "Senate Acquits Clinton," *Congressional Quarterly Weekly Report,* February 13, 1999, 361–367.

120. Quoted in John Bresnahan and Amy Keller, "Senate Acquits President; Neither Article Gets Majority; Censure Effort Goes Nowhere," *Roll Call,* February 15, 1999, 1.

121. Ibid.

122. Quoted in Drehle, "Hushed Galleries, Somber Senators, Powerful Moment," A1.

123. Ibid.

124. Ibid.

125. Ibid.

126. Quoted in Michael E. Myers, "Sen. Feinstein, Long Considered a Swing Vote, not Persuaded by House Managers' Arguments," *The Hill,* January 27, 1999, 4.

127. Ibid.

128. Richard L. Berke, "G.O.P. Unity Gets Priority over an Issue," *New York Times,* January 27, 1999, A18.

129. Ibid.

130. The most utilized measure of presidential influence and effectiveness in the Senate involves calculating in various ways the number of times annually that the Senate supports

the president's publicly expressed positions in recorded floor votes. There are shortcomings associated with *Congressional Quarterly*'s presidential support index, however. For instance, it does not distinguish between major and minor issues or between conflictual or consensual issues in the Senate. In addition, the index generally accepts statements or indications of support or opposition from the president, when measures subject to floor votes may not correctly reflect true presidential intentions. The index also does not correctly measure various nuances, such as the full extent of a president's achievements or setbacks. It is important, therefore, to see the presidential support index as "a rough indication of the state of relations between the president and Congress." See Norman J. Ornstein, Thomas E. Mann, and Michael J. Malbin, *Vital Statistics on Congress: 1999–2000* (Washington, D.C.: American Enterprise Institute, 2000), 191.

131. An obvious explanation is that *Congressional Quarterly*'s presidential support index for the Senate includes a number of presidential nominations, and at that only those that make it to the floor. These nominees for executive and judicial positions are normally, though not invariably, confirmed by the Senate. In 1997 and 1998, for example, President Clinton's Senate victory records were enhanced because he won confirmation of all forty-five nominees who were voted on, while a group of controversial nominees remained bottled up in committee. When recomputed without these nominations, his Senate scores for those years were 57.1 percent and 47.1 percent, respectively—far more modest, though still well above his House scores.

132. Roger H. Davidson and Colton C. Campbell, "The Senate and the Executive," in *Esteemed Colleagues: Civility and Deliberation in the U.S. Senate,* ed. Burdett A. Loomis (Washington, D.C.: Brookings Institution, 2000), 217.

133. Ibid.

134. Ibid., 197–200. As indicated in the cited study, presidential support indexes measure only those votes actually taken on the floor and those votes differ between the two chambers. A presidential initiative defeated by the House may never reach the Senate floor; or the Senate may vote on some modified version of a presidential initiative that was originally rejected by the House. In either case, the Senate ends up with a more positive presidential support record than the other body.

135. Steven Kull, *Expecting More Say: The American Public on Its Role in Government Decisionmaking* (Washington, D.C.: Center on Policy Attitudes, 1999), 26.

136. Quoted in Frank Ahrens, "Robert Byrd's Rules of Order; For the Senator, a Tough Job Demands a Strong Constitution," *Washington Post,* February 11, 1999, C1.

137. Loomis, "Explaining Impeachment," 337–338.

138. Ibid.; and R. K. Baker, "Examining Individualism versus Senate Folkways in the Aftermath of the Clinton Impeachment."

7. CONCLUSION: LESSONS LEARNED

1. Burdett A. Loomis, *The Contemporary Congress,* 3d ed. (Boston, Mass.: Bedford/St. Martin's, 2000), 199.

2. Interview with Representative Zoe Lofgren, May 2, 2001.

3. Robert Dallek, "Impeachment," in Encarta Online Encyclopedia, http:encarta.msn.com, accessed June 26, 2002.

4. Ibid.

5. Roger H. Davidson, "Congressional Parties, Leaders, and Committees: 1900, 2000, and Beyond," in *American Political Parties: Decline or Resurgence?*, ed. Jeffrey E. Cohen, Richard Fleisher, and Paul Kantor (Washington, D.C.: CQ Press, 2001), 187–208.

6. Robert Dallek, "A Historian Looks at Lessons of Impeachment," *The Hill,* January 12, 2000, 11. Almost half of the committee Republicans won their seats in 1994 or 1996. See Don Carney, "Hyde Staying above Clinton Fray but Tries to Raise Panel Profile," *Congressional Quarterly Weekly Report,* March 7, 1998, 564.

7. Loomis, *The Contemporary Congress.*

8. Ibid., 201.

9. See Gerald M. Pomper, "The Presidential Election," in *The Election of 2000,* ed. Gerald M. Pomper (New York: Chatham House, 2001), 125–154; and James W. Ceasar and Andrew E. Busch, *The Perfect Tie: The True Story of the 2000 Presidential Election* (Lanham, Md.: Rowman & Littlefield, 2001).

10. Peter Charles Hoffer, "Legislatures and Impeachment," in *Encyclopedia of the American Legislative System,* vol. 3, ed. Joel H. Silbey (New York: Scribner's, 1994).

11. Quoted in Michael J. Remington, "Impeachment," in *The Encyclopedia of the United States Congress,* vol. 2, ed. Donald C. Bacon, Roger H. Davidson, and Morton Keller (New York: Simon & Schuster, 1995), 1105.

12. Terry Sullivan, "Impeachment Practice in the Era of Lethal Conflict," *Congress and the Presidency* 25 (Autumn 1998): 117.

13. Ibid.

14. Dallek, "A Historian Looks at Lessons of Impeachment."

15. Ibid.

16. Ibid.

17. Colton C. Campbell and Roger H. Davidson, "Coalition Building in Congress: The Consequences of Partisan Change," in *The Interest Group Connection: Electioneering, Lobbying, and Policymaking in Washington,* ed. Paul S. Herrnson, Ronald G. Shaiko, and Clyde Wilcox (Chatham, N.J.: Chatham House, 1998), 116–136.

18. Barbara Sinclair, *Majority Leadership in the U.S. House* (Baltimore, Md.: Johns Hopkins University Press, 1983). The reforms embodied in the 1970 Legislative Reorganization Act, and later emanating from the House Democratic Caucus, were driven by the Democratic Study Group (DSG), then the largest informal group in the House, consisting of mainstream national Democrats. The DSG sought to revitalize their party and to counter the conservative coalition of Republicans and conservative, mostly southern, Democrats who then dominated in the House. Collectively, the reforms and caucus actions of the 1970s were designed to redistribute influence in the House, downward toward the subcommittee level of the legislative process (and the majority rank and file), as well as upward toward the centralized party leadership, in order to make the committee system more accountable both to the Speaker and to the Democratic caucus as a whole.

19. Thomas M. Franck, ed., *The Tethered Presidency: Congressional Restraints on Executive Power* (New York: New York University Press, 1981).

20. American Political Science Association, Committee on Political Parties, "Toward a More Responsible Two-Party System," *American Political Science Review* 44 (Supplement 1950).

21. Majorie Randon Hershey and Paul Allen Beck, *Party Politics in America,* 10th ed. (New York: Addison-Wesley Educational Publishers, 2003).

22. Ibid., 300.

23. James G. Gimpel, *Legislating the Revolution: The Contract with America in Its First Hundred Days* (Boston, Mass.: Allyn & Bacon, 1996).

24. Quoted in Ed Gillespie and Bob Schellhas, eds., *Contract with America: The Bold Plan by Rep. Newt Gingrich, Rep. Dick Armey, and the House Republicans to Change the Nation* (New York: Random House/Times Book, 1994).

25. Hershey and Beck, *Party Politics in America,* 295.

26. Richard E. Neustadt, *Presidential Power and the Modern Presidents: The Politics of Leadership from Roosevelt to Reagan,* 3d ed. (New York: Free Press, 1990), 29. See also Charles O. Jones, *The Presidency in a Separated System* (Washington, D.C.: Brookings Institution, 1994).

APPENDIXES

1. Richard F. Fenwo, Jr., "Observation, Context, and Sequence in the Study of Politics, *American Political Science Review* 80 (1986), 3–16.

2. Ibid.

Bibliography

INTERVIEWS

Representative Charles Canady, 21 December 1999.
Representative Chris Cannon, 9 March 2000.
Representative Howard Coble, 7 March 2000.
Senator Thad Cochran, 20 June 2002.
Representative Barney Frank, 1 May 2001.
Representative Martin Frost, 20 June 2002.
Representative Lindsey Graham, 8 March 2000.
Representative Asa Hutchinson, 9 March 2000.
Representative Henry J. Hyde, 8 March 2000.
Representative Peter T. King, 18 June 2002.
Representative Nick Lampson, 20 June 2002.
Representative Zoe Lofgren, 2 May 2001.
Representative Jerrold Nadler, 3 May 2001.
Representative David E. Price, 19 June 2002.
Representative Mark Souder, 18 June 2002.

BOOKS AND ARTICLES

Abramowitz, Alan I., and Kyle L. Saunders. 2000. "Ideological Realignment and U.S. Congressional Elections." Presented at the Annual Meeting of the American Political Science Association, Washington, D.C., August 31–September 3.
Ahrens, Frank. 1999. "Robert Byrd's Rules of Order; For the Senator, a Tough Job Demands a Strong Constitution." *Washington Post,* 11 February: C1.
———. 1999. "The Unyielding Robert Byrd." *Washington Post.* 11 February: C1.
Aldrich, John H., and David W. Rohde. 2000. "The Consequences of Party Organization in the House: The Role of the Majority and Minority Parties in Conditional Party Government." In *Polarized Politics: Congress and the President in a Partisan Era,* ed. Jon R. Bond and Richard Fleisher. Washington, D.C.: CQ Press.
American Political Science Association. 1950. "Toward a More Responsible Two-Party System." *American Political Science Review* 44 (Supplement). Washington, D.C.
Arnold, R. Douglas. 1990. *The Logic of Congressional Action.* New Haven, Conn.: Yale University Press.

Bach, Stanley. 1988. *Some Devices for Post-Cloture Delay in the Senate.* CRS Report No. 88-1298 GOV. Washington, D.C.: Congressional Research Service.

Bach, Stanley, and Steven S. Smith. 1988. *Managing Uncertainty in the House of Representatives: Adaptation and Innovation in Special Rules.* Washington, D.C.: Brookings Institution.

Bacon, Donald C. 1995. "Violence in Congress." In *The Encyclopedia of the United States Congress,* vol. 3. Ed. Donald C. Bacon, Roger H. Davidson, and Morton Keller. New York: Simon & Schuster.

Baker, Peter. 2000. *The Breach: Inside the Impeachment and Trial of William Jefferson Clinton.* New York: Scribner's.

———. 1999. "Lobbing Softballs and Sympathetic Queries; In Trial's New Phase, Senators Ask Questions through Chief Justice." *Washington Post,* 23 January: A13.

Baker, Peter, and Juliet Eilperin. 1998. "Clinton Impeached; House Approves Articles Charging Perjury, Obstruction; Mostly Partisan Vote Shifts Drama to Senate." *Washington Post,* 20 December: A1.

———. 1998. "Divided House Debates Impeachment; Republicans Are Poised Today to Force Senate Trial of Clinton." *Washington Post,* 19 December: A01.

Baker, Peter, Juliet Eilperin, Guy Gugliotta, John F. Harris, Dan Morgan, Eric Pianin, and David Von Drehle. 1999. "The Train That Wouldn't Stop; Key Players Thwarted Attempts to Derail Process." *Washington Post,* 14 February: A1.

Baker, Richard Allan. 2001. "To Arrest an Impeached Senator." *Series of Historical Minutes.* United States Senate Historical Office. Washington, D.C.: *http://www.senate.gov/learning/min.*

———. 2001. "Senate Adopts First Impeachment Rules." *Series of Historical Minutes.* United States Senate Historical Office. Washington, D.C.: *http://www.senate.gov/learning/min.*

———. 2001. "The Senate Votes on a Presidential Impeachment." *Series of Historical Minutes.* United States Senate Historical Office. Washington, D.C.: *http://www.senate.gov/learning/min.*

———. 2001. "The Senators Expelled." *Series of Historical Minutes.* United States Senate Historical Office. Washington, D.C.: *http://www.senate.gov/learning/min.*

———. 1988. *The Senate of the United States: A Bicentennial History.* Malabar, Fla.: Robert E. Krieger Publishing.

Baker, Ross K. 2002. "Examining Individualism versus Senate Folkways in the Aftermath of the Clinton Impeachment." In *U.S. Senate Exceptionalism,* ed. Bruce I. Oppenheimer. Columbus: Ohio State University Press.

———. 1995. *House and Senate,* 2d edition. New York: W. W. Norton.

Balz, Dan. 1998. "One Week Defines 'Partisan'; Politics of Anger Has Staying Power." *Washington Post,* 18 December: A1.

Barone, Michael, and Richard E. Cohen, with Charles E. Cook, Jr. 2001. *The Almanac of American Politics, 2002.* Washington, D.C.: National Journal.

Barone, Michael, and Grant Ujifusa. 1999. *The Almanac of American Politics, 2000.* Washington, D.C.: National Journal.

Barry, John M. 1989. *The Ambition and the Power.* New York: Viking.

Baxter, Tom, and Rebecca Carr. 1999. "Barr Presentation Interrupted by Trial's First Objection." Cox News Service. Lexis-Nexis.

Bazan, Elizabeth B. 1998. *Impeachment: An Overview of Constitutional Provisions, Procedure, and Practice.* CRS Report No. 98-186 A. Washington, D.C.: Congressional Research Service.

Bazan, Elizabeth B., Nancy Lee Jones, and Jay R. Shampansky. 1999. *Compendium of Precedents Involving Evidentiary Rulings and Applications of Evidentiary Principles from Selected Impeachment Trials.* CRS Report No. RL30042. Washington, D.C.: Congressional Research Service.

Benedict, Michael Les. 1973. "A New Look at the Impeachment of Andrew Johnson." *Political Science Quarterly* 88: 349–367 .

———. 1973. *The Impeachment and Trial of Andrew Johnson.* New York: W.W. Norton.

Berger, Raoul. 1971. "High Crimes and Misdemeanors." *Southern California Law Review* 44 (Winter): 719–758.

Berke, L. Richard. 1999. "G.O.P. Unity Gets Priority over an Issue." *New York Times,* 27 January: A18.

Bessette, Joseph M. 1994. *The Mild Voice of Reason: Deliberative Democracy and American National Government.* Chicago, Ill.: University of Chicago Press.

Beth, Richard S. 1998. *Censure of Executive and Judicial Branch Officials: Past Congressional Proceedings.* CRS Report No. 98-983 GOV. Washington, D.C.: Congressional Research Service.

Binder, Sarah A. 2001. "Congress, the Executive, and the Production of Public Policy: United We Govern?" In *Congress Reconsidered,* 7th edition. Ed. Lawrence C. Dodd and Bruce I. Oppenheimer. Washington, D.C.: CQ Press.

———. 1996. "The Disappearing Political Center." *Brookings Review* 15: 36–39.

———. 1996. "The Partisan Basis of Procedural Choice: Allocating Parliamentary Rights in the House, 1789–1990." *American Political Science Review* 90: 8–20.

Binder, Sarah A., and Steven S. Smith. 1997. *Politics or Principle? Filibustering in the United States Senate.* Washington, D.C.: Brookings Institution.

Biskupic, Joan. 1999. "Enter the Chief Justice; Rehnquist to Transform Senate into Jury." *Washington Post,* 7 January: A1.

———. 1999. "In a Court He Doesn't Rule, Chief Justice Now Finds His Role." *Washington Post.* 23 January: A13.

———. 1999. "Rehnquist Departs Trying Experience." *Washington Post,* 13 February: A33.

———. 1998. "For High Court's Stern Taskmaster, a New Role in Senate Trial." *Washington Post,* 22 December: A12.

Black, Charles L., Jr. 1974. *Impeachment: A Handbook.* New Haven, Conn.: Yale University Press.

Blaney, Joseph R., and William L. Benoit. 2001. *The Clinton Scandals and the Politics of Image Restoration.* Westport, Conn.: Praeger Publishers.

Bresnahan, John. 1999. "Each Party Plans Precise Queries for Next Phase." *Roll Call,* 18 January: 1, 30.

———. 1999. "Republicans Debate Options on Fact Bills; Democrats Call Any Version Unconstitutional." *Roll Call,* 4 February: 1.

———. 1998. "Secretary of the Senate Receives Impeachment Articles." *Roll Call,* 21 December: 14.

Bresnahan, John, and Amy Keller. 1999. "Senate Acquits President; Neither Article Gets Majority; Censure Effort Goes Nowhere." *Roll Call,* 15 February: 1.

Broder, David S., and Dan Balz. 1999. "A Year of Scandal with No Winners; Public Trust in Institutions Has Suffered, but Long-Term Damage Remains in Doubt." *Washington Post,* 13 February: A1.

Brown, Khalilah L. 2000. "Towing the Party Line, Towing the Color Line: African-American Women in Congress and the Impeachment Process." Presented at the Annual Meeting of the American Political Science Association, Washington, D.C., August 31–September 3.

Bullock, Charles E., III, and David W. Brady. 1983. "Party, Constituency, and Roll-call Voting in the U.S. Senate." *Legislative Studies Quarterly* 8(1): 29–43.

Burden, Barry C. 2001. "The Polarizing Effect of Congressional Primaries." In *Congressional Primaries and the Politics of Representation,* ed. Peter F. Galderisi, Marni Ezra, and Michael Lyons. Lanham, Md.: Rowman & Littlefield.

Burnham, Walter Dean. 1982. *The Current Crisis in American Politics.* New York: Oxford University Press.

———. 1970. *Critical Elections and the Mainsprings of American Politics.* New York: Norton.

———. 1967. *The American Party Systems.* New York: Oxford University Press.

———. 1965. "The Changing Shape of the American Political Universe." *American Political Science Review* 59: 7–28.

Bushnell, Eleanore. 1992. *Crimes, Follies, and Misfortunes: The Federal Impeachment Trials.* Urbana, Ill.: University of Illinois Press.

Butler, Anne M., and Wendy Wolff. 1995. *United States Senate: Election, Expulsion, and Censure Cases, 1793–1990.* Washington, D.C.: Government Printing Office.

Campbell, Colton C., and Roger H. Davidson. 1998. "Coalition Building in Congress: The Consequences of Partisan Change." In *The Interest Group Connection: Electioneering, Lobbying, and Policymaking in Washington,* ed. Paul S. Herrnson, Ronald G. Shaiko, and Clyde Wilcox. Chatham, N.J.: Chatham House.

Campbell, Colton C., and Paul S. Herrnson. 2004. "Lessons from the Battlefield." In *War Stories from Capitol Hill,* ed. Colton C. Campbell and Paul S. Herrnson. Upper Saddle River, N.J.: Prentice-Hall.

Campbell, Colton C., and Nicol C. Rae, eds. 2001. *The Contentious Senate: Partisanship, Ideology, and the Myth of Cool Judgment.* Lanham, Md.: Rowman & Littlefield.

Cannon, Clarence. 1936. *Cannon's Precedents of the United States House of Representatives.* Washington, D.C.: Government Printing Office.

Carlson, Peter. 1998. "130 Years Ago, Parallels up to a Boiling Point." *Washington Post,* 13 December: A1.

Carney, Dan. 1998. "Hyde Staying above Clinton Fray but Tries to Raise Panel Profile." *Congressional Quarterly Weekly Report,* 7 March: 563–568.

———. 1998. "Impeachment: Seeking Closure." *Congressional Quarterly Weekly Report,* 7 November: 2986–2988.

Ceaser, James W., and Andrew E. Busch. 1997. *Losing to Win: The 1996 Elections and American Politics.* Lanham, Md.: Rowman & Littlefield.

Chappie, Damon, and Amy Keller. 1998. "Now It's Decision Time: Members Face Intense Pressure after Judiciary Committee Passes Articles of Impeachment against President Clinton." *Roll Call,* 14 December: 1, 18.

Chappie, Damon, and Ethan Wallison. 1998. "Leaders Planning Structure of Debate." *Roll Call,* 17 December: 1, 17.

Chester, Giraud. 1945. "Contemporary Senate Debate: A Case Study." *Quarterly Journal of Speech* 31: 407–411.

Clines, Francis X. 1999. "Partisan Parade in the Capitol Corridors." *New York Times,* 28 January: A23.

Cohen, William S. 1997. "Farewell Address." In *Lessons and Legacies: Farewell Addresses from the Senate,* ed. Norman J. Ornstein. New York: Addison-Wesley.

Congressional Quarterly, Inc. 1998. *Almanac,* vol. 54. Washington, D.C.: Congressional Quarterly, Inc.

———. 1991. *Guide to Congress,* 4th edition. Washington, D.C.: Congressional Quarterly, Inc.

Connelly, William F., Jr., and John J. Pitney, Jr. 1994. *Congress' Permanent Minority? Republicans in the U.S. House.* Lanham, Md.: Rowman & Littlefield.

Conner, George E., and Bruce I. Oppenheimer. 1993. "Deliberation: An Untimed Value in a Time Game." In *Congress Reconsidered,* 5th edition. Ed. Lawrence C. Dodd and Bruce I. Oppenheimer. Washington, D.C.: CQ Press.

Constitution, Jefferson's Manual, and the Rules of the House of Representatives. 1993. 102nd Cong., 2d sess., H. Doc. 102-405. Washington, D.C.: Government Printing Office.

Converse, Phillip E. 1964. "The Nature of Belief Systems in Mass Publics." In *Ideology and Discontent,* ed. David E. Apter. New York: Free Press.

Cooper, Joseph. 1991. *The Origins of the Standing Committees and the Development of the Modern House.* Houston, Tex.: Rice University Studies Monograph.

Cooper, Joseph, and Garry Young. 2002. "Party and Preference in Congressional Decision Making: Roll Call Voting in the House of Representatives, 1889–1999." In *Party, Process, and Political Change in Congress: New Perspectives on the History of Congress,* ed. David W. Brady and Mathew D. McCubbins. Palo Alto, Calif.: Stanford University Press.

Cox, Gary W., and Mathew D. McCubbins. 1993. *Legislative Leviathan: Party Government in the House.* Berkeley, Calif.: University of California Press.

Currie, James T. 1988. *The United States House of Representatives.* Malabar, Fla.: Robert E. Krieger.

Dallek, Robert. 2002. "Impeachment." In *Encarta Online Encyclopedia.* http://encarta.msn.com. 26 June.

———. 2000. "A Historian Looks at Lessons of Impeachment." *The Hill,* 12 January: 11.

Davidson, Roger H. 2001. "Congressional Parties, Leaders, and Committees: 1900, 2000, and Beyond." In *American Political Parties: Decline or Resurgence?,* ed. Jeffrey E. Cohen, Richard Fleisher, and Paul Kantor. Washington, D.C.: CQ Press.

———. 2001. "The 2000 Elections: A New Gilded Age?" In *Congressional Parity: Where Do We Go from Here? Extension of Remarks,* ed. Burdett A. Loomis. Lawrence: University Press of Kansas.

———. 1999. "Building the Republican Regime: Leadership and Committees." In *New Majority or Old Minority? The Impact of Republicans on Congress,* ed. Nicol C. Rae and Colton C. Campbell. Lanham, Md.: Rowman & Littlefield.

———. 1995. "Congressional Committees in the New Reform Era: From Combat to the Contract." Presented at the Annual Meeting of the Midwest Political Science Association, Chicago, Ill., April 28–30.

———. 1985. "Senate Leaders: Janitors for an Untidy Chamber?" In *Congress Reconsidered,* 3d edition. Ed. Lawrence C. Dodd and Bruce I. Oppenheimer. Washington, D.C.: CQ Press.

Davidson, Roger H., and Colton C. Campbell. 1997. "Deliberation in Congress: Past Traditions and Future Directions." Presented at the Annual Meeting of the American Political Science Association, Washington, D.C., August 28–31.

———. 2000. "The Senate and the Executive." In *Esteemed Colleagues: Civility and Deliberation in the U.S. Senate,* ed. Burdett A. Loomis. Washington, D.C.: Brookings Institution.

Davidson, Roger H., and Walter J. Oleszek. 2000. *Congress and Its Members,* 7th edition. Washington, D.C.: CQ Press.

———. 2002. *Congress and Its Members,* 8th edition. Washington, D.C.: CQ Press.

Deering, Christopher J. 2001. "Principle or Party? Foreign and National Security Policymaking in the Senate." In *The Contentious Senate: Partisanship, Ideology, and the Myth of Cool Judgment,* ed. Colton C. Campbell and Nicol C. Rae. Lanham, Md.: Rowman & Littlefield.

Deering, Christopher J., and Steven S. Smith. 1990. *Committees in Congress,* 2d edition. Washington, D.C.: CQ Press.

Deschler, Lewis. 1977. *Deschler's Precedents of the United States House of Representatives.* 94th Cong., 2d sess., H. Doc. 661. Washington, D.C.: Government Printing Office.

Dettmer, Jamie. 1999. "The Impeachment." *Insight on the News,* 11 January: 7.

Dewar, Helen, and Peter Baker. 1999. "Clinton Fate Is Debated in Private; Censure Agreement Still Elusive." *Washington Post,* 10 February: A1.

———. 1999. "Senate Votes Rules for President's Trial; Proceedings to Begin Next Week; Decision on Witnesses Deferred." *Washington Post,* 9 January: A1.

"Do Republicans Have a Death Wish?" 1998. *The Hill,* 9 December: 10.

Dodd, Lawrence C., and Bruce I. Oppenheimer. 2001. "Congress and the Emerging Order: Assessing the 2000 Elections." In *Congress Reconsidered,* 7th edition. Ed. Lawrence C. Dodd and Bruce I. Oppenheimer. Washington, D.C.: CQ Press.

Doherty, Carroll J. 1998. "Riding the Omnibus off into the Sunset." *Congressional Quarterly Weekly Report,* 17 October: 2794–2796.

Dorsen, David. 1999. "Impeachment Partisanship Strikes at the Constitution." *The Hill,* 20 January: 9.

Doyle, Charles. 1998. *Impeachment Grounds: A Collection of Selected Materials.* CRS Report No. 98-882 A. Washington, D.C.: Congressional Research Service.

———. 1998. *Impeachment Grounds: Part 1: Pre-Constitutional Convention Materials.* Congressional Research Service Report No. 98-893 A. Washington, D.C.

———. 1998. *Impeachment Grounds: Part 2: Selected Constitutional Convention Materials.* CRS Report No. 98-894 A. Washington, D.C.: Congressional Research Service.

———. 1998. *Impeachment Grounds: Part 3: Hamilton, Wilson, and Story.* CRS Report No. 98-895 A. Washington, D.C.: Congressional Research Service.

———. 1998. *Impeachment Grounds: Part 4A: Articles of Past Impeachments.* CRS Report No. 98–896 A. Washington, D.C.: Congressional Research Service.

———. 1998. *Impeachment Grounds: Part 4B: Articles of Past Impeachments.* CRS Report No. 98-897. Washington, D.C.: Congressional Research Service.

———. 1998. *Impeachment Grounds: Part 5: Selected Douglas/Nixon Inquiry Materials.* CRS Report No. 98-898 A. Washington, D.C.: Congressional Research Service.

———. 1998. *Impeachment Grounds: Part 6: Quotes from Sundry Commentators.* CRS Report No. 98-899 A. Washington, D.C.: Congressional Research Service.

Drew, Elizabeth. 1997. *Whatever It Takes: The Real Struggle for Political Power in America.* New York: Viking.

———. 1996. *Showdown: The Struggle between the Gingrich Congress and the Clinton White House.* New York: Simon & Schuster.

Duverger, Maurice. 1964. *Political Parties: Their Organization and Activity in the Modern State,* 3d edition. London, Methuen.

Ellis, Richard E. 1992. "Impeachment." In *The Oxford Companion to the Supreme Court of the United States,* ed. Kermit L. Hall. New York: Oxford University Press.

Epstein, Leon D. 1967. *Political Parties in Western Democracies.* New York: Praeger.

Erickson, Robert S., and Gerald C. Wright. 2002. "Voters, Candidates, and Issues in Congressional Elections." In *Congress Reconsidered,* 7th edition. Ed. Lawrence C. Dodd and Bruce I. Oppenheimer. Washington, D.C.: CQ Press.

Eulau, Heinz, and Vera McCluggage. 1984. "Standing Committees in Legislatures: Three Decades of Research." *Legislative Studies Quarterly* 9: 195–270.

Evans, C. Lawrence, and Walter J. Oleszek. 2001. "Message Politics and Senate Procedure." In *The Contentious Senate: Partisanship, Ideology, and the Myth of Cool Judgment,* ed. Colton C. Campbell and Nicol C. Rae. Lanham, Md.: Rowman & Littlefield.

———. 1997. *Congress under Fire: Reform Politics and the Republican Majority.* New York: Houghton Mifflin.

Farrand, Max. 1966. *Records of the Federal Convention.* New Haven, Conn.: Yale University Press.

Farrar-Myers, Victoria A., and Diana Dwyre. 2001. "Parties and Campaign Finance." In *American Political Parties; Decline or Resurgence?,* ed. Jeffrey E. Cohen, Richard Fleisher, and Paul Kantor. Washington, D.C.: CQ Press.

Fenno, Richard F., Jr. 1990. *Watching Politicians: Essays on Participant Observation.* Berkeley, Calif.: IGS Press.

———. 1986. "Observation, Context, and Sequence in the Study of Politics." *American Political Science Review* 80: 3–16.

———. 1978. *Home Style: House Members in Their Districts.* New York: HarperCollins.

———. 1973. *Congressmen in Committees.* Boston, Mass.: Little, Brown.

Fields, Howard. 1978. *High Crimes and Misdemeanors: The Dramatic Story of the Rodino Committee.* New York: W. W. Norton.

Fiorina, Morris P. 1986. "Legislator Uncertainty, Legislative Control, and the Delegation of Legislative Authority." In *Regulatory Policy and the Social Sciences,* ed. Roger G. Noll. Berkeley: University of California Press.

———. 1977. *Congress: Keystone of the Washington Establishment.* New Haven, Conn.: Yale University Press.

Foerstal, Karen. 1998. "Elections Expected to Produce Modest Gains for Republicans." *Congressional Quarterly Weekly Report,* 24 October: 2866–2867.

Foley, Michael. 1980. *The New Senate: Liberal Influence on a Conservative Institution, 1959–1972.* New Haven, Conn.: Yale University Press.

Gerhardt, Michael J. 2000. *The Federal Impeachment Process: A Constitutional and Historical Analysis.* Chicago, Ill.: University of Chicago Press.

Gettinger, Stephen. 1998. "An Alternative to Impeachment." *Congressional Quarterly Weekly Report,* 7 March: 566.

Gillespie, Ed, and Bob Schellhas, eds. 1994. *Contract with America: The Bold Plan by Rep.*

Newt Gingrich, Rep. Dick Armey, and the House Republicans to Change the Nation.
New York: Random House/Times Books.

Gimpel, James G. 1996. *Fulfilling the Contract: The First Hundred Days.* Boston, Mass.: Allyn & Bacon.

———. 1996. *Legislating the Revolution: The Contract with America in Its First Hundred Days.* Boston, Mass.: Allyn & Bacon.

Ginsburg, Benjamin, and Martin Shefter. 1991. *Politics by Other Means: The Declining Importance of Elections in America.* New York: Basic Books.

Goldstein, Amy, and Dan Balz. 1998. "The President and Monica Lewinsky: An Unusual but Ambiguous Connection." *Washington Post,* 8 February: A01.

Granstaff, William. 1999. *Losing Our Democratic Spirit: Congressional Deliberation and the Dictatorship of Propaganda.* Westport, Conn.: Praeger.

Greenblatt, Alan. 1998. "Negative Campaigning: Denounced, Denied—and Indispensable." *Congressional Quarterly Weekly Report,* 31 October: 2950–2951.

Grimes, Warren S. 1991. "Hundred-Ton-Gun Control: Preserving Impeachment As the Exclusive Removal Mechanism for Federal Judges." *UCLA Law Review* 38. Accessed on Lexis-Nexis: http://web.lexis-nexis.com/universe/document?_m=dea49a50170c30066 a6b4ed3c7b53d76&_docnum=20&wchp=dGLbVlb-lSlAl&_md5=2deeebdabb5986757 a40cd56f5a0e4d4.

Grunwald, Michael, and Helen Dewar. 1999. "Strains Drive Hill toward Gridlock: Parties Stress Difference, No Deals." *Washington Post,* 1 August: A1.

Gugliotta, Guy, and George Lardner, Jr. 1998. "Arguments the Same, Only Places Switched; Bipartisanship Eluded Hill in Watergate." *Washington Post,* 2 October: A16.

Gugliotta, Guy, and Eric Pianin. 1999. "Acquittal Nears Majority on Both Articles." *Washington Post,* 12 February: A1.

———. 1999. "Perjury Charge Is Faltering; Some Republicans Remain Skeptical of House's Case." *Washington Post,* 7 February: A1.

Guth, James L. 2000. "Clinton, Impeachment, and the Culture Wars." In *The Postmodern Presidency: Bill Clinton's Legacy in U.S. Politics,* ed. Steven E. Schier. Pittsburgh: University of Pittsburgh Press.

Hall, Richard. 1996. *Participation in Congress.* New Haven, Conn.: Yale University Press.

Halstead, T. J. 1998. *An Overview of the Impeachment Process.* CRS Report No. 98-806 A. Washington, D.C.: Congressional Research Service.

Harris, Fred R. 1997. *Deadlock or Decision: The U.S. Senate and the Rise of National Politics.* New York: Oxford University Press.

———. 1995. *In Defense of Congress.* New York: St. Martin's.

Herrnson, Paul S. 1998. *Congressional Elections: Campaigning at Home and in Washington,* 2d edition. Washington, D.C.: CQ Press.

Hill, Kevin A. 1995. "Does the Creation of Majority Black Districts Aid Republicans? Analysis of the 1992 Congressional Elections in Eight Southern States." *Journal of Politics* 57: 384–401.

Hill, Kevin A., and John E. Hughes. 1998. *Cyberpolitics: Citizen Activism in the Age of the Internet.* Lanham, Md.: Rowman & Littlefield.

Hill, Kevin A., and Nicol C. Rae. 2000. "What Happened to the Democrats in the South? U.S. House Elections, 1992–1996." *Party Politics* 6: 5–22.

Hinds, Asher C., ed. 1907. *Hinds' Precedents of the House of Representatives,* 5 vols. Washington, D.C.: Government Printing Office.

Hoffer, Peter Charles. 1994. "Legislatures and Impeachment." In *Encyclopedia of the American Legislative System,* vol. 3. Ed. Joel H. Silbey. New York: Scribner's.

Hoffer, Peter C., and N. E. H. Hull. 1984. *Impeachment in America, 1635–1805.* New Haven, Conn.: Yale University Press.

Hofstadter, Richard A. 1955. *The Age of Reform: From Bryan to FDR.* New York: Knopf.

Hook, Janet. 1998. "Divisiveness Rules As Debate Opens." *Los Angeles Times,* 19 December: A1.

Hritzuk, Natasha. 2000. "The Impeachment of President Bill Clinton: Background." In *Presidential Power: Forging the Presidency for the Twenty-first Century,* ed. Robert Y. Shapiro, Martha Joynt Kumar, and Lawrence R. Jacobs. New York: Columbia University Press.

Hsu, Spencer S. 1999. "The Jurors; Senate's Partisan Lines Don't Foreclose Partnerships." *Washington Post,* 31 January: A20.

Huckabee, David C., Paul S. Rundquist, and Thomas H. Neale. 1998. *Impeachment: Frequently Asked Questions.* CRS Report No. 98-919 GOV. Washington, D.C.: Congressional Research Service.

Huitt, Ralph K. 1954. "The Congressional Committee: A Case Study." *American Political Science Review* 48: 340–365.

Hunter, James Davison. *Culture Wars: The Struggle to Define America.* New York: Basic Books.

"Impeachment of the President." 1999. *Congressional Digest.* Washington, D.C.: Congressional Quarterly, Inc.

Jacobson, Gary C. 2001. "Congress: Elections and Stalemate." In *The Elections of 2000,* ed. Michael Nelson. Washington, D.C.: CQ Press.

———. 2000. "Party Polarization in National Politics: The Electoral Connection." In *Polarized Politics: Congress and the President in a Partisan Era,* ed. Jon R. Bond and Richard Fleisher. Washington, D.C.: CQ Press.

———. 2000. "Public Opinion and the Impeachment of Bill Clinton." *British Elections and Parties Review* 10: 1–31.

———. 1999. "Impeachment Politics in the 1998 Congressional Elections." *Political Science Quarterly* 114: 31–51.

Jamieson, Kathleen Hall. March 1999. "Civility in the House of Representatives: The 105th Congress." Report prepared by the Annenberg Public Policy Center, University of Pennsylvania.

Jones, Charles O. 1999. *Clinton and Congress: 1993–1996: Risk, Restoration, and Reelection.* Norman: University of Oklahoma Press.

Kagay, Michael R. 1999. "Presidential Address: Public Opinion during Presidential Scandal and Impeachment." *Public Opinion Quarterly* 63(3): 449–463.

Kaiser, Robert G. 1998. "In Debate, Divided They Stand; House Members Reach for High—Not Common—Ground on Impeachment." *Washington Post,* 19 December: A27.

Kamen, Al. 1999. "United He Falls." *Washington Post,* 28 April: A23.

Katz, Jeffrey L. 1999. "Exit Strategies Divide Senate." *Congressional Quarterly Weekly Report,* 30 January: 249.

———. 1998. "Shakeup in the House." *Congressional Quarterly Weekly Report,* 7 November: 2989–2991.

Katz, Jeffrey L., and Carroll J. Doherty. 1998. "New GOP Leaders' Watchword Is Realism, Not Revolution." *Congressional Quarterly Weekly Report,* 21 November: 3161–3166.

Keller, Amy. 1999. "Chaplain Reflects on Impeachment Lessons." *Roll Call,* 12 April: 1, 18.

————. 1998. "Judiciary GOP Releases Four Draft Articles." *Roll Call,* 10 December: 1, 14, 15.

————. 1998. "Two of Four Articles Go to Senate for Trial." *Roll Call,* 21 December: 1, 26.

Kiewiet, D. Roderick, and Mathew D. McCubbins. 1991. *The Logic of Delegation: Congressional Parties and the Appropriations Process.* Chicago, Ill.: University of Chicago Press.

King, David C. 1997. *Turf Wars: How Congressional Committees Claim Jurisdiction.* Chicago, Ill.: University of Chicago Press.

Kirpatrick, Jeane J. 1976. *The New Presidential Elite: Men and Women in National Politics.* New York: Sage Foundation.

Kolodny, Robin. 1999. "Moderate Success: Majority Status and the Changing Nature of Factionalism in the House Republican Party." In *New Majority or Old Minority? The Impact of Republicans on Congress,* ed. Nicol C. Rae and Colton C. Campbell. Lanham, Md.: Rowman & Littlefield.

————. 1998. *Pursuing Majorities: Congressional Campaign Committees in American Politics.* Norman: University of Oklahoma Press.

Kosczuk, Jackie. 1997. "Coup Attempt Throws GOP off Legislative Track." *Congressional Quarterly Weekly Report,* 19 July: 1671–1674.

————. 1996. "Democrats' Resurgence Fueled by Pragmatism." *Congressional Quarterly Weekly Report,* 4 May: 1205–1210.

Kravitz, Walter. 1993. *American Congressional Dictionary.* Washington, D.C.: Congressional Quarterly, Inc.

Krehbiel, Keith. 1991. *Information and Legislative Organization.* Ann Arbor: University of Michigan Press.

————. 1986. "Unanimous Consent Agreements: Going along in the Senate." *Journal of Politics* 48: 541–464.

Kull, Steven. 1999. *Expecting More Say: The American Public on Its Role in Government Decisionmaking.* Washington, D.C.: Center on Policy Attitudes.

Labovitz, John R. 1978. *Presidential Impeachment.* New Haven, Conn.: Yale University Press.

Ladd, Everett Carll, Jr., with Charles C. Hadley. 1978. *Transformations of the American Party System: Political Conditions from the New Deal to the 1970s,* 2d edition. New York: Norton.

Lanoue, David J., and Craig F. Emmert. 1999. "Voting in the Glare of the Spotlight: Representatives' Votes on the Impeachment of President Clinton." *Polity* 32(2): 253–269.

Lawrence, Chris. 2000. "Impeaching the President: Representatives' Behavior on a Highly Salient Issue." Presented at the Annual Meeting of the American Political Science Association, Washington, D.C., August 31–September 3.

Layman, Geoffrey. 2001. *The Great Divide: Religious and Cultural Conflict in American Party Politics.* New York: Columbia University Press.

Loomis, Burdett. 2002. "Explaining Impeachment: The Exceptional Institution Confronts the Unique Experience." In *U.S. Senate Exceptionalism,* ed. Bruce I. Oppenheimer. Columbus: Ohio State University Press.

————. 2001. "Senate Leaders, Minority Voices: From Dirksen to Daschle." In *The Contentious Senate: Partisanship, Ideology, and the Myth of Cool Judgment,* ed. Colton C. Campbell and Nicol C. Rae. Lanham, Md.: Rowman & Littlefield.

————. 2000. *The Contemporary Congress,* 3d edition. Boston, Mass.: Bedford/St. Martin's.

Lucas, Stephen E. 1995. "Debate and Oratory." In *The Encyclopedia of the United States Congress*, vol. 1. Ed. Donald C. Bacon, Roger H. Davidson, and Morton Keller. New York: Simon & Schuster.

Maas, Arthur. 1983. *Congress and the Common Good.* New York: Basic Books.

MacNeil, Neil. 1963. *Forge of Democracy: The House of Representatives.* New York: David McKay.

Maraniss, David, and Michael Weisskopf. 1996. *Tell Newt to Shut Up!* New York: Touchstone.

Marcus, Ruth. 1999. "With Precedents As a Guide; Senators' Decisions, As Well As Rules, Will Affect Process." *Washington Post,* 14 January: A17.

———. 1998. "Panel Unclear on Impeachment Role: Lawmakers to Clash in Attempt to Define Standards and Constitutional Duties." *Washington Post,* 6 December: A8.

Martinez, Gebe, and Jackie Koszcuk. 1999. "Tom Delay: The Hammer That Drives the House GOP." *Congressional Quarterly Weekly Report,* 5 June: 1322–1328.

Maskell, Jack. 1998. *Censure of the President by the Congress.* CRS Report No. 98-843 A. Washington, D.C.: Congressional Research Service.

———. 1998. *Independent Counsel Provisions: An Overview of the Operation of the Law.* CRS Report No. 98-282A. Washington, D.C.: Congressional Research Service.

Masterson, William H. 1969 [1954]. *William Blount.* Westport, Conn.: Greenwood Press.

Matthews, Donald R. 1960. *U.S. Senators and Their World.* Chapel Hill: University of North Carolina Press.

Mayhew, David R. 1974. *Congress: The Electoral Connection.* New Haven, Conn.: Yale University Press.

Merida, Kevin. 1999. "The Senate Vigil of a House Democrat." *Washington Post,* 22 January: C1.

Mitchell, Alison. 1999. "Congress Returns to a Shadow Cast by Impeachment." *New York Times,* 4 January: A1.

———. 1999. "The President's Trial: The Assessment." *New York Times,* 28 January: A24.

———. 1999. "The Trial of a President: The Overview; Senate, in Unanimity, Sets Rules for Trial." *New York Times,* 9 January: A1.

Morris, Irwin L. 2002. *Votes, Money, and the Clinton Impeachment.* Boulder, Colo.: Westview Press.

Myers, E. Michael. 1999. "After the Summing Up, Hyde Reflects on Trial." *The Hill,* 20 January: 12.

———. 1999. "Sen. Feinstein, Long Considered a Swing Vote; Not Persuaded by House Managers' Arguments." *The Hill,* 27 January: 4.

Neal, Terry M. 1999. "As Jury, Senate Is Full of Conflicts; Lawmakers Vow Impartiality Despite Personal Connections." *Washington Post,* 15 January: A18.

Neustadt, Richard E. 1990. *Presidential Power and the Modern Presidents: The Politics of Leadership from Roosevelt to Reagan,* 3d edition. New York: Free Press.

Nichols, Stephen M. 2002. "Schiff Defeats Rogan in California's 27th District Race." In *The Roads to Congress, 2000,* ed. Sunil Ahuja and Robert Dewhirst. Stamford, Conn.: Wadsworth.

O'Donnell, Norah M., and John Mercurio. 1999. "Managers React with Disappointment and Resignation." *Roll Call,* 15 February: 9.

Oleszek, Walter J. 2001. *Congressional Procedures and the Policy Process,* 5th edition. Washington, D.C.: CQ Press.

Oliver, Robert T. 1965. *History of Public Speaking in America.* Boston: Allyn and Bacon.

O'Neill, Thomas P. 1987. *Man of the House.* New York: St. Martin's.

Ornstein, Norman J. 2000. "Civility, Deliberation, and Impeachment." In *Esteemed Colleagues: Civility and Deliberation in the U.S. Senate,* ed. Burdett A. Loomis. Washington, D.C.: Brookings Institution.

Ornstein, Norman J., and Tomas E. Mann, ed. 2000. *The Permanent Campaign and Its Future.* Washington, D.C.: The AEI Press.

Ornstein, Norman J., Thomas E. Mann, and Michael J. Malbin. 2000. *Vital Statistics on Congress: 1999–2000.* Washington, D.C.: American Enterprise Institute.

————. 1998. *Vital Statistics on Congress: 1997–1998.* Washington, D.C.: American Enterprise Institute.

Ornstein, Norman J., Robert L. Peabody, and David W. Rohde. 1997. "The U.S. Senate: Toward the 21st Century." In *Congress Reconsidered,* 6th edition. Ed. Lawrence C. Dodd and Bruce I. Oppenheimer. Washington, D.C.: CQ Press.

————. 1985. "The Senate through the 1980s: Cycles of Change." In *Congress Reconsidered,* 3d edition. Ed. Lawrence C. Dodd and Bruce I. Oppenheimer. Washington, D.C.: CQ Press.

Osborne, B. Jonathan. 1999. "Media Coverage Mixed Blessing for Managers." *The Hill,* 20 January: 11.

Ostrogorski, Moisei I. 1974. *Democracy and the Party System in the United* States. New York: Arno Press, 1974.

Patterson, James T. 1967. *Congressional Conservatism and the New Deal: The Growth of the Conservative Coalition in Congress.* Lexington: University of Kentucky Press.

Patterson, Samuel C. 1979. "The Semi-sovereign Congress." In *The New American Political System,* ed. Anthony King. Washington, D.C.: American Enterprise Institute.

Peabody, Robert L. 1981. "Senate Party Leadership from the 1950s to the 1980s." In *Understanding Congressional Leadership,* ed. Frank H. Mackaman. Washington, D.C.: CQ Press.

Pershing, Ben. 1998. "Rules Trace Articles' Path from Chamber to Chamber." *Roll Call,* 21 December: 15.

Pianin, Eric, and Guy Gugliotta. 1999. Senate's Fiercest Partisan Battle Possible over 'Findings of Fact.'" *Washington Post,* 4 February: A7.

————. 1998. "Likelihood of Impeachment Grows in House; Republicans See Clinton As Arrogant, Unrepentant." *Washington Post,* 6 December: A1, A9.

Pitkin, Hanna F. 1978. *The Concept of Representation.* Berkeley: University of California Press.

Pitney, John J., Jr. 2001. "War on the Floor." In *Congressional Parity—Where Do We Go from Here? Extensions of Remarks,* ed. Burdett A. Loomis. Lawrence: University Press of Kansas.

Posner, Richard A. 1999. *An Affair of State: The Investigation, Impeachment, and Trial of President Clinton.* Cambridge, Mass.: Harvard University Press.

Price, David E. 2000. *The Congressional Experience,* 2d edition. Boulder, Colo.: Westview Press. "Quantifying the Impeachment Proceedings." 1999. *Washington Post,* 13 February: A32.

Quirk, Paul J., and Joseph Hinchcliffe. 1996. "Domestic Policy: The Trials of a Centrist Democrat." In *The Clinton Presidency: First Appraisals,* ed. Colin Campbell and Bert A. Rockman. Chatham, N.J.: Chatham House.

Rae, Nicol C. 2000. "Clinton and the Democrats: The President As Party Leader." In *The Postmodern Presidency: Bill Clinton's Legacy in U.S. Politics,* ed. Steven E. Schier. Pittsburgh: University of Pittsburgh Press.

———. 1998. *Conservative Reformers: The Republican Freshmen and the Lessons of the 104th Congress.* Armonk, N.Y.: M. E. Sharpe.

———. 1994. *Southern Democrats.* New York: Oxford University Press.

Rae, Nicol C., and Colton C. Campbell. 2000. "Ignoring Electoral Outcomes: House Judiciary Committee Republicans and the Clinton Impeachment." Presented at the Annual Meeting of the Midwest Political Science Association, Chicago, Ill., April 28–30.

Randon Hershey, Majorie, and Paul Allen Beck. 2003. *Party Politics in America,* 10th edition. New York: Addison-Wesley Educational Publishers.

Ranney, Austin, and Willmoore Kindall. 1974. *Democracy and the American Party System.* Westport, Conn.: Greenwood Press.

Remington, Michael J. 1995. "Impeachment." In *The Encyclopedia of the United States Congress,* vol. 2. Ed. Donald C. Bacon, Roger H. Davidson, and Morton Keller. New York: Simon & Schuster.

Ripey, Thomas B. 1998. *Standard of Proof in Senate Impeachment Proceedings.* CRS Report No. 98-990 A. Washington, D.C.: Congressional Research Service.

Ripley, Randall B. 1985. "Power in the Post–World War II Senate." In *Studies of Congress,* ed. Glenn R. Parker. Washington, D.C.: CQ Press.

Ritchie, Donald A. 1991. *Press Gallery: Congress and the Washington Correspondents.* Cambridge, Mass.: Harvard University Press.

Rohde, David W. 1991. *Parties and Leaders in the Postreform House.* Chicago, Ill.: University of Chicago Press.

Rothenberg, Stuart. 1999. "Is Clinton 'Vendetta' the Opening GOP Needs to Recover?" *Roll Call,* 15 February: 6.

———. 1998. "Will Impeachment Be GOP Version of The Health Care Debacle?" *Roll Call,* 14 December: 6.

"Scenes from Senate Trial." 1999. *The Hill,* 20 January: 1.

Schier, Steven E. 2000. *By Invitation Only: The Rise of Exclusive Politics in the United States.* Pittsburgh, Pa.: University of Pittsburgh Press.

Schmidt, Susan, and Michael Weisskopf. 2000. *Truth at Any Cost: Ken Starr and the Unmaking of Bill Clinton.* New York: HarperCollins.

Schmitt, Eric. 1999. "Obstruction Charge Drove Managers' Witness Choices." *New York Times,* 28 January: A1.

———. 1999. The President's Trial: The Overview: Democrats Urge Censure Measure but G.O.P. Balks." *New York Times,* 8 February: A1.

———. 1999. "The President's Trial: The Proceedings; Senate Unity on Reprimand is Elusive." *New York Times,* 5 February: A23.

Schneider, Jerrold E. 1979. *Ideological Coalitions in Congress.* Westport, Conn.: Greenwood Press.

Seliger, Martin. 1976. *Ideology and Politics.* New York: Free Press.

"Sen. Byrd: 'Impeachment Is a Sword of Damocles'; Quotes from Senators and Other Key Players in the Senate." 1999. *Roll Call,* 15 February: 1.

Shafer, Byron E. 1991. *The End of Realignment?: Interpreting American Electoral Eras.* Madison: University of Wisconsin Press.

Silbey, Joel H. 1991. *The American Political Nation, 1838–1893*. Palo Alto, Calif.: Stanford University Press.

———. 1967. *The Shrine of Party: Congressional Voting Behavior, 1841–1852*. Pittsburgh: University of Pittsburgh Press.

Sinclair, Barbara. 2001. "The Senate Leadership Dilemma: Passing Bills and Pursuing Partisan Advantage in a Nonmajoritarian Chamber." In *The Contentious Senate: Partisanship, Ideology, and the Myth of Cool Judgment*, ed. Colton C. Campbell and Nicol C. Rae. Lanham, Md.: Rowman & Littlefield.

———. 2000. *Unorthodox Lawmaking: New Legislative Processes in the U.S. Congress*, 2d edition. Washington, D.C.: CQ Press.

———. 1999. "The President As Legislative Leader." In *The Clinton Legacy*, ed. Colin Campbell and Bert A. Rockman. Chatham, N.J.: Chatham House.

———. 1997. *Unorthodox Lawmaking: New Legislative Processes in the U.S. Congress*, 1st edition. Washington, D.C.: CQ Press.

———. 1996. "Trying to Govern Positively in a Negative Era." In *The Clinton Presidency: First Appraisals*, ed. Colin Campbell and Bert A. Rockman. Chatham, N.J.: Chatham House.

———. 1995. *Legislators, Leaders, and Lawmaking: The U.S. House of Representatives in the Postreform Era*. Baltimore, Md.: Johns Hopkins University Press.

———. 1989. *The Transformation of the United States Senate*. Baltimore, Md.: Johns Hopkins University Press.

———. 1983. *Majority Leadership in the U.S. House*. Baltimore, Md.: Johns Hopkins University Press.

Skocpol, Theda. 1997. *Boomerang: Health Care Reform and the Turn against Government*. New York: W. W. Norton.

Smith, Steven S. 1993. "Forces of Change in Senate Party Leadership and Organization." In *Congress Reconsidered*, 5th edition. Ed. Lawrence C. Dodd and Bruce I. Oppenheimer. Washington, D.C.: CQ Press.

———. 1989. *Call to Order: Floor Politics in the House and Senate*. Washington, D.C.: Brookings Institution.

———. 1989. "Taking It to the Floor." In *Congress Reconsidered*, 4th edition. Ed. Lawrence C. Dodd and Bruce I. Oppenheimer. Washington, D.C.: CQ Press.

Snyder, Alan K. 2001. *Mission Impeachable: The House Managers and the Historic Impeachment of President Clinton*. Vienna, Va.: Allegiance Press.

Specter, Arlen, with Charles Robbins. 2000. *Passion for Truth: From Finding JFK's Single Bullet to Questioning Anita Hill to Impeaching Clinton*. New York: William Morrow.

Stathis, Stephen W., and David C. Huckabee. 1998. *Congressional Resolutions on Presidential Impeachment: A Historical Overview*. CRS Report No. 98-763 GOV. Washington, D.C.: Congressional Research Service.

Stewart, James. 1996. *Blood Sport: The President and His Adversaries*. New York: Simon & Schuster.

Stoddard, A. B. 1999. "Lott Relied on Key Senators As Link to House." *The Hill*, 17 February: 1.

Stoddard, A. B., and Philippe Shepnick. 1999. "Managers Weigh 'Jane Doe' Witnesses." *The Hill*, 20 January: 1, 40.

Sullivan, Terry. 1998. "Impeachment Practice in the Era of Lethal Conflict." *Congress and the Presidency* 25(2): 117–128.

Sundquist, James L. 1983. *Dynamics of the Party System: Alignment and Realignment of Political Parties in the United States.* Washington, D.C.: Brookings Institution.

———. 1981. *The Decline and Resurgence of Congress.* Washington, D.C.: Brookings Institution.

Swift, Elaine L. 1996. *The Making of an American Senate: Reconstitutive Change in Congress, 1787–1841.* Ann Arbor: University of Michigan Press.

Taylor, Andrew. 1998. "Is Livingston the Manager the House Needs?" *Congressional Quarterly Weekly Report,* 14 November: 3050–3054.

"Testing of a President; Clinton's Responses to Questions from the House Judiciary Committee." 1988. *New York Times,* 28 November: A12.

Thomas, David Y. 1908. "The Law of Impeachment in the United States." *American Political Science Review* 2(3): 378–395.

Tocqueville, Alexis de. 1988. *Democracy in America.* Edited by J. P. Mayer. Translated by George Lawrence. New York: Harper & Row.

Toobin, Jeffrey. 2000. *A Vast Conspiracy: The Real Story of the Sex Scandal That Nearly Brought Down a President.* New York: Random House.

Uslaner, Eric M. 1999. *The Movers and the Shirkers: Representatives and Ideologues in the Senate.* Ann Arbor: University of Michigan Press.

———. 1993. *The Decline of Comity in Congress.* Ann Arbor: University of Michigan Press.

VandeHei, Jim. 1999. "Managers Working on Witness List; Many Want Clinton." *Roll Call,* 18 January: 28.

———. 1999. "Speaker Hastert Spending His Time on House Agenda, Not Impeachment." *Roll Call,* 18 January: 8.

VandeHei, Jim, and John Bresnahan. 1999. "House Managers Set to Argue for Witnesses, Extended Trial." *Roll Call,* 14 January: 1, 16.

Van Dongen, Rachel, and Norah M. O'Donnell. 1998. "Is Vote 'Political Suicide'?" *Roll Call,* 17 December: 9, 14.

Van Tassel, Emily Field, and Paul Finkelman. 1999. *Impeachable Offenses: A Documentary History from 1787 to the Present.* Washington, D.C.: Congressional Quarterly, Inc.

Volcansek, Mary L. 1993. *Judicial Impeachment: None Called for Justice.* Urbana: University of Illinois Press.

Von Drehle, David. 1999. "Hushed Galleries, Somber Senators, Powerful Moment." *Washington Post,* 13 February: A1.

Voorhis, Jerry. 1947. *Confessions of a Congressman.* Westport, Conn.: Greenwood Publishers.

Wallison, Ethan. 1999. "House GOP Moderates Just Glad It's Over." *Roll Call,* 15 February: 14.

Walsh, Edward. 1998. "The Bitterness of Being in the Minority; House Democrats Watch Helplessly As Republican Juggernaut Rolls On." *Washington Post,* 19 December: A27.

Weatherford, J. McIver. 1985. *Tribes on the Hill: The U.S. Congress Rituals and Realities,* revised edition. South Hadley, Mass.: Bergin & Garvey.

Weingast, Barry, and W. Marshall. 1988. "The Industrial Organization of Congress." *Journal of Political Economy* 91: 775–800.

West, Paul. 1999. "In the Senate, a Solemn Ritual; Chamber Now Enters Unchartered Waters." *Baltimore Sun,* 8 January: 1A.

Wildavsky, Aaron B. 1991. *The Rise of Radical Egalitarianism.* Washington, D.C.: American University Press.

————. 1971. *The Revolt against the Masses and Other Essays in Politics and Public Policy.* New York: Basic Books.

Wilson, James Q. 1962. *The Amateur Democrat: Club Politics in Three Cities.* Chicago: University of Chicago Press.

Wilson, Woodrow. 1956. *Congressional Government.* New York: Meridian.

Wolfe, Alan. 1998. *One Nation, After All: What Middle-Class Americans Really Think About: God, Country, Family, Racism, Welfare, Immigration, Homosexuality, Work, the Right, the Left, and Each Other.* New York: Viking.

Wolfensberger, Donald R. 2000. *Congress and the People: Deliberative Democracy on Trial.* Washington, D.C.: Woodrow Wilson Center Press; Baltimore, Md.: Johns Hopkins University Press.

————. 1998. "History Shows 'Censure Peradventure' Is a Better Punishment for Clinton." *Roll Call,* 3 December: 5.

Wright, Gerald C., Jr. 1977. "Constituency Response to Congressional Behavior: The Impact of the House Judiciary Committee Impeachment Votes." *Western Political Quarterly* 30: 401–410.

GOVERNMENT DOCUMENTS AND PUBLICATIONS

Congressional Record. 1970. 91st Cong., 2d sess., vol. 116, pt. 1.

Congressional Record. 1970. 91st Cong., 2d sess., vol. 116, pt. 2.

Congressional Record. 1998. 105th Cong., 2d sess., vol. 144, pt. 1.

Congressional Record. 1999. 106th Cong., 1st sess., vol. 145, pt. 2.

U.S. Congress. Senate. 1933. *Proceedings of the United States Senate in the Trial of Impeachment of Harold Louderback, United States District Judge for the Northern District of California.* 73d Cong., 1st sess., S. doc. 73. Washington, D.C.: Government Printing Office.

U.S. Congress. Senate. 1986. *Procedure and Guidelines for Impeachment Trials in the United States Senate,* revised edition. 99th Cong., 2d sess., S. Doc. 99-33. Washington, D.C.: Government Printing Office.

U.S. Congress. House. Committee on House Administration. 1994. *History of the United States House of Representatives, 1789–1994.* 103d Cong., 2d sess. Washington, D.C.: Government Printing Office.

U.S. Congress. Senate. 1986. *Procedure and Guidelines for Impeachment Trials in the United States Senate.* 99th Cong., 2d sess., S. Doc. 99-33. Washington, D.C.: Government Printing Office.

U.S. Senate. Historical Office. *www.senate.gov/learning/learn_history.html.*

Index

Abraham, Spencer, 203(n94)
Abuse of power, 4, 26(table), 70, 97, 118, 119(table), 154, 176–177
Abuse of trust, 137
ACA. *See* Americans for Constitutional Action
Activists, 12, 13, 94
ADA. *See* Americans for Democratic Action
Adams, John, 42, 50–51(table)
Albert, Carl, 27
Allard, Wayne, 200–201(n34)
American Political Science Association, 10–11, 156
Americans for Constitutional Action (ACA), 58, 59(table)
Americans for Democratic Action (ADA), 58, 59(table), 86, 87(table)
"Anti-Republican" attitude, 42
Archbald, Robert W., 35–38(tables), 44
Armey, Dick, 101
Ashurst, Henry F., 45

Bad policy decisions, 26(table)
Baker, Howard H., Jr., 126, 127
Baker, Peter, 106, 123, 137
Baker, Ross K., 127, 129, 135, 200–201(n34)
Barr, Bob, 59(table), 60, 66–67(tables), 107, 116, 133
Barrett, Thomas M., 92
Bayard, Thomas, 50–51(table)
Bazen, Elizabeth A., 33
Belknap, William W., 35-38(tables), 47(table)
Bennett, Robert F., 136, 138, 144, 147
Bentsen, Ken, 116–117
Berman, Howard, 62, 87(table), 103
Biased conduct, 42

Biden, Joseph R., 29, 143
Binder, Sarah A., 144
Blount, William, 31–32, 34, 35–41(tables), 40
Blumenthal, Sidney, 3, 5, 71–72, 138
Boehlert, Sherwood, 198(n86)
Bomb threat (1999), 147
Bonior, David E., 115
Bono, Mary, 59(table), 66–67(tables)
Bork, Robert, 16, 126
Boucher, Rick, 87(table), 88, 90, 92, 110
Boxer, Barbara, 131
Breaux, John B., 125
Bribery, 25, 34, 46, 48
  and conspiracy to solicit a bribe, 34, 46
Broaddrick, Juanita, 110, 130
Brooks, Jack, 87(table)
Bryan, Richard H., 147
Bryant, Ed, 59(table), 66–67(tables)
Bryce, James, 53
Buchanan, James, 50–51(table)
Budget deficit, 76–77
Bumpers, Dale, 137
Bunning, Jim, 131
Burr, Aaron, 43, 52
Burton, Dan, 21, 81
Bush, George H. W., 15, 26–27(tables), 48, 76, 94, 126
  congressional support, 149(table)
Bush, George W., 153
Butler, M. Caldwell, 59(table)
Buyer, Stephen E., 59(table), 66–67(tables), 110
Byrd, Robert C., 126, 127, 128, 133, 138, 142, 143, 150

Calhoun, John C., 112
Cameron, Simon, 50–51(table)
Campaign finance, 5, 13

Canady, Charles T., 55, 56–57, 59(table), 60–61, 62, 63, 65, 66–67(tables), 68, 71, 100

Candidate-centered campaigns, 125

Cannon, Christopher B., 59(table), 61, 66–67 (tables), 70–71

Cannon, Joseph G., 9, 15

Cannon Revolt (1910–1911), 15, 184(n50)

Carter, Jimmy, 125, 149(table), 150

Castle, Mike, 108, 198(n86)

Censure, 4, 49–52, 65, 69–70, 91–92, 93(fig.), 101, 102–103, 108, 118–120, 142, 147, 153, 190(n108). *See also* Finding of fact

Central Intelligence Agency (CIA), 48

Chabot, Steve, 59, 66–67(tables)

Chafee, John H., 146, 147

Chase, Samuel, 35–41(tables), 42–43

Chester, Giraud, 112

CIA. *See* Central Intelligence Agency

Civil rights, 9, 10, 12

Civil War reconstruction, 43

Claiborne, Harry E., 31, 35–41(tables), 38–41(table), 45–46

Clay, Henry, 49, 112

Cleland, Max, 145

Cleveland, Grover, 27(table)

Clinton, Bill (William Jefferson)
  attorney, 133
  campaign fundraising, 21, 79–80, 107
  and censure, 101, 102–103, 118–120, 142, 147, 153. *See also* House Judiciary Committee, and censure of Clinton
  and congressional support, 148–149, 150
  and Democrats, 75, 77, 80, 81, 82–83, 86, 88, 92, 93(fig.), 97, 109, 111, 115, 118, 119(table), 125, 127, 142, 147–148
  impeachment acquittal (1999), 5, 146–148
  impeachment and House Judiciary Committee, 59(table), 60–74, 88–90, 92, 97, 101
  impeachment by House of Representatives, 1, 2, 4, 29, 38–41(tables), 53, 56, 60, 86, 88, 91, 97, 98, 114–118, 119(table), 151, 174–177

impeachment opposition by public, 1–2, 61, 63, 84, 90, 93, 95, 97, 155
  and "Jane Does," 110
  and Paula Corbin Jones, 2, 3, 4, 70, 80, 83
  as moderate, 19
  policies, 19–20, 21, 75, 76–77, 78–79, 80, 99
  questions from House Judiciary Committee, 4, 102, 105–106, 161–174
  scandals. *See* Jones, Paula Corbin; Lewinsky, Monica; White House Travel Office; Whitewater land deal
  secretary. *See* Currie, Betty
  and Starr grand jury, 3, 4, 61, 83
  and Starr Report release, 85
  trial by Senate (1999), 1, 4–5, 31, 35–41 (tables), 122–123, 132–148, 151, 177–180
  trial by Senate preliminary, 126–132
  veto, 78–79
  videotape of testimony, 61–62, 83, 84
  See also Lewinsky, Monica; "New Democrat"

Clinton, Hillary Rodham, 3, 75, 81, 131

Coates, Dan, 106

Coble, Howard, 56, 57, 58, 59(table), 60, 66–67(tables), 68, 70, 152

Cochran, Thad, 122, 123, 126, 127, 141

Cohen, William S., 17, 19, 59(table)

Collins, Susan, 136, 141, 146, 147, 203(n94)

Confederates, 43

Congress
  assertiveness, 154–155
  committee chairs, 11, 12, 20
  decision making, 6, 111–113
  elections, 12, 76
  and presidential support, 148–150, 204–205(nn130–131, 134)
  redistricting, 14, 103
  and reelection, 55–56, 98, 103
  See also Democrats; House of Representatives; Republicans; Senate

Congressional Quarterly, 17, 58
  Presidential Support Index, 204–205(nn130–131, 134)

Congressional Record, 28, 113, 142

Connor, George E., 112

"Conservative coalition" (1930s–1970s), 10, 11–12, 14–15, 94, 125
Conservatives, 10, 12. *See also under* Democrats; Republicans
Conservative states, 153
Constitution
    Amendment 22, 155
    and censure, 190(n108)
    violation of, 27(table), 63
    See also under Impeachment
"Contract with America," 20, 78, 126, 156
Conyers, John, Jr., 87(table)
Court orders defied, 27(table)
"Court-packing," 9, 10
Court TV (television channel), 132
Cox, Archibald, 186(n23)
Craig, Gregory, 89, 103, 135–136
Craig, Larry E., 141, 142
Crapo, Michael D., 131
Crédit Mobilier scandal (1872), 52
Currie, Betty, 3, 71, 202(n65)
Cutler, Lloyd, 102

D'Amato, Alfonse M., 21
Danielson, George E., 87(table)
Daschle, Tom, 20, 79, 126, 127, 133
Dash, Sam, 102
Davidson, Roger H., 7, 52
Decision contrary to law, 42
Deering, Christopher J., 56
Defense of Marriage Act (DOMA), 79
Delahay, Mark, 35–41(tables)
Delahunt, William, 60, 97(table), 92
Delay, Tom ("The Hammer"), 68, 07, 101, 104–105, 106, 107, 109, 111, 117, 120, 152
Democratic Study Group (DSG), 206(n18)
Democrats
    and George H. Bush, 94
    centrist, 125
    and Clinton impeachment vote, 4, 6, 7, 63, 70, 102, 117, 136, 145–146, 147, 153, 177–180, 198(n87)
    as congressional majority, 11, 19
    as congressional minority, 78, 80
    conservative, 86, 88, 95
    constituency, 93, 95
    grassroots, 12
    and House Democratic Caucus, 15, 206(n18)

interest groups, 13
    liberal, 12, 77, 80, 81, 85, 152
    midterm elections (1862–1998), 78(table)
    midterm elections (1994), 77–78
    moderate, 86, 88, 109
    "New," 19, 77
    Northern, 12
    and party unity, 17, 18(fig.)
    and Reagan, 94
    and redistricting, 4
    and Senate deposition procedures, 138, 139–140(fig.)
    Southern, 10, 12, 14, 88, 95, 125
    Southern Black, 12
    and Starr Report, 61–62, 83
    and support of presidents, 149–150
    See also Ideology; *under* Clinton, Bill; House Judiciary Committee
Dennis, David W., 59(table)
DeWine, Mike, 203(n94)
Dingell, John, 61, 62
Direct primary, 9, 14
"Disorderly behavior," 40
Dodd, Christopher J., 135, 138
Dole, Robert J., 19, 20, 66–67, 79, 126
DOMA. *See* Defense of Marriage Act
Domenici, Pete V., 128, 141
Donohue, Harold D., 87(table)
Dorgan, Byron L., 136
Douglas, William O., 23, 189–190(n105)
Drinan, Robert F., 87(table)
Drunkenness, 33, 42
DSG. *See* Democratic Study Group
Dukakis, Michael, 76
Durbin, Richard J., 130, 143
Duverger, Maurice, 10, 13

Edwards, William D., 87(table)
Eilberg, Joshua, 87(table)
Eisenhower, Dwight D., 149(table)
Election
    1862–1998 (midterm), 78(table), 86
    1994 (midterm), 77, 98
    1996, 66–67(tables), 80, 95
    1998 (midterm), 2, 4, 56, 64–68, 78(table), 90, 91, 99, 120
    2000, 96, 157
    turnout, 103
English, George, 35–41(tables)

English, Phil, 198(n86)
Epstein, Julian, 88
Epstein, Leon, 10

Failure of moral leadership, 26(table)
Faircloth, Duncan McLauchlin ("Lauch"), 21
"Fairness Document" (Lofgren), 88
False statements to grand jury, 34, 141
FBI. *See* Federal Bureau of Investigation
Federal Bureau of Investigation (FBI), 48
    files "theft," 20, 82
Federalist
    No. 52, 98
    No. 65, 1, 7, 23
    No. 68, 24
Federalists, 32, 42
Feingold, Russell D., 138, 145
Feinstein, Diane, 142, 143, 148
Fenno, Richard F., Jr., 11, 56, 103, 127, 144, 195(n2)
Finding of fact, 141
Finkelman, Paul, 41
Fish, Hamilton, Jr., 59(table)
Fiske, Robert, 20, 21, 82, 132, 185(n77)
Flannery, John, 88, 90
Flowers, Walter, 87(table)
Flynt, Larry, 114
Ford, Gerald R., 23, 148, 149(table)
Foster, Vincent, 20, 82
Frank, Barney, 75, 81, 83, 84, 85, 86, 87(table), 89, 91, 92
Freedmen's Bureau Act (1865), 43
Free trade, 80
Froelich, Harold, 59(table)
Frost, Martin, 76, 99–100

Gallegly, Elton, 59(table), 66–67(tables)
Garland, A. H., 50–51(table)
Gekas, George W., 59(table), 66–67(tables), 202(n65)
Gephardt, Richard, 62, 79, 84, 86–87, 89, 93, 117
Gerhardt, Michael J., 52
Gingrich, Newt, 4, 15–16, 20, 68, 76, 85, 90–91, 98–101, 104, 116, 155, 156
Goldwater, Barry, 12, 67
Goode, Virgil H., Jr., 198(n87)
Goodlatte, Bob, 59(table), 66–67(tables)

Gore, Al, 21, 77, 96, 153
Gorton, Slade, 128–130, 146, 203(n94)
Gorton-Lieberman plan, 128–130
Government shutdown (1995), 78–79, 98
Graham, Bob, 6, 138, 141
Graham, Lindsey O., 6, 58, 59–60, 61–62, 66–67(tables), 68, 69, 70, 71–72, 74, 102, 103, 106, 107, 147
Gramm, Phil, 134, 135, 142
Gramm-Kennedy plan, 134, 135
Grassley, Charles E., 142
Great Society, 76
Grimes, Warren S., 53
Gurney, Joseph ("Uncle Joe"), 8

Hagel, Chuck, 203(n94)
Hall, Ralph M., 198(n87)
Hamilton, Alexander, 1, 7, 23, 24, 25, 30, 43, 50–51(table)
Harkin, Tom, 133, 142
Hastert, Dennis J., 4
Hastings, Alcee L., 32, 35–41(tables), 38–41(tables), 46, 47(table), 188(n60)
Hastings, Warren, 24
Hatch, Orrin G., 128
Helms, Jesse, 21, 82, 185(n77)
Hendricks, Thomas Andrews, 131
"High crimes and misdemeanors," 25, 42, 43, 115
Hoar, George F., 44
Hogan, Lawrence J., 59(table)
Hollings, Ernest F. ("Fritz"), 29
Holt, Rush, 91
Holtzman, Elizabeth, 87(table)
Hoover, Herbert, 26–27(tables)
Houghton, Amo, 198(n86)
House Appropriations Committee, 56, 57, 100
House Banking Committee, 21, 81–82
House Commerce Committee, 57
House Ethics Committee, 85
House Government Operations Committee, 21, 81
House Judiciary Committee
    articles of impeachment, 4, 106, 174–177
    bipartisan group, 69–70, 84, 94
    and censure of Clinton, 65, 69–70, 92–93, 102–103, 109–110

chairmen. *See* Hyde, Henry J.; Rodino, Peter W., Jr.
created (1813), 27
Democrats on, 70, 75–76, 84, 85–86, 87, 88–91, 152
impeachment charges, 25, 27, 28, 29, 33, 46, 48, 60–74, 84, 151
impeachment inquiry (1998), 4, 56–60, 63, 70, 85, 88, 90–91, 101
impeachment resolutions tabled, 48
members (1974, 1998), 59(table), 87(table), 94. *See also individual names*
Minority Counsel, 88
partisanship, 6, 7, 53–54, 57–60, 68, 72, 84, 85, 86, 87(table), 102
Republican ideology, 59(table), 86
Republicans on, 56–60, 64, 65, 66–67(tables), 68–74, 84, 85, 86, 88, 89, 101, 106, 110, 116
House of Representatives
and censure, 49–52, 91–92, 93(fig.), 101, 102–103, 108–109
committees, 9, 14–15, 20, 21, 28, 56, 57
and debate and deliberation, 111–114, 197(n53)
Democratic Caucus, 15, 78, 81, 78, 81, 86, 206(n18)
Democratic majority, 19, 76, 91, 114
Democratic minority, 75, 80, 95, 120–121
and impeachment, 26–30, 33, 46–48, 189–190(n105). *See also* House Judiciary Committee
impeachment of Clinton. *See impeachment subentries under* Clinton, Bill
impeachment trial managers, 29, 31, 33, 123, 127, 134, 136, 144, 145, 147, 202(n65)
partisanship, 7, 15, 16–19, 81, 93, 94, 95, 98, 103, 117, 118, 121, 123, 135–136, 148, 152–153, 157
and popular will, 55
and presidential support, 148–150
and proportional representation, 14
Republican majority, 16, 20, 77, 80, 96, 155
Republican minority, 15–16
Resolution 581, 88

scandals, 19
Select Committee on the Impeachment of the President (pre-1813), 27, 43
speakers. *See* Gingrich, Newt; Hastert, Dennis J.; Livingston, Robert L.; O'Neill, Thomas P.
House Rules Committee, 15, 184(n50)
and impeachment, 25, 27
House Ways and Means Committee, 15, 56, 57
Huckabee, David C., 25
Humphreys, West H., 35–41(tables), 47(table)
Hungate, William L., 87(table)
Hutchinson, Asa, 59(table), 61, 65, 66–67(tables), 69, 102, 107, 131
Hutchinson, Edward, 59(table)
Hutchinson, Tim, 131
Hutchison, Kay Bailey, 146, 203(n94)
Hyde, Henry J., 4, 55, 58–59, 62, 63, 70, 66–67(tables), 68, 73, 85, 86, 88, 89, 90, 98, 100, 101, 102, 109, 115, 119, 151, 152

Ideology, 6, 7, 10, 11, 12, 14, 19, 53, 104, 156, 181(n11)
activists, 12–13, 19, 157
of House Judiciary Committee Democrats, 87 (table)
of House Judiciary Committee Republicans, 59(table), 86
of Senate, 123, 125, 148
See also Political partisanship and polarization
Impeachable offense, 23, 87, 88
as criminal not political, 43
as political, 53
Impeachment
articles of, 28, 30, 34, 44, 97, 117–118, 119(table), 150, 174–180, 198(nn86,87)
cases, 33–48
charges against presidents, 7, 8, 25, 26–27, 33, 35–41(tables), 43–44, 84, 115
and "civil officers of the United States," 23–24, 25, 29, 30, 35–41(tables), 189–190(n105)
consideration time, 34, 36–41(tables), 47(table), 160–161, 180

Impeachment, *continued*
  Constitution on, 25, 29, 31, 32–33, 42,
    115, 144, 147, 150
  convictions, 46
  first, 31–32, 34, 35–41(tables)
  Alexander Hamilton on, 1, 7, 24, 30
  Thomas Jefferson on, 154
  on moral grounds, 115, 150
  nature of, 154
  origins of, 24–25
  and perjury based on sex, 115
  as political, 1, 2, 17, 52–54, 74, 89, 150,
    151, 154
  procedures, 28–30, 154
  as remedy to protect the nation, 116
  See also Censure; Finding of fact; *under*
    Clinton, Bill; House Judiciary
    Committee; House of
    Representatives; House Rules
    Committee; Senate
Incitement to revolt, 33
Incumbency, 9, 11
Independent Counsel. *See* Starr, Kenneth
Inglis, Bob, 59(table), 66–67(tables)
Inhofe, James M., 148
Inouye, Daniel K., 132
Inslee, Jay, 91
Institutional patriotism, 127
Interest groups, 13, 15, 22, 72, 157. *See
  also* Political action committees
Internal Revenue Service (IRS), 48
Internet, 14, 84
Interventionism, 9
Iran-Contra scandal (1986), 52, 108
Iraq, 114, 115
IRS. *See* Internal Revenue Service
Isolationism, 9

Jackson, Andrew, 49, 50–51(table), 141,
  203 (n88)
Jackson-Lee, Sheila, 29–30, 87(table)
Jamieson, Kathleen Hall, 113
Jefferson, Thomas, 34, 42, 154
Jeffersonian-Republicans, 32, 42
Jeffords, James M., 146, 147, 203(n94)
Jenkins, J. G., 50–51(table), 66–67(tables)
Jenkins, William L., 59(table)
Johnson, Andrew, 7–8, 25, 26–27(tables),
  30, 35–41(tables), 43–44, 47(table),
  53, 107, 131, 155

Johnson, Lyndon B., 12, 149
Johnson, Nancy, 198(n86)
Jones, Paula Corbin, 2, 3, 70, 80, 83
  settlement, 4
Jones v. Clinton (1997), 2, 132
Jordan, Barbara, 87(table)
Jordan, Vernon E., Jr., 3, 5, 83, 138
Judicial Watch, 81
Judiciary Act (1801), 42

Kastenmeier, Robert W., 87(table)
Kendall, David, 133
Kennedy, Anthony M., 32
Kennedy, Edward M., 128, 132, 134, 135
Kennedy, John F., 116, 149
Kennedy, Patrick J., 116–117
Kerrey, Bob, 83
Kickbacks, 34
Kim, Jay, 198(n86)
King, David C., 28
King, Peter, 97, 102, 105, 198(n86)
Kolodny, Robin, 17
Kyl, Jon, 132, 148, 203(n94)

Labovitz, John, 23, 52
LaHood, Ray, 117
Latta, Delbert L., 59(table)
Lautenberg, Frank, 132
Leach, Jim, 21, 82, 198(n86)
Leahy, Patrick J., 130, 135, 148
Leaking of information, 48
Legislative Reorganization Act (1970),
  206(n18)
Levin, Carl M., 131
Levin, Sander, 131
Lewinsky, Monica, 1, 2–3, 4, 5, 22, 56, 60,
  61, 71–72, 80, 81, 83, 130, 137, 139
Liberals, 10, 12
Lieberman, Joseph I., 83, 127, 128–130,
  141
  on Clinton, 129, 143
Lincoln, Abraham, 154–155
Linder, John, 99, 100
Livingston, Robert L., 4, 100–101, 105,
  109, 112, 114, 117
Locke, John, 8
Lofgren, Zoe, 75, 86, 87(table), 88, 89, 90,
  91, 95, 151
Loomis, Burdett A., 143, 144, 146, 150,
  153

Lott, Trent, 59(table), 67, 79, 126, 127, 130, 133, 134, 135, 138, 146–147
Louderback, Harold, 29, 35–41(tables), 44–45
Lowell, Abbie, 89, 102
Lugar, Richard G., 128, 203(n94)

Machine politics, 8–9
Mack, Connie, 148
Madison, James, 30, 97
"Manifest injury to the country," 42
Mann, James R., 87(table)
Maraziti, Joseph J., 59(table)
Mason, George, 25
Matthews, Donald R., 127
Mayhew, David R., 11, 103
Mayne, Wisley, 59(table)
McCain, John, 135, 203(n94)
McClory, Robert, 59(table)
McCollum, Bill, 59(table), 66–67(tables)
McConnell, Mitch, 135
McGovern, George, 12
McHale, Paul, 198(n87)
McHugh, John, 198(n86)
Meehan, Martin T., 87(table)
Meek, Carrie P., 6, 182(n13)
Mezvinsky, Edward, 87(table)
Michel, Robert, 20
Middle class, 12
Mikulski, Barbara, 146
Minorities proportional representation, 4
Misconduct, 26(table)
Mitchell, George, 126
Moorhead, Carlos J., 59(table)
Morella, Connie, 198(n86)
Morris, Dick, 79
Morris, Irwin L., 5
Morrison v. Olson (1988), 132
Morton, Oliver Hazard P.T., 131
Moynihan, Daniel Patrick, 83, 127
Murphy, George L., 198(n3)

Nadler, Jerrold, 81, 82–83, 85, 87–88, 115–116
Nationalization of politics, 13
Neal, Terry M., 131
New Deal, 9, 10, 76, 155
"New Democrat," 19, 77, 78
News media, 14, 68, 81, 88, 106, 108, 125, 157

Nickles, Don, 148
Nixon, Richard M., 26–27, 28, 33, 35–41(tables), 48, 50–51(table), 59(table), 63, 67, 84, 86, 87(table), 94, 143, 151–152, 155, 189–190(n23)
    and Congressional support, 149(table)
    resignation (1974), 48
Nixon, Walter L., Jr., 32, 35–41(tables), 46

Obstruction of justice, 4, 5, 27(table), 48, 83, 115, 118, 119(table), 175–176
    vote by Senate, 146–147, 177–178, 180
O'Connor, Sandra Day, 32
Ogilvie, Lloyd J., 137
Oleszek, Walter, 52
Oliver, Robert T., 112
O'Neill, Thomas P. ("Tip"), 6, 15
Oppenheimer, Bruce I., 112
Owens, Wayne D., 87(table)

PACs. *See* Political Action Committees
Packwood, Bob, 138
Patronage, 8
Pease, Edward A., 59(table), 66–67(tables), 110
Peck, James H., 32, 35–41(tables), 47(table)
Perjury, 4, 5, 10, 105, 115, 117, 118(fig.), 119(table), 136, 174–175, 180
    vote by Senate, 146, 177–178
Perot, Ross, 76, 80
Pickering, John, 35–41(tables), 41–42, 131
Pinckney, Charles Cotesworth, 30
Pitney, John J., Jr., 17
Political Action Committees (PACs), 5, 13, 72, 103, 104
Political culture, 8, 98–99
Political "mobilization," 103–104, 157
Political participation, 2, 13, 157
Political parties, 8–9, 157
    and congressional voting, 9
    cross-party alliance. *See* "Conservative coalition"
    and government reform, 156
    unity, 9–10, 17, 18(fig.), 124(fig.)
    and voter loyalty, 77, 103–104
    weakness and decline, 9, 10–11, 103
    in Western Europe, 10
    See also Ideology

Political partisanship and polarization, 1, 2, 5–6, 7–8, 14–17, 57–60, 81, 82, 94, 97, 110–111, 125, 143, 156–157. *See also* partisanship *under* House Judiciary Committee; House of Representatives; Senate
Polk, James K., 49, 50–51(table)
Presidential power, 155
Presidential term limits, 155
Price, David E., 97, 98, 109
Primaries. *See* Direct primary
Profanity, 42
Progressive reformers, 9

Quayle, Dan, 106

Radical Republicans, 43, 44
Radio, 14
Railsback, Thomas F., 59(table)
Rangel, Charles B., 87(table)
Reagan, Ronald, 15, 26–27(tables), 48, 94, 125
    Congressional support, 149(table)
    policies, 126
Rebellion against the nation, 33
Redistricting. *See under* Congress
Reed, Jack, 147
Reed, Thomas Brackett ("Czar"), 8
Regula, Ralph, 198(n86)
Rehnquist, William, 32, 132–133, 137, 146, 147
Remington, Michael J., 24
Reno, Janet, 3, 83
"Republican Revolution" (1994), 76, 98
Republicans
    and Clinton impeachment vote, 63, 88, 97, 99, 102, 104, 108, 111, 117, 118, 119(table), 120, 136, 144, 146–147, 177–180, 198(n86), 203(n94)
    as congressional majority, 16, 20, 94
    conservative, 12, 15, 21–22, 58, 67, 104, 148, 152
    constituency, 94–95
    grassroots, 12, 99
    interest groups, 13, 22
    Jeffersonian, 32, 42
    and Andrew Johnson, 7–8
    midterm election (1994), 77, 78(table)
    midterm elections (1862–1998), 78(table)
    moderate, 58, 108, 152
    and party unity, 17, 18(fig.), 148
    Radical, 43, 44
    and redistricting, 14
    Southern conservative, 12, 67, 125, 152, 153
    Speakers (1828–1948), 8, 9
    and Starr Report, 60–61
    voting behavior, 5–7, 10, 63, 88, 146–147
    Western conservative, 152
    women and Clinton impeachment, 108
    See also "Conservative coalition"; Ideology; *under* House Judiciary Committee
Revlon Corporation, 3
Richardson, Elliot L., 186(n23)
Ricks, Augustus J., 50–51(table)
Ripey, Thomas B., 33
Ritter, Halstead, 35–41(tables), 45, 47(table)
Rodino, Peter W., Jr., 28, 58, 84, 86, 87(table), 89, 94, 152
Rogan, James E., 59(table), 66–67(tables), 73, 116
Rohde, David W., 12
Roosevelt, Franklin Delano, 10, 155
Roosevelt, Theodore, 155
Rothman, Steven R., 87(table)
Ruckelshaus, William D., 186(n23)
Ruff, Charles, 144
"Rules of Procedure and Practice in the Senate when Sitting on Impeachment Trials" (*Senate Manual*), 30
Rutherford Institute, 2

Sandman, Charles W., 59(table)
Santorum, Rick, 148
Sarbanes, Paul S., 87(table)
"Saturday Night Massacre," 26, 186(n23)
Scalia, Antonin, 32
Schier, Steven E., 103
Schippers, David, 89
Schumer, Charles E., 87(table), 131, 141
Scott, Robert C., 87(table), 90
Secret Service, 3, 48
Sedition Acts (1798), 42
Seiberling, John F., 87(table)
Self-interest, 5

Senate
  "candy desk," 123, 198(n3)
  and censure, 49–52
  "centrists," 125
  collective disarray, 125
  committees, 9
  culture, 123, 127–128, 150, 200–201
    (n34)
  Democratic majority, 19, 126
  election, 14
  "Golden Age" (1810–1859), 134
  impeachment consideration of time, 34,
    40–41 (table), 47(table), 134, 180
  impeachment jurors, 131, 133
  impeachment presiding officer. See
    Rehnquist, William
  impeachment private deliberation, 142,
    203(n94)
  impeachment role and rules, 30–33, 34,
    40, 44, 45, 121, 127, 131, 133,
    139(fig.)
  parliamentarian, 17, 133, 184(n66)
  partisanship, 16, 17–19, 122, 123–126,
    150, 157
  and party unity, 124(fig.)
  and presidential support, 148–149,
    204–205(n130)
  Republican majority, 20, 77, 126
  registry, 133
  votes for impeachment needed, 129, 141
  witness deposition, 138
  See also Clinton, Bill, impeachment
    acquittal; Clinton, Bill, trial by
    Senate; Clinton, Bill, trial by Senate
    preliminary
Senate Banking Committee, 21
Senate Governmental Affairs Committee,
    21
Senate Manual, 30
Senility, 33, 42
Seniority rule, 9, 12
Sensenbrenner, James F., 45, 59(table),
    66–67(tables)
Sessions, Jeff, 144
Sentelle, David, 21, 82
Shaw, E. Clay, Jr., 100
Shays, Christopher, 110, 198(n86)
Shelby, Richard C., 146
Sinclair, Barbara, 15, 80, 104, 112, 125
Smith, Gordon H., 203(n94)

Smith, Henry P., III, 59(table)
Smith, Israel, 131
Smith, John, 131
Smith, Lamar S., 59(table), 66–67(tables)
Smith, Samuel, 131
Smith, Steven S., 56, 112, 144
Snowe, Olympia J., 141, 146, 147,
    203(n94)
Socialist parties, 10
Souder, Mark, 106–107, 108, 110, 111,
    198(n86)
Specter, Arlen, 122, 133, 136, 146, 147,
    203(n94)
Stanton, Edwin, 43
Starr, Kenneth
  as House Judiciary Committee witness,
    4, 102, 105
  Independent Counsel (1998), 1, 4, 21,
    60, 70, 82, 83, 102, 116, 120, 132,
    148, 152
  investigation costs, 82
  and "Jane Does," 110
  and neutrality, 102
  Report, 1, 4, 21, 61–62, 69, 83–84, 85,
    110, 180
  taped conversations from Linda Tripp, 3
  Whitewater testimony, 3–4
  See also Lewinsky, Monica
Stathis, Steven W., 25
Statutory law violation, 27(table)
Stenholm, Charles W., 198(n87)
Stevens, John Paul, 32
Stevens, Ted, 146, 203(n94)
Subversion of government, 48
Supreme Court, 2, 10, 16, 30
  chief justices and impeachment, 31, 32
  size, 42
Swayne, Charles, 35–41(tables), 44

Tampa Tribune, 68
Tax evasion, 34, 45
Taylor, Gene, 61, 198(n87)
Taylor, Zachary, 49
Teapot Dome scandal (1924), 52
Television, 14, 132
Terrorist attack (9/11/01), 157
Test Oath Law (1867), 43
Thomas, Clarence, 16, 32, 108, 126
Thomas, David Y., 25
Thompson, Fred, 21, 146

Thornton, Ray, 87(table)
Thurmond, Strom, 132, 135
Torricelli, Robert G., 143
Toucey, Isaac, 50–51(table)
"Toward a More Responsible Two-Party System" (American Political Science Association), 11, 156
Tower, John, 108
Treason, 25
"Triangulation" strategy, 79, 95
Tripp, Linda, 2–3, 116
Truman, Harry S, 26–27(tables), 189–190(n105)
Tyler, John, 26–27(tables), 49, 50–51(table)

"Unfaithfulness to the Union," 41
United Nations
  arms inspectors, 114
  Charter violation, 27(table)
U.S. v. Brig Eliza (1802), 42

Van Tassel, Emily Field, 41
Victor v. Nebraska (1994), 145
Volcansek, Mary L., 24
Voting Rights Act (1965), 12, 14

Wade, Benjamin F., 131, 201(n51)
Wag the Dog (film), 114
Waldie, Jerome R., 87(table)
Walker, Robert S., 104
Walsh, Lawrence, 108
Warner, John, 133, 146
Washington, George, 8
Washington Post, 106
Watergate scandal (1972), 48, 52, 84, 94, 186(n23)
Waters, Maxine, 87(table), 90
Watt, Melvin, 87(table)
Waxman, Henry A., 81
Weatherford, J. McIver, 128
Webster, Daniel, 49, 112
Welles, Gideon, 50–51(table)
Wexler, Robert, 87(table)
White House Travel Office, 20, 81
Whitewater land deal, 1, 4, 20–21, 81, 82
Wiggins, Charles E., 59(table)
Williams, George H., 44
Wilson, Woodrow, 155
Withholding of information, 26(table), 48
Wright, James C., 16

Young, Andrew, 189–190(n105)